THE FUTURE OF
ASTROLOGY

Also by A. T. Mann

The Round Art
Life★Time Astrology
The Divine Plot: Astrology, Reincarnation, Cosmology
    and History
The Mandala Astrological Tarot

THE FUTURE OF ASTROLOGY

Edited by A.T. Mann

UNWIN HYMAN
London   Sydney

First published in Great Britain by Unwin Hyman, an imprint
of Unwin Hyman Ltd, 1987.

UNWIN HYMAN LTD
Denmark House, 37–39 Queen Elizabeth Street,
London SE1 2QB

and

40 Museum Street, London WC1A 1LU

Allen & Unwin Australia Pty Ltd
8 Napier Street, North Sydney, NSW 2060, Australia

Allen & Unwin New Zealand Ltd with the
Port Nicholson Press
60 Cambridge Terrace, Wellington, New Zealand

British Library Cataloguing in Publication Data
The Future of astrology.
1. Astrology
1. Mann, A.T.
133.5   BF1708.1
ISBN 0-04-133023-4

Printed in Great Britain by Biddles Ltd, Guildford, Surrey

Contents

Preface

Astrology is a science in itself and contains an illuminating
body of knowledge. It taught me many things and I am greatly
indebted to it.
                                                    Albert Einstein

Astrology originally included the sciences of astronomy, geometry,
mathematics, psychology and medicine. It was central to the ancient
civilizations of Babylonia, Chaldea, Egypt, Greece, Rome and medieval
Europe. But, with the advent of scientific materialism in the eighteenth
century astrology was rejected by church and university. Despite the rapid
decline into mere fortune-telling, it continued to exert a profound influence
over many of the greatest thinkers. Isaac Newton, Galileo, Jung and
Einstein all practised astrology, though largely in secret for fear that its
mysteries would compromise their 'serious' scientific work in the public
eye.

In recent years, astrology has undergone a resurgence in popular
interest along with new generations questioning the wisdom of a
scientifically run civilization rapidly heading towards destruction in
personal relations, ecology and politics. It represents an alternative view of
the universe which is relativistic and ecological. Astrology can be a central
tool for the integration of the individual and the outside world, as
expressed in the ancient dicta: 'as above, so below' and 'the microcosm is
the macrocosm'.

The New Paradigm for Astrology

The combination of a questioning generation and the accessibility of
personal computers, together with the spread of psychotherapy, has
created a 'new paradigm', a new way of thinking about astrology and the
world. Astrology's bad press in past centuries had led to its value being
overlooked and confined merely to prediction, but there are many other
aspects which are of great worth.

Astrology is an important tool for psychotherapists in the process of
describing and clearing the confusion in people's lives. Its symbolic

language is very useful in identifying with, and integrating, aspects of life ranging from parental behaviour, sexuality, mental life and worldview. Medical astrology, which was an essential part of the education of early doctors such as Paracelsus, is being rediscovered and investigated in large-scale research projects. Astrology is also being used in economic prediction and for counselling businesses and business people. And, most importantly, astrology is being viewed as a fundamental way of looking at the physical universe and its laws, as the quotation from Einstein demonstrates.

A recent study in *Astro★Talk* (vol. 3, June 1986) mentions that in the United States alone there are over 50 million people who feel that they know enough about astrology to talk about it, while the German school of Cosmobiology estimates that about 30 million people in West Germany know their Sun-sign. It is good news that there is massive interest in astrology, but conversely an overwhelming number of people in the street only know astrology through the daily Sun-sign columns in newspapers. Nevertheless, an astrological revolution is going on.

The Future of Astrology is a presentation of essays by many of the most influential and best known astrological theorists, practitioners and researchers of our time. All have addressed themselves to the direction in which astrology is heading. Their responses are varied, and represent many of the primary areas of interest in the subject today, including science versus astrology, computers, research, the politics of astrology, counselling, psychology and astrology, new theories about astrological mechanisms, a reassessment of astrological history, astro-economics, astrology as a healing art, prediction, and many more. All the essays are for the general reader as well as for the professional astrologer, and there is a minimum of technical terms or discussion.

In addition to the essays, each participant has permitted the publication of a brief biography, bibliography, photograph and birth information, from which their horoscope has been calculated. This allows those with astrological knowledge access to the astrology of the astrologers. The bibliographies provide other books by each astrologer.

The Astrological Revolution

A few brave individuals in the early part of the twentieth century have almost single-handedly brought astrology into the modern era. Foremost of these is Dane Rudhyar, who has brought a unique insight to bear on astrology and integrated it with other important areas of human concern. Rudhyar was a psychologist, humanist, artist, metaphysician and musician who combined astrology with the fledgling field of psychology to create a 'humanistic astrology'. His pioneering has led to many astrologers training as psychotherapists. Although Rudhyar died in 1985, he is represented by an essay written in 1933 which is seminal to modern astrological thought and is as modern as today.

Leyla Rael-Rudhyar was married to Dane Rudhyar for many years, and is an influential humanistic and transpersonal astrologer living in San Francisco.

The historian of science and computer systems designer, Robert Hand, is a truly original thinker in modern astrology, living in Massachusetts. In addition to developing very sophisticated astrological software through his company, Astrolabe, Robert is a profound and inquiring student of the history of astrology and revolutionary science. He is at once a traditionalist, scientist, humanist and metaphysician with great influence and intelligence.

John Addey devoted his life to astrology as a researcher and co-founder of the Astrological Association in London. Up until his death in 1982, he did research into astrological mechanisms with the intention of creating an astrological science based upon the principle of harmonics.

The French psychologist and statistician Michel Gauquelin, although raised by an astrologer father, attempted to disprove astrology in his doctorial dissertation at the Sorbonne in the early 1950s. Then he discovered that there was an irrefutable statistical basis for astrology, which he has since expanded – to the consternation of other scientists. In collaboration with his wife Françoise, Gauquelin created a firm scientific foundation for astrology and forced both scientists and astrologers to approach the subject in new and more challenging ways. Gauquelin is at the forefront of those who are attempting to bring astrology into the domain of modern science.

Charles Harvey is President of the Astrological Association and director of the Urania Trust in England, a translator of the German works of Ebertin, and a protégé of John Addey in the harmonic tradition. He is also a firm supporter of mundane astrology, which is the astrology of countries and world events.

The logarithmic time-scale developed by A. T. Mann is an integration of astrology with biology and psychology through the phenomenon of 'biological time'. By further making an analogy between the movement of the planets in time with the spiral genetic code, astrology becomes a way for decoding our psycho-genetic world, a possible connection of science, psychology and metaphysics.

Dennis Elwell has been a provocative and amusing voice in English astrology for more than thirty years. He is a leader of those who oppose any attempt to integrate astrology with science, and has proposed an alternative way of seeing the world.

Jim Lewis runs his Astro★Carto★Graphy business from San Francisco. The techniques which he has refined provide a graphic representation of the positions of the planets superimposed on a world map, which allows one to determine the astrological qualities in operation at particular places and times, both in the past and future. He is a founder of AFAN, the networking astrological organization in the US.

Dr Karen Hamaker-Zondag is a well-known Dutch Jungian analyst who runs her own school and writes extensively about the integration of Jungian psychology with astrology.

Alan Oken is a prolific author and linguist who presents the traditions of esoteric astrology and psychological doctrine of the Tibetan D. K., as transmitted by the works of Alice A. Bailey.

Bruno and Louise Huber were secretaries to Roberto Assagioli, the founder of psychosynthesis, and they run the very influential Institute for Astrological Psychology in Switzerland, as well as being co-organizers of the biannual World Congress of Astrology held in Zurich. The Hubers have taught many thousands of astrologer-psychologists who work with the horoscope, using a wide range of techniques, particularly visualization, meditation, guided imagery and experiential work. The Huber method is characterized by the attribution of the sequence of houses to the life process around the horoscope.

Barry Lynes is a primary advocate and expert on astro-economics and is president of Astro★America, an ecological lobbying group based in New England. He is concerned with the political, legal and moral position of astrology in our world, and attempts to expose suppressive measures by authorities.

Roger Elliot appeals to the popular astrological market with his Star★Life computer horoscopes and yearly predictive booklets. He is, however, a serious researcher of the uses of computer technology in modern astrology, particularly for graphic representations of the horoscope in colour.

The many varied, stimulating and provocative views contained in *The Future of Astrology* are bound to intrigue the reader, and the obvious insight and scholarship of current astrological thought is far beyond the misleading simplicity of newspaper astrology with which most people are familiar. It is the editor's sincere hope that these essays will lead more people to learn about the practising of the profound art and science of astrology.

A. T. Mann
Cranbrook, Kent

THE FUTURE OF
ASTROLOGY

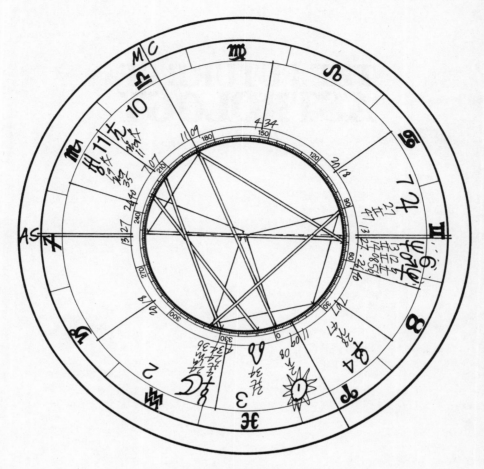

DANE RUDHYAR

23 March 1895   00:30:39 am GMT   Paris, France

Dane Rudhyar

For over sixty years Dane Rudhyar has attempted to transform the character of the assumptions and patterns of thinking structuring our way of life and our Western culture. His accomplishments in the fields of music, philosophy, astrology, psychology, painting and literature have earned him the accolade of twentieth-century 'Renaissance Man'. But Rudhyar prefers the term 'Seed Man', for, he says, we are not living in a classical age in which a culture flowers, but in a period in which the end of one culture-cycle interpenetrates the beginning of the next and comes, as it were, to seed in and through a relatively few promethean pioneers.

Rudhyar began his multifaceted public life in Paris, France, his birthplace, at the age of 17, when some of his piano compositions and a book on music were published. He came to America in 1916 at the age of 21 for the performance of some of his ultra-modern orchestral works at the Metropolitan Opera in New York – possibly the first such performance in the United States. In the 1920s, when most musicians considered oriental music 'barbaric noise', he was among the first to stress its validity and importance both in Eastern cultures and to the West. His vital interest in oriental and occidental philosophies has never waned; on its basis he has formulated a dynamic and compelling 'philosophy of wholeness' which while including both Asian and Western concepts is limited to neither and thus represents a true synthesis of East and West.

As an outgrowth of his interest in oriental music and philosophy, in the early 1930s, Rudhyar turned his attention and synthesizing mind to the ancient art of astrology. Initially, he hoped to integrate it with the depth psychology of C. G. Jung, the philosophy of Holism of Jan Smuts, and the philosophical implications of modern physics. In thirty published books and over a thousand articles, he has transformed astrology into a meaningful psychospiritual frame of reference within which modern men and women can understand and meet constructively the unprecedented psychological and social challenges facing them.

Rudhyar died in 1985 at the age of 90.

Dane Rudhyar Bibliography

The Astrology of Personality (1936)
New Mansions for New Men (1938)
Astrological Signs (The Pulse of Life) (1943)
The Lunation Cycle (1946)
An Astrological Study of Psychological Complexes (1966)
An Astrological Triptych (1968)
The Practice of Astrology (1968)
Astrological Timing: The Transition to the New Age (1969)
Person-Centred Astrology (1970)
Astrological Themes for Meditation (1972)
My Stand on Astrology (1972)
The Astrological Houses: The Spectrum of Individual Experience (1972)
An Attempt at Formulating Minimal Requirements for the Practice of Natal Astrology (1973)
An Astrological Mandala (1973)
The Astrology of America's Destiny (1975)
From Humanistic to Transpersonal Astrology (1975)
The Galactic Dimension of Astrology: The Sun is Also a Star (1975)
Astrology and the Modern Psyche (1976)
Astrological Insights into the Spiritual Life (1979)
The Astrology of Transformation (1980)
Astrological Aspects: A Process-Oriented Approach, with Leyla Rael (1980)

1

Whence, Why and Whither

DANE RUDHYAR

A great deal of unnecessary confusion seems to exist in the mind of most people concerning the great and ancient *mystery-knowledge* which today is called astrology. It is with deliberate intention that I use the rather involved term mystery-knowledge; for it seems the best to define the true and millennia-old system of life-interpretation which has been lowered by many to the level of mere fortune-telling.

Astrology ought not to be considered as a means for the gratification of an idle curiosity as to possible future events; it should not either be thought of as an ordinary science, to be approached with the analytical and experimental point of view of the material scientist. It is a knowledge which is rooted fundamentally in the mystery of the spiritual laws of life. It is a spiritual, not a materialistic, knowledge – one which has been largely lost for centuries, or when not lost, materialized, but which appears to be now revitalized as a means to lead humanity to change its mind concerning life and man's relationship to his true destiny, as well as to all his fellows.

Astrology undoubtedly began as a mystery-knowledge and not as an experimental science, and its beginnings cannot be traced for they seem to be simultaneous with the birth of civilization.

Here, however, we begin at once to be on dangerous ground and to write about the beginnings of astrology would require that we discuss the origin of civilization and of Man as a thinking spiritual being on earth, a vast subject which depends for its development on one's philosophy of life or beliefs. Modern science sees Man developing from the animal and thinks of the growth of civilization as a slow progress from dumb barbarism to the light of the present day. But men, who live and think by the light of the traditional mystery-knowledge which is at the back of all true spiritual teachings and religions, say that such a slow progress is true only in regard to the intellectual aspect of civilization, not to the spiritual aspect of knowledge or consciousness. They claim that at the dawn of civilization in fabled continents of old there were great 'Knowers', masters of all

5

'mystery-knowledge' – of which astrology is only one branch – and that these Knowers taught the principles of civilization to mankind.

Man, in the mass – animal-like in his intellect – had then to build up slowly, painstakingly, his own many cultures on the basis of those principles of civilization which constitute the substance of the true and eternal mystery-knowledge on this planet of ours. Astrology, when free from superstitions and accretions which disfigure its eternal countenance, is a changeless system of laws of cosmic relationship, of pure abstract relationship. It is not an evolving science, as is the case with astronomy, yet in some ways it is influenced by the condition of development of astronomical knowledge – just as civilization is influenced by the state of cultural development in any race, nation or continent.

This is the first consideration to have in mind in order to understand the history of astrology; for astrology has seemed to evolve and to alter its teachings only in so far as the science of astronomy evolved. Astronomy was one thing in China, another in India, another in Alexandria, another in the nineteenth century. Astrology is outwardly transformed to adjust its changeless laws of relationship to the ever-changing astronomical and cultural conceptions of each era. Thus Chinese astrology differs from Hindu or medieval European astrologies as to the symbolism, nomenclature, aspects, outer emphasis, etc.

Astrology proper, as a mystery-knowledge, is the core of all these various period-astrologies which claim to be more or less experimental sciences based upon astronomical investigation, the general state of the race-minded, and of culture at the time considered. Chinese philosophy, which brought forth the ethical principles of collective behaviour, led to a sort of ethical astrology which sees in stars the elements of the perfect harmony of Heaven, the duplication of which on earth is the main goal of Chinese wisdom. In India, where a more individualistic philosophy ruled and men strove to live lives of yoga, of training the life-force on all planes, astrology was more deeply concerned with the solar and lunar cycles and their effects upon the tides of this creative life-power within the individual.

In Egypt, astrology was the foundation of magical practices and ceremonial rites, and astronomy was brought to great perfection for practical religious uses; while in ancient Chaldea the stars were the very gods of the universal religion, and men attuned their souls to the life-force within the stars, learning the secrets of their inner cosmic nature by self-absorption into the beams of light of the star worshipped.

In all these ancient cultures, astrology was of practical daily use in the conduct of life; social, conjugal, national or personal. Man's ideal was to live lives in harmony with the pattern of divine perfection, the glory of which was made manifest in the skies. Free will and individualistic self-expression were practically unknown. Astrology was the one science of perfect living, and as such permeated all human activities, regulating the functioning of collectivities, of state and family.

With the Graeco-Roman culture a new keynote of human development was struck. The intellectual faculties began to predominate. Man began to feel superior to all forces of life, to erect himself as ruler of all life-energies. Thus the axiom, which gradually became endowed with a peculiar and rebellious significance: the wise man rules his stars; the fool is bound by their decrees.

Medieval astrology is the outcome of Greek intellectualism combined with influences of Eastern mysticism and alchemical knowledge, part of which had been reshaped by the original Arabian sense of abstract relationship. It depends for its laws and methods of interpretation almost solely on the writings of Ptolemy, who lived in the second century AD and who based its symbolism upon the geocentric astronomy which was then taken for granted by the masses, but not by the Initiates.

The most profound astrologers of medieval times were men whose spiritual philosophy can be best called *alchemy*. Alchemy was not for them what most people believe it was; the chimerical art of making gold out of lead. It was a secret process of spiritual development which revealed the practical application of Christian mysticism. Astrology was thus concerned with the working out of alchemical regeneration, and its symbolism pointed to hidden mysteries and laws governing the process of practical regeneration.

Outwardly, it is true, astrology was also used to prognosticate events, especially those of national importance. Every court had its official astrologer, and even the Roman Catholic Church used — and probably still uses — astrology to guide its policies.

With the nineteenth century and the tremendous development of modern science, a change was bound to come in astrology. Medieval astrology had to be reshaped to conform to new astronomical concepts; the Sun had to be put in a central, all important place as symbol of the highest in man, the influence of stars and constellations had to be ignored — were they not too distant to affect man? — and a scientific structure coupled with a spiritual system of interpretation had to be worked out.

Alan Leo, a devoted student of the modified theosophy that grew from the teachings of leaders who succeeded Madame Blavatsky, but personalised her original instructions, has been the most influential person in directing modern astrology towards the condition of a spiritual science. While accepting the basis of Ptolemaic astrology, he strove to lift the whole structure of astrological thought by linking it to his understanding of theosophy and Hindu philosophy. There were many who worked in this direction, like Sepharial, who attempted to increase the value of astrological data and discover or rediscover rules and ideas to make astrology more accurate or scientific.

With the advent of the philosophy of relativity, of radioactivity and of radio; with substance vanishing into waves, and time and space playing queer tricks upon each other and everybody else — it was inevitable that astrology, after again becoming influential in the lives of many, should also tend to become more ethereal and abstract – and in a new way, scientific.

This obviously has just begun, and the trend is noticeable only in close quarters. Marc Edmund Jones has brought astrology to the level of a most abstract system of knowledge pervaded by relativism and deeply embedded in intellectual speculation, though also most keenly effective in a regenerated 'horary' system. On the other hand, the radio engineer Johndro has evolved an astrology in which star-rays play a conspicuous part and the principles of radio waves are used to justify astrological predictions.

We have only mentioned a few of the most striking tendencies and a few names that are, in our estimation, most characteristic. Evangeline Adams has done much to popularize astrology and to force its practical workings upon the attention of businessmen; while Max Heindel and his movement have been effective in bringing astrology to good repute and in stressing the healing possibilities of the art when in clean and pure hands.

We must now conclude by briefly stating what would seem to be the outstanding message of astrology to future mankind.

We see astrology as the basis of a new and truly spiritual psychology; and by 'psychology' we mean the *science of soul-formation, or soul integration* – the science which teaches the 'I' in man how and when to build his spiritual temple, the 'temple of the living God', which is spoken of in the scriptures. We see in planets and stars (as astrology considers them) symbolical representations of soul-energies within every man. These soul-energies wax and wane, interrelate and mentally affect each other. A human soul is a complex network of psychological–mental processes which must be harmonized, chorded, made organic, if man is to become master of himself and of life, a 'Perfect' One.

Astrology shows us how to work out soul-harmony, how to build the inner soul-organism into which the Breath of Spirit will descend when it has become 'viable' after a definite period of interior spiritual gestation. It shows us, by extension and analogy, how the collective life of a group, a nation, and ultimately humanity, can be made organic, harmonious and efficient.

Astrology, if properly understood and applied, can bring order to the usual chaos of human life, individual and collective. Wherever there is a principle of unification – a will, or individual purpose, an 'I' – trying to bring into a state of coherence and integration a mass of more or less independent elements – there astrology can teach the way to the necessary integration.

Anyone will see after a moment of thought that life itself is such a process of integration. A seed becomes a plant by integrating to its organic will the chemicals of the soil and the moisture of its surroundings. A nation becomes a powerful state by assimilating slowly all the human elements that live within its boundaries, by permeating them with a national consciousness. Assimilation of the many life-elements by the one will; integration of inchoate substance into an organic body in which the Individual Spirit acts – such is the universal process.

Astrology reveals the law of the universal process. It deals with life itself, with its most fundamental and general operations. Its value is not that we should know what events are in store for us, but rather that 'we', as individual selves, should accept the task of becoming 'immortal souls', by harmonizing the many forces, inner and outer, which every year, every month presents to us; which so often tear us to pieces!

Astrology should bring order to a chaotic humanity, unable at present to understand, assimilate and much less integrate the energies which it has summoned. Astrology might be called a sort of *spiritual technology*, for it should be in charge of the organization of man's consciousness and of man's soul. It is a technique for organizing life, and is therefore unlimited. Wherever life manifests in a form, there astrology can and should operate – whether in the growth of plants and crops – or in the growth of human cultures and souls.

Astrology is the mystery-knowledge which teaches fulfilment, completion, harmony and order. It is thus the foundation of all cosmic operations and is rooted in the so rarely understood 'harmony of the spheres'. Astrology will bring to men the knowledge of harmonious relationship.

Leyla Rael Bibliography

The Lunation Process in Astrological Guidance (1979)
Astrological Aspects: A Process-Oriented Approach, with Dane Rudhyar (1980)
Shambhala Astrological Calendar, 1980–85
The Essential Rudhyar (1983)

2

Dane Rudhyar and the Astrology of the Twentieth Century

LEYLA RAEL

> Rudhyar's *Astrology of Personality* is the greatest step forward in Astrology since the time of Ptolemy. It represents the birth of a new epoch.
>
> Paul Clancy, founder and editor of *American Astrology*

Indeed it did. This statement appears on the flyleaf of the first edition of *Astrology of Personality*, which was the very first attempt to link astrology with depth psychology, especially the formulation and terminology of Jung, and with Smut's philosophy of Holism. Many students of astrology are surprised to learn that this seminal work was written and published in 1936, long before they had ever set eyes on an ephemeris, perhaps even before they were born – or, conversely, are surprised that the ideas in it were formulated so recently. For so many, notions that Rudhyar was the first to advance in this book, and in the thousand articles and twenty books on astrology that followed, have become so integral to twentieth-century astrology that they are taken for granted and students may be unaware of their origin. In a field marked by a notable absence of quotation marks and references to other authors, and a remarkable proliferation of redundant texts, imitation without credit seems to be the highest form of flattery. Perhaps an even more thorough indication of the total acceptance of one's ideas is to have them taken for granted – not because they are unimportant but because, once formulated and read, it is inconceivable for the reader to proceed without them.

This is not to say that Rudhyar's work has been without its critics and detractors, or even that the totality of his approach has been fully understood or accepted by even a sizeable minority of astrologers today. However, virtually no astrologer practising today is unaffected by Rudhyar's work. Ideas which he was the first to formulate (and often the only one to develop fully, consistently, and coherently) have been 'in the air' for nearly half a century, during which time he wrote and lectured prolifically. Today, even the most event-oriented astrologer (a term which Rudhyar himself coined in contrast to his person-centred approach) counsels clients – that is, points out the client's responsibility, indeed purpose in life, to grow and learn from whatever happens, however dire or sublime. This in itself marks a definitive departure from traditional astrological practice.

Of course, one could say that the time had come for such a change and that it doesn't really matter who originated it. Indeed, such a need is primary and collective, and the individual who responds to it is only the vehicle through which the answer comes. Yet the answer is a particular formulation, shaped by a vehicle who is not merely a passive channel without personal history, feelings, characteristics, and concerns, and the answer he or she offers may be fully adequate, partial, or distorted. Is the scope and focus of the individual's mind adequate to the task? Does he or she possess the necessary discipline and dedication, or is he or she derailed by criticism, non-comprehension, or disappointment? To answer these questions, history must evaluate the efforts of a particular human being, Dane Rudhyar, for it was Rudhyar's work that inaugurated 'the birth of a new epoch' in astrology – or as Rudhyar himself might say, the beginning of a new phase in its cyclic development.

A new phase in its cyclic development – this notion is at the core of Rudhyar's approach to both astrology and human living. A true Promethean spirit (born with the Sun in Aries and the nodes of Uranus contacting the birth-horizon), Rudhyar sought to reawaken a sense of dynamism in astrology and human living. He envisioned every set of astrological symbols – signs, planets, houses, aspects – as phases of cyclic processes which are lived and experienced, step by step, from birth to death. This departed from the more traditional approach that took each symbol separately, as a discrete category of qualities, issues, actions, or events.

While the signs of the zodiac had been pictured previously as symbolic phases of the hero's equally symbolic journey, Rudhyar's *Pulse of Life* brought the inner journey of each sign into sharper focus psychologically and psycho-spiritually. It also reinterpreted the symbolic foundation of the zodiac itself by linking it with the waxing and waning lengths of days and nights throughout the year, thereby revealing a hitherto unexplored dimension of rich symbolism (this later became the philosophical underpinnings for a meta-astrological cosmology and *Weltanschauung* that Rudhyar developed much later in *The Rhythm of Wholeness*).

Rudhyar treated the heliocentric order of the planets' orbits as a cycle in which the planets acquired their basic meanings. He also showed how even rulerships, which are usually considered unconnected categorical affinities, are the product of relating the planets' correct heliocentric sequence to the cycle of the zodiac. He worked extensively with the cycles and meanings of the outer planets, Uranus, Neptune, and Pluto, and was the first to define these trans-Saturnians as 'planets of the unconscious' and 'messengers of the galaxy'. He was also the first to examine fully the Pluto–Neptune cycle, calling the period of Pluto's penetration of Neptune's orbit (now in full swing with Pluto approaching perihelion in Scorpio in 1988) a cosmic 'fecundation' of the solar system. Also along mundane lines, he rectified and promoted the Sagittarius rising chart for the American people – a thankless task until recently, when a new generation of astrologers is accepting this chart's validity. And if it weren't for Rudhyar's request to publish the Sabian Symbols in *Astrology of Personality*, the index cards containing these valuable, intriguing (and sometimes maddeningly cryptic) revelations might have lain indefinitely in Marc Edmond Jones' safe deposit box.

Regarding aspects, Rudhyar replaced the study of separate interplanetary relationships within the context of two planets' overall cycle together, strongly differentiating the meaning of aspects occurring in a cycle's waning half from those taking place while the cycle waxes. He also gave new meanings to the less familiar aspects such as quintiles (72 degrees), septiles (51 degrees), noviles (40 degrees), and so on.

For Rudhyar, the houses represent 'the spectrum of individual (and individualizing) experience', while the signs of the zodiac represent the spectrum of generic human nature. He therefore accentuated the primary significance of the houses on the background of the zodiac – the reverse of the way the relationship had been seen and interpreted before (this is why he advocates using a chart wheel with printed, equally spaced spokes for house cusps, rather than a form with the zodiac printed and houses unequally superimposed). To make more concrete the life journey through the houses, he invented the technique of the 'point of self', a symbolic clockwork hand that moves through the houses and over the natal angles and planets once every twenty-eight years, seven years per quadrant, regardless of the number of zodiacal degrees between horizon and meridian (it's often amazingly accurate!). This was perhaps an attempt to neutralize some of the problems surrounding different intermediate house cusps generated by various house systems. At a time when most astrologers were content to take Placidus for granted, Rudhyar pointed out the inadequacies of all existing systems of domification – Campanus, the one he favours, included – and issued a challenge to younger astrologers that has yet to be met even in this age of microprocessors and computer graphics: to invent a three-dimensional representation, a 'birth-globe', including all frames of reference (horizon, meridian, prime vertical, ecliptic, and equator) and positions in relation to them (altitude, azimuth, longitude, latitude, right ascension and declination).

These matters are perhaps too technical to pursue here. Suffice it to say that Rudhyar rethought every component of the birth-chart, taking nothing for granted. He also reformulated the meaning of the chart as a whole and redefined the role of the astrologer. He was the first to speak explicitly about the astrologer–client relationship and to stress the astrologer's psychological responsibility to the client. He called the birth-chart a *mandala* that can illumine the *meaning* of a person's life, as the life unfolded its natal potentials through a number of highly significant cycles, from birth to death.

By 'mandala' Rudhyar referred to both the Jungian and Hindu meanings of the term. He meant an integrating symbol, a multidimensional, psychically charged formula of organization representing the potential growth, integration, and transformation of the total person – not simply a flat map indicating fated events or character traits or flaws. Rudhyar would be the first to allow that some events and circumstances of life do indeed carry a sense of fated inevitability, but they are also charged with great meaning, the depths of which a person must plumb in order to grow, develop and ultimately transform himself or herself.

By 'natal potentialities' Rudhyar did not mean mere possibilities or trends, especially not the kind that could (or should) be dealt with statistically. (While statistics may be useful in establishing for the scientific mentality the general validity of astrology, Rudhyar, along with the vast majority of statisticians, recognizes that statistics deal with large numbers and have little if any useful bearing on individual cases.) For Rudhyar, the difference between possibilities and potentialities resides in the root of the latter term, which means power. Possibilities may or may not happen, and it is relatively unimportant whether they do or do not become actual. Potentialities, on the other hand, have within themselves power – the power of purpose, telos, indeed of destiny. Rudhyar has not shrunk from this term, even though (as Liz Greene has eloquently reminded us recently) it conjures up the ghost of a deterministic past which many astrologers wish would rest in peace. For Rudhyar, the power of one's life potentials have been invested in one, in one's birth, by the greater whole of which one is a part – humanity, the earth, and ultimately the whole universe. One's birth and life is a potential answer to the need of this greater whole, and the birth-chart is a potent symbol of both the need and the way it can best be fulfilled.

This may (and to many astrologers does) sound too grandiose to be applied to the issues facing most individuals in their daily lives. Not so. There is no individual problem which cannot be defined – and thereby made worth meeting consciously, courageously, and nobly – in archetypal terms or as a theme or product of collective change. Moreover, anything an individual experiences is inherently *human*. Elation, rage, grief, guilt, illness, love: all are universally human experiences represented by the same astrological symbols that appear in all horoscopes. To see through the apparent opacity and particularity of individual circumstances, no matter how dire or everyday, to the core of the human spirit striving to know itself, to integrate its myriad facets, and ultimately to transfigure itself – according to the way evoked by the individual birth-chart – this is the very concrete challenge of Rudhyar's approach. It is also why individuals seek the services of astrologers rather than (or in addition to) the advice of statisticians or psychotherapists. They want to be inspired by an extraordinary perspective; they want to see their personal situation in a metapersonal, cosmic context. Astrologers do, after all, traffic with 'the stars' and deal in such intangibles as karma, faith and inspiration. Thus instead of merely describing what is (which the client already knows, often too well) or speculating about what may or may not come to pass, Rudhyar's approach aims at helping human beings know and fulfil the purpose for which they were born; it helps individuals gain this self-knowledge by interpreting the concrete issues of their lives in archetypal terms. 'What is' is acknowledged, respected and understood as a phase – not 'merely' a phase like pimples in adolescence but a necessary, integral step – in the process of actualizing what is 'trying' to be.

Thus for Rudhyar nothing in a chart, progressions, or transits is in itself good or bad, fortunate or unfortunate; neither is any event or circumstance in life. Everything astrological and existential (that is, in real life) is what it is because it needs to be that way in the context of a more encompassing situation or cycle. This is not to say that all events and circumstances are, can be, or should be made, pleasant, easy, or even uplifting, or that a particular difficulty necessarily had to happen. Rudhyar has lived sufficiently long and deeply, through many crises, difficulties and disappointments, to appreciate the profound mysteries and ambiguities of life, karma, and causation, especially those inherent in suffering. A pollyanna approach trivializes his own striving and follows this statement with other equally significant thoughts: what matters is the significance we bestow upon events; only by giving meaning to events do we make them real; events do not happen, we happen to them; we make events constructive or destructive according to the meaning we give them, the place we let them occupy in our lives; we must therefore know what we are, actually and potentially, and how we can be stretched and our capacities for being enhanced, expanded and transformed, rather than what events per se may be.

Thus instead of encouraging the prediction of events Rudhyar exhorts their constructive interpretation. It is much easier to predict catastrophe (and to bring it about through self-fulfilling prophecy) than it is to interpret trauma constructively – and to evoke in oneself or in a client the imagination and the will to make the interpretation actually produce constructive action and growth. Of course, the predicting astrologer may impress a client by foretelling an event, especially a dire one which does not come to pass because the astrologer also counsels a way to avoid it. But Rudhyar's approach does not advocate avoidance of any kind. It seeks to create an open, courageous, and understanding attitude with which to meet the difficult and traumatic – as well as the exalting – and to actualize the potentials hidden therein.

In order to promote this understanding, Rudhyar reinterpreted many astrological techniques, indications and configurations, especially those which previously had been given primarily negative definitions. Early on, he redefined the meaning of the nodes of the Moon, eclipses and retrograde planets, each in terms of its own cyclic celestial phenomena. As far as I am concerned, he is the only astrologer-philosopher ever to formulate a cogent cohesive explanation justifying the use and illumining the meaning of secondary progressions. (Even though professional astrologers have told me that Rudhyar's ideas are too difficult for them to understand, I tell this explanation to my clients regularly and it never fails to elicit an 'Ah Ha'! response from them.)

Among the many techniques and cycles Rudhyar has studied and written about, the progressed lunation cycle is, I believe, his greatest gift to the practising astrologer. My own approach to counselling was exponentially transformed by its use, and I do not believe I could practise effectively without it. It was only when I began to use the progressed lunation cycle as a background for studying whole lives – clients' and persons whose biographies I borrowed from the library – that I began to really understand what Rudhyar was getting at in his more theoretical or inspirational writings.

Briefly, the progressed lunation cycle is the series of aspects formed throughout the life between the progressed Sun and progressed Moon. The eight phases of the cycle are called by the names of the phases of the Moon – new moon, crescent, first quarter, gibbous, full moon, disseminating, last quarter, and balsamic or seed phase. Each phase (lasting about 3½ years) represents a particular principle or step in cyclic development; successive cycles (lasting about 29½ years corresponding in progressed time to the 29½ days of a lunation) represent levels of personal, social and individual development. While a full lunation lasts 29½ years for everyone, the chronological age at which phases and cycles begin varies from person to person, depending upon the exact soli-lunar angle at birth and the relative speeds of motion of the progressed Sun and Moon. Dates of phase changes and new lunations can be calculated as exactly as one pleases, but that is not the point. The point is the way in which the life events fit into the phases and overall cycles. If the astrologer understands the principles behind the sequence of phases well enough and can explain them simply to the client (I use the metaphor of the growth of a plant from seed, through germination, to flower, then through fruit back to seed), he or she will also see the same principles of unfoldment operating (or being violated) throughout the client's life in the form of events and other developments – and the client will get the picture too. Together, the astrologer, who knows the archetypal meanings and relationships of the phases (and the transits that occur within them), and the client, who knows his or her history, can allow the connections between events and the coherence of the entire pattern to emerge.

Clients especially appreciate this technique and type of approach because no one else ever invites them to view their whole life in a structured, non-judgemental, purposeful way. It is the best way I have found to accomplish what Rudhyar challenges us to do: to see a life as a whole, as a structured process of unfolding from birth to death.

I have not exhausted the list of notable firsts and 're's' that mark Rudhyar's long and distinguished career as an astrological thinker and writer, nor have I touched upon his activities as a composer, poet, painter, novelist and philosopher. His 90 years on earth were full and productive indeed. He used to say that 84, the Uranus return, would be an appropriate time for him to leave. But after his Uranus return, in 1979, Rudhyar wrote a major text on music and several important musical compositions (and attended and helped prepare for performances of some of them), a long autobiography (as yet unpublished), two booklets published by the Rudhyar Institute for Transpersonal Activity (RITA), and two major volumes on philosophy (*Rhythm of Wholeness* and *Towards the Fullness of Human Experience*). He also supervised the translation of twenty of his books into French (lesser numbers have appeared in Dutch, German, Spanish, Italian and Portuguese). In his spare time he wrote as many letters as his failing eyesight allowed, received occasional visitors, washed more dishes than I did, pottered in the garden (he had a special love for flowers, with which he surrounded himself while working), and fed the birds and black squirrels that live in our backyard (he said that they are semi-trained, they probably tell their friends that they have fully trained him!). He was remarkably philosophical and graceful about accepting the adversities and indignities of aging (in a body working out a sixth-house conjunction of Pluto, Mars and Neptune to begin with).

I was extraordinarily privileged to share the last ten years of Rudhyar's life. We are all blessed to partake of the harvest of his life's work. Each of his many first and 're's' represents a seed generously tossed into the furrow his Arian nature has ploughed in the planetary mind-field. Even though some of us may be inclined to thin the crop by uprooting plants that seem to us weak (while others may be undiscriminating in their zeal to spread fertilizer), let us all realize that we tend the same garden. May its soil prove as fertile under our care as it has under Rudhyar's.

In another sense, each of us represents, or can represent, one of the kernels Rudhyar has awakened to seedhood. May we, like golden sunflowers, ourselves heavy with yet another generation of seed, stand tall, not in mere imitation or reflection of the sun, but in the genuine radiance of understanding. For this, after all, is what Rudhyar's life and work have been all about: understanding life, parenthood and the meaning of human existence – understanding the role astrology can play

17

in human development, what it can contribute, what it is for.

'What is astrology for?' This is the most significant question posed, and, again, he was the first to do so. Each of us answers this question in our own way. Rudhyar, ever respectful of all truly individualized answers, would have it no other way. As he has freely scattered seeds, let our understanding and appreciation of his performance of this task be as generous as his gifts to us.

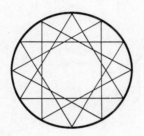

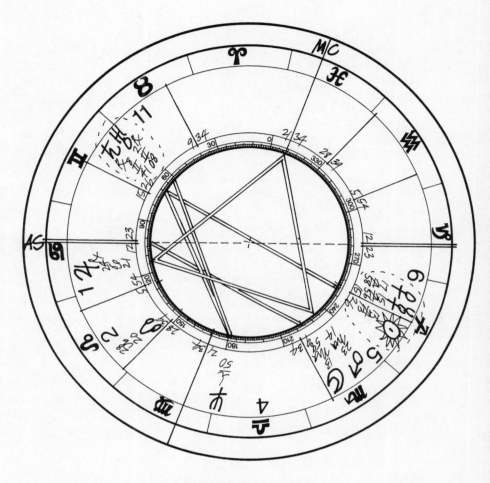

ROBERT HAND

5 December 1942   7:30:11 pm EWT   Plainfield, New Jersey

Robert Hand

Robert Hand has studied astrology since 1960, his original impetus coming from his father, Wilfred Hand, who successfully applied astrological techniques to stock-market forecasting. He became a full-time professional astrologer in 1972 practising first in New York and later in Boston and Cape Cod. He now makes his home on Cape Cod in Massachusetts. He has lectured extensively in the United States, Canada, Europe, Australia, New Zealand and India.

Currently Robert Hand is the president of Astro-Graphics Services, Inc, which markets various astrological products under the name of Astrolabe. These products include astrological computer software, astrological graphics products, periodicals and with the publication of Bruce Schofield's *Timing of Events*, books as well.

Robert Hand Bibliography

Planets in Composite (1975)
Planets in Transit (1976)
Planets in Youth (1977)
Horoscope Symbols (1981)
Essays on Astrology (1984)

3

Astrology as a Revolutionary Science

ROBERT HAND

This paper should not be construed in any way as belittling the significance of any form of humanistic or spiritual uses of astrology. I believe, along with many others, that astrology has a great contribution to make to the welfare of humanity as a counselling tool and a device for expanding human awareness. But the time has come for us to examine the bases of astrology in a scientific manner; to cast aside obscurantist attitudes and to reveal to the world the usefulness and spiritual merit of what we are exploring. If we do not, then what we have to offer will be for naught.

The Merits of Astrology as It Is

Independent of the validity of astrology being based on any objectively real physical effects or founded on any real planetary energy that influences human lives, astrology has value. This is something not generally acknowledged or realized even by many astrologers.

First of all, its symbolic language has roots in the collective psyche of the human race. If it did not, it would not have survived. And as such it has the ability to communicate something about people that they find meaningful. One of the widespread superstitions held by scientists is that the people hold beliefs (which scientists call superstitions) that are valueless, unreal and contradicted by everyday experience. Such beliefs are far less common among the races of humanity that is generally supposed. For any system to survive it must give people some genuine value, even though it may not be based on anything like modern scientific understanding. Astrology has survived for thousands of years on this basis. What modern system of psychology can say the same?

Secondly, the language of astrology is a particularly potent one. Two astrologers can convey the essence of a personality more clearly and concisely than the practitioners of any other discipline. When I say that an individual has Mars conjunct Saturn on the Midheaven square his Uranus rising in the first house, that code contains a huge amount of information. We know that such a personality type has little tolerance for others' criticism, that he may have spent his early life rebelling against a repressive father figure and that he tends to be irritable in a way that expresses itself in sudden outbursts of anger. We can also make educated guesses as to probable medical problems that may arise in the course of life.

We did not even begin to develop the possibilities of that simple configuration, yet even in this example the reader can see how much more concisely astrology expresses psychological patterns than English or psychological jargon.

Astrology also has a unique ability to describe a human being in non-judgemental terms. (This does not mean that individual astrologers might not express certain symbols more negatively than others.) Compare the Freudian term 'anal-retentive' with the astrological equivalent, 'a difficult expression of a strong Saturn or Capricorn symbolism'. Most Saturnian types are not genuine anal-retentives, but I suspect that all anal-retentives are strong Saturn types. Psychological terminology is loaded with implicit judgements, despite any protest of neutrality, while astrology is genuinely neutral in its language.

Herein lies the real value of astrological language, independent of the real nature of astrological influences. An astrologer can counsel and nurture with great insight, depth and support. Astrologers are genuine counsellors.

Being more sceptical of the usefulness of academic training than most, I believe that astrologers should study standard counselling techniques to find out what other counsellors are doing, but not necessarily to 'learn' how to counsel. Other paradigms of counselling language are impoverished with respect to astrology and an uncritical acceptance of standard counselling paradigms may only lead to a weakening of the effectiveness of the astrology.

Astrologers provide a type of counselling service that would otherwise not be available, and they can take pride in this. (There are horror stories of particularly bad counselling techniques being used by astrologers, but my experience with 'legitimate' professional counsellors is that the horror stories are just as frequent. The ability to counsel seems to be an intrinsic talent which training may hone but not create where it is absent.)

Astrology – A Science?

Readers of my book *Essays on Astrology* (1984) know that I am aware that astrology is not a science or even a pseudo-science. Neither is medicine! There are true sciences behind medicine such as physiology and anatomy, but medicine is a craft. There is much in the art of healing that would not stand up to rigorous scientific analysis, yet is still effective. A craft is a set of techniques designed to achieve a practical result in the real world. Sciences are not aimed at practical results. Technologies and crafts may be scientific, that is, they may use the results of scientific study to become more effective, but they are not of themselves sciences. A craft can be quite effective without being based on science. Almost all technologies and crafts in use prior to the mid-nineteenth century were non-scientific. Craftsmen got more useful information by trial and error than by studying the sciences. The sciences simply were not powerful enough to provide useful information. At that point in history the sciences learned from the crafts.

Strong upper-class affiliations were at first a major barrier to the sciences learning from the crafts. Many of the earliest practitioners felt that crafts were 'vulgar empiricism', not true high science which is attained through pure reason. This kind of science reached its peak with Descartes who created mathematics that were valid and a natural philosophy that was almost totally invalid! Fortunately, in the late seventeenth century many scientists overcame their prejudices. Many even came from the artisan classes. The result was that the crafts were studied and the sciences learned from them.

However, some of this snobbery is still with us and is part of our problem with the sciences. Universities are not only seats of learning, they are also places in which the select few are admitted to study under the elite.

Astrology is a craft without a science. It is important to realize however, that this need not be the case since astrology contains a latent science. A fairly large segment of the astrological community opposes this, in part because astrologers are afraid that their techniques will be invalidated by scientific studies. There is also a very real fear that a scientific approach to astrology will destroy the spiritual aspect of astrology that we all agree is essential. I understand and accept both of these fears. I am no more interested in having my favourite technique invalidated than anyone else. And I certainly recognize the spiritual dangers within the sciences, as I hope to make abundantly clear.

But astrologers should be aware that so far research, even by the debunkers, has not debunked anything. Scientific investigation has rendered some astrological techniques highly suspicious, but that is all. There are both good and bad reasons for this.

One good reason is that before scientific testing may be brought to bear on a new field of study like astrology, methods have to be developed which are suitable for investigating the new field. One cannot simply transfer a methodology from one field to another without significant alterations. Some astrological ideas are surviving such research tests, mainly through the work of the Gauquelins.

Among the bad reasons is that many astrological ideas are so poorly formulated and mushy in their thought content that no one can tell what they really mean in terms of observable consequences. Many astrological 'hypotheses' are too unclear to be testable. We must tighten up our thinking considerably.

But the main reason why we need a true science of astrology is that such a science would transform not only the other sciences but the very basis of our culture's attitude towards Man, God and Nature. If the fundamental assumptions of astrology at any level are validated then the metaphysical foundations of the sciences and of our culture are wrong! And it is the metaphysical assumptions of modern science and their broader cultural counterparts, not the intrinsic nature of scientific inquiry, that are threatening the world we live in.

The Roots of the Problem

It is of interest here to delve into the hoary past. The material under discussion is to a great extent derived from Joseph Campbell, the leading student today of the history of religion and mythology. (Primarily from his four-volume work, *The Masks of God*.)

My use of the word 'religion' in what follows is an expanded one. I do not mean what one does on a Sunday or Saturday, but the entire body of beliefs by which one establishes a relationship with the ultimate ground of being, what the late E. R. Goodenough called the *mysterium tremendum*. It governs one's day-to-day dealings with reality as well as whatever one's views may be on the nature of 'God'. Religion is a combination of metaphysics, ontology, epistemology, moral code, behavioural patterns and a simple reality system. It is often, but by no means exclusively, mythological in its expression. Non-mythological religions are very prominent in our own time, although it might be more accurate to say that the mythologies of these religions are more hidden than absent. Early in human history religions reached a very high level of sophistication. The view of most modern Westerners that they consist of naive collections of superstitions is not borne out by studies of contemporary primitive peoples. If one looks at the religious concepts of so-called primitive shamans, as opposed to the popular religions of their peoples (popular religions always being rather primitive even now among the so-called advanced peoples of the West), the sophistication of these beliefs is astounding.

Modern representations of the earlier types of religion also survive, in fact are thriving today among advanced peoples. And these are extremely advanced philosophically, in many ways to a greater degree than modern religions. Taking Hinduism as an example of the older type of religion and Christianity as an instance of the newer type, it is possible with little or no compromise in one's religious beliefs to be a modern scientist and a Hindu. However, it is very difficult to be a fundamentalist Christian, as all Christians were until the nineteenth century, and practise modern science.

I call the older religions Type I religions denoting that they came earlier in time than the later Type II, but they are definitely not more primitive. This type includes Hinduism, Buddhism, and Taoism. In the West none of these has survived as major religions, but Hermeticism (from which astrology, as we know it, comes) and Neoplatonism are examples from the past which have not lost their influence entirely. There are also very strong strains of Type I in Kabbalism, Sufism and Quakerism. Mystics (in the true sense of the word) almost always move towards Type I forms of belief.

Type I religions have a number of common characteristics:

1. *No single moment of Creation* – The universe is alternately created and destroyed. This idea is most explicit in Hinduism although it is found in Kabbalism as well.

2. *Cyclical Time* – Time moves in circles which is related to the previous idea. There is no beginning and end to the great wheel. We are in time and the object of transcendence is to get off the wheel completely – to get out of time altogether.

3. *No clear boundary between self and unself* – Mysticism does not mean mystification, but recognizing that the apparent diversity of creation is an illusion and that we are all at one with each other and the ground of being. The mystical principle de-emphasizes the ego which is, among other things, an awareness of the isolation of the self from the unself.

4. *Definition of reality* – The universe is an illusion, therefore individuals can legitimately differ in their views of what is real and what is not. There is no definition of orthodoxy and consequently no definition of heresy.

5. *Experience of the Divine* – There are priests and doctrines, but every believer is able to experience the divine directly, and there are paths available for this purpose. Various systems of yoga and meditation are found in Type I religions. But looking out at the world and trying to understand it empirically makes little sense because the world is an illusion.

6. *The Diffusion of Consciousness and Spirit* – Consciousness and spirit are diffused throughout the universe and are not limited to one God, human beings and a number of demonic entities. Type I religions look polytheistic from our point of view, although they believe that the apparent multiplicity of gods are all aspects of one being. Nature is something to be worked with and lived in, not dominated and mistreated as dumb, brutish or a machine.

7. *The Nature of Paradise* – The final state of being is not at the end of history, for history is outside time and will never end. The circular image of time going nowhere represents the inherent meaningless of our plane of existence. As the wheel turns, we continuously incarnate and reincarnate until we attain moksha, liberation, enlightenment or nirvana. These are always nearby and at the same time far away, but the distance is in terms of consciousness, not time.

The Birth of Type II Religions

Somewhere around 500 BC a new religion came into being in Persia, taught by the prophet, Zoroaster. This was the first Type II religion. It had Type I roots, but in the course of its development it became a completely new kind of religion. Zoroastrianism has the distinction of being the first religion to persecute on purely doctrinal grounds. The object of their attention was Zervanism, a Type I religion that worshipped the principle of infinite, unending time, Zervan, which was also the Persian term for the planet Saturn. Fortunately the Achaemenid emperors realized that religious persecution was not compatible with holding together a multinational empire, and Zervanism was tolerated.

At the time of Zoroaster there lived near the Mediterranean sea coast a tribe of primitive monolatrists. (Monolatry is the practice of worshipping one god to the exclusion of others while recognizing that there are other gods. It is their monolatry that was primitive, not the general level of their culture.) The tribe was abducted en masse to Babylon when Jerusalem was conquered by the second Babylonian Empire. There the Judaeans encountered a rather advanced Type I system of star-worship involving astrology and number mysticism.

It is apparent from Daniel and other books of the Bible that the Judaeans used number mysticism and astrology, but they also despised it. They had no problem with using the stars to interpret the will of God, but with the idea of worshipping the stars as gods, because only their god was important. The Bible prohibits only the kind of astrology practised by the Babylonians and other peoples of the region. When the Persians conquered Babylon, the Judaeans were exposed to Zoroastrianism with its one god of light and goodness in eternal warfare with the spirit of evil. The Judaeans decided that they and the Persians were worshipping the same god, it being much easier to adopt the religion of your liberators than that of your oppressors. The Persians allowed those Judaeans who wished, to return and rebuild Jerusalem. The ethical monotheism of Judaism comes directly from the fusion of Yahweh with Ahura-Mazda. From Judaism comes Islam and Christianity. Thus were born the Type II religions.

Let us review the major tenets of Type II religion in the same way that we did with Type I.

1. *Creation is a unique act which occurs only once* — At the end of time there is a unique moment of destruction. In Christianity it is the Last Judgement.
2. *Time is linear* — Nothing is repeated, there is no second chance.
3. *Self and unself are separate* — The individual is an isolated unit, different from, in kind, and alien to all of nature. This is the opposite of the mystical view, and it has serious consequences.
4. *There is only one reality* — Any deviation from the truth flaws the whole and makes the world corrupt and evil. Thus the universe becomes the

history of warfare between truth and evil. All Type II religions like Zoroastrianism are dualistic, even though they deny it. Their view of the power of evil exalts it to such an extent that it is close in power to that of good. This dilemma has caused no end of tortuous reasoning in Christianity. If God is wholly good then he cannot be the whole of the universe since there is observably evil in the universe. This is the problem of evil. There is no such problem in Type I religions.

5. *God is external to the self* – Like all aspects of the unself, therefore one must look outside oneself to find God. More reliance is placed on divinely sanctioned writings and priests. Even though a few favoured individuals may hear the word of God within, it is only a kind of psychic ear that operates, not a sign that God dwells within.

6. *There is no diffusion of consciousness and spirit* – They are to be found in only three types of entity: God; his angels and saints; human beings and diabolical entities. Matter is inherently dead and can only be animated by one of the three types of entities. (What to do with animals becomes an interesting problem.) Because Nature is dead it is easy to treat it callously and cruelly.

7. *Paradise is a definite place and time.*

The Evolution of Type II Religions in the West

Judaism gave birth to two successful Type II religions, first Christianity and then Islam. (There were quite a few others as well, such as the various Gnostic sects and, more lastingly, Manichaeanism. But none of these had anything like the impact of Christianity and Islam.)

The gospel according to John implies that Christianity began as a Type I resurgence within Judaism with the mystical Word or *logos* at the centre of all being. But in the hands of St Paul and his successors that element was nearly expunged, except for various mystics who periodically restated the essential unity of humanity and God. These either had to keep a very low profile during their lives or face the stake. Mainstream Christianity developed into the vast political structure that we see the remnants of today. God is somehow 'out there', there is only one truth (as witness the endless feuds and schisms among the various branches) and time is linear, with the heavenly kingdom at the end. Islam never became quite as monolithic as Christianity, perhaps because it was spared the horrendous union of the Latin legal tradition, with its hairsplitting concern with detail, and the intense, monotheistic fanaticism of the Judaic tradition. Islam has the latter but not the former, but even so it has had its share of theological conflict.

In some respects Type II religion is a significant step backwards. But it was not merely a serious mistake in the history of the human race. It has had a vitally important function.

In Type II religion, the individual is not distinct from the surrounding universe and the ultimate nature of reality is not clearly defined. Both these tend to discourage the development of the strong individualism and egoism that has characterized the West. Yet I believe that the development of the ego has been a necessary step in the development of the consciousness of the race, just as it is in the growth of the individual. (I must acknowledge here that I do believe that in the very long run there is some kind of overall evolution of consciousness in history. I do not think that history is merely tracing very large circles. Maybe it is a bit more like an ascending helix.)

The God of Type II is a 'jealous God', that is, he (note the fact that it has a sex) is an ego. With Yahweh egoism enters history as a cosmic principle. His separateness from us and our separateness from nature force human consciousness to go on its own and develop a very clear and definite concept of the self. As a result, Type II ego-consciousness has developed to an extreme degree in the West. We have developed ego-consciousness to the point where we identify our being almost entirely with the experience of having an ego.

In Puritanism and Calvinism, the deity is simply the ultimate ego and that makes him separate from us. All egos are separate from us. One is reminded of Shaw's famous quip, 'God created Man in his own image, and Man returned the compliment!'

After the peak of alienation of Man from God in the sixteenth and seventeenth centuries, it became clear that if God was that far from Man we might better dispense with him altogether. Thus late Reformation Protestantism evolved into Deism and then finally agnosticism and atheism.

There is a famous anecdote concerning a conversation between Napoleon and the astronomer Laplace. Laplace was demonstrating to Napoleon that the theory of gravitation was sufficient alone to explain how the solar system was regulated. Napoleon allegedly asked Laplace where God fitted into his theories. Laplace is supposed to have replied, 'God? I have no need of that hypothesis!' The story is probably apocryphal, but it does illustrate the fate of the Father God, as the adolescent ego of the West matured into adulthood.

Life and the Universe

Primitive humans and Type I religions believe that life-energy in some form is scattered throughout the material universe. The most primitive form is *animism*, in which every rock, tree and stream has an animating spirit. In the more evolved pagan religions of antiquity the material universe is heavily populated with non-human, spiritual entities that act, move and converse much like human beings. In Type I religions the universe itself is a single entity which may be beyond our comprehension but is still nevertheless alive. The material universe, ourselves, and any other entities that may be perceived, such as gods, demigods, nymphs, dryads, etc. are aspects of the single living One. In all early religions the basic model for interpreting the universe has been that of the behaviour of living things. The worldview is organic.

Type II religions began much like the so-called pagan religions. There was a chief deity, but he was surrounded by many other types of living entities such as devas or angels. With Judaism there began a kind of contraction of the life-energy into smaller and smaller numbers of entities. All kinds of nature spirits disappeared or were converted into devils and demons. Any idea of a life-force diffused throughout nature disappeared. Gradually the material universe was converted into dead, inanimate matter manipulated by God and the Devil. Humans and animals were conceived as being particles of the divine trapped in inanimate matter.

In the Middle Ages the Church branded anyone accepting life-energy, such as the women who were nature worshippers, as agents of the Devil. Such women were closet followers of Old Religion which has many Type I elements within it, especially the idea of life-essence in matter.

Another group who differed were the alchemists, magicians and astrologers who pursued the secrets of nature. These studies lead to the conclusion that either we are tools of the stars or our consciousness is connected to the life-energy of the universe. In a way, we and the planets are one. All these groups were natural philosophers and magicians. (Please note the use of the present tense above. Natural magicians have not died out! We astrologers are natural magicians!)

The Evolution of Mechanist-Materialism

A new strain of thought in the later Renaissance was called mechanical philosophy. Although in its early stages it was nominally Christian, it was the logical outgrowth of the increasing sense of distance between God and humanity. Aside from occasional diabolical energies manifest in nature, matter was dead and God too far away for either him or his minions to be active in regulating affairs on a day-to-day level. Therefore, the behaviour of matter was explained purely in terms that did not require the intervention of life-essences. The obvious metaphor was the machine. All nature was explained in terms of machines which meant there could be no action at a distance, no mysterious 'occult' forces, no occult sympathies or antipathies, nothing but the effects of matter directly contacting matter.

The early stage of the movement was entirely theoretical. It was not yet fashionable to perform experiments, although workers like Galileo certainly pointed the way. Descartes developed a theory of natural philosophy to explain all observable nature in terms of direct action. His mathematics were brilliant; his natural philosophy almost completely wrong. His work foundered on mathematical astronomy developed by Kepler, who was more a natural magician than a follower of the mechanical school. Descartes' natural philosophy was finally superseded by another transitional figure, Isaac Newton. Newton was a member of the mechanical school, but he spent much more of his life studying alchemy than physics. Newton was severely attacked by the more extreme mechanists precisely because his principle of universal gravitation reintroduced an 'occult' property.

However, the mechanists finally accepted gravitation because it worked so well. It was tacitly decided that it was simply a mechanism which was not yet understood. It is still not completely understood. The mechanists also took over from the natural magicians the principle of observation and the empirical method took its place alongside mechanical theory.

Science as a Type II Religion

Science is one of several Type II religions about at the present. The *scientific method*, on the other hand, is not a religion, but a method for attaining knowledge. Using Hindu terminology, the scientific method is a form of jnana yoga. It is an epistemology that is quite capable of being independent of a particular religious or metaphysical viewpoint. The scientific method is a set of techniques used to interpret nature according to the precepts of the religion of Science, much as Aristotle's philosophy was used to interpret nature in terms of Christianity in the Middle Ages.

Many authors, myself included, have used the term 'Scientism' to distinguish the current religion of Science from the actual practice of inquiring about the nature of the universe. I will continue to use the word Science to denote the religion.

Scientists object to Science being called a religion. In their eyes Science has no God, and is practised independently of the issue of God. It has no churches, no established liturgy and no rigid dogma. Except for the last item, this is basically true. But this points out some of the ways in which Science is different from Christianity. But let us look at the criteria that we have already set forth for a Type II religion and see how well Science fits.

1. *Creation* – Most cosmologists believe that the universe came into being at the moment of the 'Big Bang', the one and only moment of creation. The universe will end in an entropic heat-death. ('Steady state' theorists views are more like Type I, but they are not the mainstream at present.)
2. *Time* – The mainstream of Science treats time as linear, despite the increasing complexity of relativity and quantum mechanics. The one moment of creation leads by a single path to the one point of ending.
3. *Self v. Unself* – The self and nature are clearly distinct. Science has the

same egoistic worldview as late Renaissance Christianity and is a logical outgrowth of it. Only in ecology and modern physics has the oneness of observer and observed been re-established.

4. *Definition of Reality* – First, there is only one reality, and all departures from it are in error. Science does not claim to know what reality is, but believes it is getting closer to it all the time. No other field of human endeavour is likely to do as well as Science.

Second, Science believes that the laws of nature are constant throughout time and space. We have not been able to experience this, but it is believed that the inquiries of Science are getting closer to laws which have always governed the universe and govern it everywhere. The idea that the laws of the universe may evolve and differ at various points in time and space is quite outside the established system of belief. Even statistically oriented sciences have to postulate that the laws of statistics are constant, even if other laws are only statistical tendencies. This is the Uniformitarian Hypothesis, explicitly set forth in geology but found throughout the sciences.

5. *Experience of the Divine* – The experience of the truth replaces the divine in language, and is sought entirely outside the self. Reality is 'objective' reality, which raises an interesting problem.

When one postulates that the search for truth must be carried out in the world outside the individual, and that the universe is essentially not alive, and there is no God, then one has a fundamental reality that cannot be experienced. Science has a God's-eye view of reality with a God. Human life is thus subjected to criteria that cannot arise out of human or any other kind of experience. What the individual experiences is believed to be subjective and superficial, and therefore not really true. Outside us exists an abstract idea of pure truth that is completely independent of our existence, a truth that can be comprehended only in the eyes of somebody whom we have banished from the universe. Other religions teach the existence of a transcendental reality beyond human experience, but do not claim to be able to decipher it.

I trust the reader can see the paradox here. The religion of Science divorces people from the experience of their own validity. Instead of trying to understand what they feel, they are taught to deny it. When the Virgin Mary appeared at Lourdes, it was written off by people who were not there as a mass hallucination. Are there any well-authenticated examples of mass hallucination in history? Or is this simply a judgement because it violates a belief system? Several hundred people's experience has been rejected in the name of an unperceivable abstraction of reality.

From this has arisen the cult of the expert, the child psychologist who has never been a parent, the anthropologist who makes no effort to get into the experience of cultural mores for fear that it would cloud his 'objectivity'. In many cases direct, personal experience counts as a disqualification for expertise.

6. *The Diffusion of Consciousness and Spirit* – This is simple. There is neither consciousness nor spirit in nature. It is no longer clear in the minds of psychologists that either consciousness or spirit exists even with human beings. We are just machines who hallucinate that we are conscious. If we are all machines operating solely as the consequences of environmental influences, then who is B. F. Skinner?

7. *The Nature of Paradise* – Although Science has no official conception of a paradise, it is closely allied with a set of ideas that do. It can be argued that as a whole this set of ideas so permeates Science that it qualifies as part of it.

Why study Science? Because the increase in knowledge is good. Why is it good? Because it brings about the ability of the human race to make life better and better. If scientists believed that their understanding was simply going round in meaningless circles, old ideas coming up again, having their day and being replaced in turn by other old ideas, I doubt that many would be attracted by it. Historically, institutionally and actually, in the minds of most people both in and out of the sciences, Science is closely connected to the idea of Progress. What is progress? It is the Type II idea of the paradise at the end of linear time.

There is not a single criterion in which mainstream Science fails at being a classic Type II religion. Modern science is the latest stage (along with Marxism) in the deterioration of Type II religion. Its key characteristics are that everything operates unconsciously as a machine, that the essential driving forces of the universe are dead and blind, and that consciousness, even in human beings, is an illusory epiphenomenon of the laws of physics and chemistry. It is a death cult because out of the multiplicity of nature, with an almost infinite variety of possible interpretations, it has chosen to exalt death above life and unconsciousness above consciousnes.

Christianity has at last perceived this fact but its reaction is primitive and retrogressive. It would move us back towards an older consciousness. Christianity requires belief in ideas that are contradicted by genuine experience and observation far more than Science, but given the spiritual barrenness of the scientific worldview, the resurgence of primitive forms of Christianity in our time is completely understandable.

And now we know the religion of Science and its true name, a name which I have already used in this essay, mechanist-materialism. The idea behind Science and the word itself must be enlarged to include any rigorous inquiry into truth, not merely ones that follow the canons of mechanist-materialism.

Astrology and the New Science

Astrologers have a worldview that holds that every human being is tied to the workings of the cosmos, not as a victim, but as a full participant in and manifestation of its workings. Carl Jung postulated that there are *archetypes* of the collective unconscious that link all individuals to each other and to the race as a whole. These archetypes exist both within and outside the human individual. Planetary symbols are archetypes and operate more like living entities than machines. Astrology is an art based upon the mystical idea of the unity of all human beings with the cosmos. There are other systems of thought that share this feature, but astrology is peculiar in that it is amenable to study by the scientific method once the scientific method is shorn of its connection with mechanist-materialism.

The most powerful reason for developing a science of astrology is to make a conscious attempt to overthrow the mechanist-materialist worldview. It would also be useful for the new science to improve what astrologers actually do with clients, but this is secondary. It will take a long time before a science of astrology can be of much use to the art, given the incredible complexity of practical astrology and the difficulties of creating a scientific method suitable to the new field of study.

In fact, for the foreseeable future, it would be well to keep the science and craft of astrology separate. The science can draw inspiration and ideas from the craft but it should not try to pass judgement or otherwise impinge too closely upon its practices. And at the same time the separation would benefit the new science because it would not have to deal with the whole weight of astrological tradition which undoubtedly contains much that is of little value to the new science.

The Astrological Hypothesis

The new science of astrology must not simply become another branch of mechanist-materialism. Some efforts along those lines may be seen already in the writings of the more scientifically oriented of astrology's researchers. We must assume for now and probably forever that the science of astrology will be the science of a radically different kind of reality from the sciences of mechanist-materialism. I would like here to set forth the basic metaphysical principles of the science of astrology:

1. All points in the time-space continuum are qualitatively unique.

This point is offered in distinction to the classical Newtonian view that all points in time and space are identical and essentially featureless except for their mathematical dimensions. Astrology makes it clear that there is something specific about each point in time and space.

2. Every event associated with any point in the continuum bears the quality of that moment expressed according to a symbolic language that is inherent in both nature and consciousness.

No science has ever effectively dealt with anything but mathematical quantities, certainly nothing as complex and hard to define as symbolic language. However, in the short term, the methodology of the Gauquelins offers some possible paths. In the long term, the sciences of linguistics and information theory are going to have to be tapped as well. Beyond that it is anyone's guess.

3. The quality of every point in time-space can be found by examining the relationship to every other point in time-space.

Each cross-section in time is an analytical tool, although we must improve astrology's understanding of the sequences of symbols in time as well as their relationships in space.

4. The science of astrology will focus on the planets as expression of the symbolism because planets are convenient. They are mathematically regular and predictable. Other entities can and have been used.

Astrology must be kept as astrology and not some other science of correlations. We must recognize that the astrological hypothesis is a restatement of the old doctrine of correspondences that underlies all the so-called occult arts.

5. The Laws of the Universe may or may not be constant. They may evolve gradually over time as if the universe were an organism.

Astrology is a rejection of the Uniformitarian Hypothesis as it is usually put forth. Any understanding of nature is an approximation accurate only for a given period of time. At the highest level, however, it will probably be difficult to reject Uniformitarianism. For astrology to work, the archetypes must have an overall constancy in time even if we can allow for some changes in their expression.

The Nature of the Conflict

However fallacious the assumptions and practices of the craft of astrology may be, the primary resistance to it goes far beyond its mere truth or falsity. Academicians who study astrology for historical reasons invariably feel called upon to apologize for their interest, even though it is obvious that the influence of astrology has been enormous. Neugebauer in his book *Greek Horoscopes*, a compilation of every surviving ancient Greek horoscope written down, felt it necessary to bowdlerize the texts, expunging every reference to astrology that did not also contribute to our understanding of Greek astronomy – a remarkable feat of scholarship! Reactions to astrology run the entire range from fear to loathing. And very few of these reactions seem to be to astrology as it is, but rather to some view of the subject that people have in their heads.

I have dubbed this resistance to astrology *astrophobia*, the fear that astrology might be true! It seems to have two forms, religious and scientific.

Religious astrophobia has ancient roots. As mentioned earlier, the Bible does not condemn astrology, only the worship of planets as gods instead of the 'one true God'. This is nothing more than the attitude of a Type II religion striving for a place in a world dominated at the time by Type I religions.

In the time of early Christianity, astrology became strongly associated with other religious traditions whose philosophical depth and profundity far outweighed Christianity's: Stoicism, a Type I religious philosophy, and the worship of Sol Invictus, the unconquered Sun. The latter was the official religion of the Roman Empire prior to the triumph of Christianity. Although it is usually portrayed as the pagan worship of the Sun, it was a late offshoot of the grandfather of all Type II religions, Zoroastrianism. The Sun was simply a symbol of the god of light and the good. But astrology became very closely associated with Sun worship as it had earlier with Zoroastrianism. The wise men who came to worship the infant Jesus are believed to have been Zoroastrian magi. The New English Bible translates the original Greek as 'astrologers'. This made it necessary for Christianity to discredit astrology, although it never totally did so even in its own ranks.

Astrology had the taint of paganism from that time on, and since anything that was not wholly Christian had to be wholly diabolical, astrology had that taint hanging on it as well. The point, however, is that the conflict was completely religious, rather than scientific or rational.

During the Renaissance things got even worse. Astrology and alchemy became associated with left-wing forms of Christianity, mystical sects with concrete political views. Astrology was thrown out of the universities and out of the mainstream of thought as well. Meanwhile, the mechanist-materialists closely associated themselves with the establishment after some early conflicts and disconnected themselves from astrology as strongly as possible.

Astrology did not come close to dying out because of its inherent unreasonableness. Its near death was due to political and religious factors.

The conflict today is still essentially religious even though there are legitimate scientific questions involved. Why else would an established scientific committee in America falsify the Gauquelin results when they found nothing scientifically wrong with the work? Why else would committees in Europe quietly bury their results when they successfully replicated the Gauquelin results?

The work of Michel and Françoise Gauquelin, limited in scope as it is, is one of the strongest threats to mechanist-materialism in existence. What they have found has no known mechanistic explanation and it will strain the possibilities of mechanism to find one.

The desire to disprove astrology is so strong that a perusal of the literature of conventional scientific investigations of astrology will show some of the worst science ever attempted. The 1986 Carlson paper in *Nature* magazine, flawed as it is in many respects, is of uncharacteristically high quality compared to other similar studies. We find scientists consistently going beyond their expertise, including Carlson, who is not a psychologist, in ways that would not be tolerated in any other study. We find scientists making claims about astrology that astrology does not make, and then 'refuting' them. And we even find cheating as mentioned above. (This is not to say that astrologers have done scientifically superior research, but astrologers at least have the excuse of being both ignorant and untrained in scientific methods.)

What Astrology Must Do

We must face the problem of creating the science of astrology. Addey and the Gauquelins, whatever the future may say about their work, have already made a beginning. We must strive through our work to overthrow the mechanist-materialist worldview. But stating it thus may seem too negative. Let us put it another way.

We must re-establish the idea of the universe as a living, conscious entity of which we are all manifestations – limited, but definitely manifestations. Truth is not 'out there', it is in here, out there and everywhere, and it can be sought in a variety of ways. All the people who find the truth will find it differently and the sum total of all these differences and contradictory truths is the One Truth. The universe is the universe of all possibilities, not merely of some that can be obtained by some particular, limited means.

Physicists are the advance guard of this process. Quantum mechanics, despite the name, has completely rejected the mechanist-materialist worldview although it has not yet found a substitute. There are also students of statistical psychology who are finding things that are completely incompatible with the mechanist-materialist psychology of Behaviourism. There are many others on the barricades with us, but they do not have the tradition or the philosophical underpinnings that we have.

We are going to have a difficult time not only because of external resistance but also because of internal difficulties. While we have to study existing science, especially the social sciences, for suggestions as to methods, we have to be very critical of them as well. We have to distinguish between methods whose function is to maintain mere orthodoxy and methods which are genuinely useful to our work. We also have to recognize the need for modifying existing techniques from other fields and creating completely new ones.

We also have a problem among astrologers, many of whom are antagonistic to the creation of a science of astrology. And there is some legitimacy in what they feel, as already indicated. but they have to recognize the larger issue. If astrology simply persists as it is, it will do very little for the culture as a whole. It will remain a deviant little group doing strange things within their own little world and disregarded by the rest of the world. *Meanwhile the rest of the world will go on treating nature as if it were dead, until it is*. Our existence is threatened, if not already doomed. It is far more important that we do whatever we can to help steer the world away from the death cult in whose grip it now lives. Mechanistic science cannot do anything but destroy life because it has no real comprehension of what life is. In a real sense, astrologers, helping in whatever way they can to support a science of astrology, are acting in self-defence. On the lowest level, a science of astrology may help to legitimize what we do so that people will stop trying to legislate against our activity. But on the highest level it will help to keep the world that we live in alive.

Not every astrologer can, will, or ought to become an astrological scientist. All we can ask is that everyone supports and acknowledges the effort. We must remain unified and work together at whatever level we can or there will be little else worth doing. Astrology will be a truly revolutionary science or there will be no astrology!

Two books which throw a great deal of light on the truth about the 'death' of astrology are the following:
Easlea, Brian, *Witch-Hunting, Magic and the New Philosophy*, 1980.
Berman, Morris, *The Re-Enchantment of the World*, 1984.

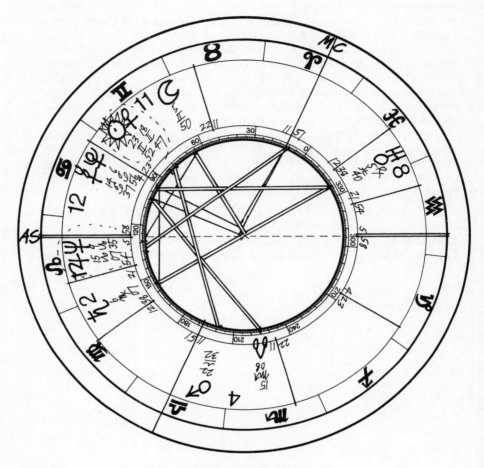

JOHN ADDEY

15 June 1920   8:17 am BST   Barnsley, Yorkshire

John Addey

John Addey was one of the great astrologers. His fundamental insight that all astrological effects can be understood in terms of the harmonics of cosmic periods has provided a unified field theory of astrology, linking it back to the best elements of the scientific tradition and revitalizing its philosophical roots in Neoplatonism and Pythagorean number theory. His visionary work in establishing the Astrological Association and the Urania Trust has provided a secure foundation and support for astrology in Britain and around the world.

At school and college Addey was a very considerable sportsman and athlete, setting records that still remain unbroken. He obtained his Master of Arts degree from St John's College, Cambridge. His serious interest in astrology began whilst he was still at school. However he was all set for a dominantly extrovert 'sporting' life when on 23 December 1943 he was suddenly stricken with ankylosing spondylitis, a form of acute paralysing rheumatism which was to leave him a life-long cripple and constantly fighting pain. Those seventeen months flat on his back, only able to read, drove him inward to the deeper study of both astrology and mystical philosophy. Under the guidance of Charles Carter, who was to be his close friend and mentor until his death in 1968, he joined the Astrological Lodge, serving as its Vice-President from 1951 to 1958. On obtaining his Diploma of the Faculty of Astrological Studies in 1951, he joined the Council of the Faculty of which he was in due course to become a guiding light and Patron. At the same time, he began to undertake professional work in addition to his teaching of severely handicapped children at the Queen Mary Hospital for Sick Children.

In 1955, his dissatisfaction with the confused and uncertain state of much in astrology led him to embark upon a programme of rigorous and systematic research which was to continue for the rest of his life, with the help of volunteers from the AA and in close co-operation with the Gauquelins. Original studies on longevity and poliomyelitis and a reanalysis of the work of Bradley and others caused him to formulate his harmonic wave theory of astrology. This led on to his complete reanalysis of the Gauquelins' work first by hand and then by computer, and the demonstration that the Gauquelins' results contain many deeper and subtler layers of significance than mere angularity. These later results will be published in 1987 and along with his other work open the way to a complete reinvigoration of astrology.

In 1958, Addey inspired Brigadier Roy Firebrace and Joan Rodgers to join him in forming the Astrological Association which was dedicated to the serious development and integration of all aspects of astrology. He was first General Secretary and then President from 21 June 1961 until 11 July 1973, when he became Patron. His editorship of the AA's *Astrological Journal* from 1952 to 1972 established it as the premier journal in the field. In 1970 he set up the Urania Trust, an educational charity dedicated to the advancement of astrology and served as its Chairman until his death. On 24 September 1945, John married Betty Poole, who was to be his life-long support and sustenance, and mother of their three children. His son Timothy John Addey (b. 25 August 1952) continues the family tradition as a student of philosophy and astrology and as a trustee of the Urania Trust.

John Addey Bibliography

Harmonics in Astrology (1976), Cambridge Circle, USA and L. N. Fowler, also in Danish, French, Italian and Japanese.
Harmonics Anthology (1976), Cambridge Circle.
Selected Writings (1976), AFA.
The Discrimination of Birthtypes (1974), Cambridge Circle.
The New Study of Astrology (1987), The Urania Trust.

4

Astrology Reborn

JOHN ADDEY

(Delivered as the second C. E. O. Carter Memorial Lecture to the Astrological Association Conference at Cambridge, September 1971.)

Astrology is evidently about to undergo a rebirth and a period of new growth. It will be no ordinary rebirth and no ordinary period of growth. From being an outcast from the fraternity of sciences, it seems destined to assume an almost central role in scientific thought.

What reasons are there for saying this? In all science there is, or should be, an interplay between the inner and outer, between the idea and the fact, between the conceptual and observational orders. In the larger sense the conceptual dominates the observational, if only because we make our observations and select and interpret our facts in the light of what we believe – in the light of our conception of the kind of reality we are dealing with.

Nevertheless, the external aspect of science plays an important role too, because the changing conditions of the phenomenal world continually require science to be re-expressed and adapted to the solution of new problems.

Another point to notice is this: all human progress is from thesis, through antithesis to a new and higher synthesis. The period of thesis tends to be dogmatic and authoritative, to rely heavily on tradition and to look more to the unchanging world of ideas and so to enjoy a consequently greater stability. The period of antithesis tends to be more sceptical and to try and test the inherited teachings and traditions against actual experience. From the interplay of these two should come a higher and more complete synthesis which represents, in terms of that cycle, maturity and balance.

In order to see where we now stand scientifically in relation to this process, we must review, very briefly, the history of Western thought during the past two millennia.

Before the Renaissance there had been a long period in which a certain

43

view of the universe (within and without, spiritual and material) had prevailed. It was a thoroughly ordered view of things. Theocentric and hierarchical in conception, it was above all rational, in the true sense, for it saw all things proceeding from a Divine First Cause, through secondary and subsidiary causes to the last and least of manifested things.

The whole essence of this system was its orderly procession from unity into multiplicity. Every part was subordinated to a larger whole which, being dynamic, expressed itself through the parts of which it was the parent and origin. Without the presubsistent whole the parts would not have existed, nor would have had any reason for existing. It was a system in which matter was considered to be passive, receptive and inert, and in which spirit was considered to be active, creative, dynamic and the source of all intelligibility in the worlds of form.

Between spirit and matter, this worldview conceived of a third principle which is called Soul, which was partly like one and partly like the other and was the intermediary by which the realities of the higher and inner were communicated to, and manifested in, the outer and lower.

This was the great thesis which men inherited at the time of the Renaissance. It had been enunciated by Pythagoras and Plato (though it was not original to them), fortified with other elements in the thought of antiquity and taken up by Christian philosophers and theologians to provide a continuous tradition of thought, which retained its essential character right down to the Middle Ages.

This was the tradition of which the true astrology has always been an integral part, for in its hierarchy of productive principles the primary cosmic substances had a necessary place. In the words of the Platonists the heavenly bodies were 'the first-born thoughts of God'; 'born', that is, in the sense that they were the primary lives of the manifested universe. Astrology was as homogeneous with the thought of Pythagoras and Plato as it was with that of St Thomas Aquinas and St Albertus Magnus in the thirteenth century.

But sooner or later, if man is to progress, thesis must be followed by antithesis. That which has become the settled dogma must be challenged, at whatever cost, or human thought crystallizes into rigid forms which stifle progress and in the later Middle Ages this rigidity had, indeed, set in.

Just as the thesis had been that the spiritual and unmanifested world was the primary reality, so the antithesis must needs be that the manifest and material world was real. And so, at the beginning of the so-called Renaissance, men began to turn their observational powers with an altogether new enthusiasm upon the world about them. Increasingly, they began to place their confidence in observed facts and to reach inductively from these observations to their own conclusions about the nature of things.

In the absolute, if not the immediate sense, this was a retrogressive step, for in abandoning a hierarchy of principles rooted in intelligible causes, they overthrew the basis of all higher philosophy and, indeed, of all rational thought. For how can reason flourish where matter, the very principle of unreason, is taken as the starting-point of science?

To quote A. N. Whitehead from *Science and the Modern World:*

> Science has never shaken off its origin in the historical revolt of the later Renaissance. It has remained a predominantly anti-rationalistic movement, based upon a naive faith. What reasoning it has wanted it has borrowed from mathematics which is a surviving relic of Greek rationalism, following the deductive method . . . Of course the historical revolt was fully justified. It was wanted. It was more than wanted: it was an absolute necessity for healthy progress . . . It was a sensible reaction; but it was not protest on behalf of reason.

Empirical scientists and their converts have constantly declared that astrology is an irrational subject – in contrast, of course, to their own brand of science which they deem to be rational. But this is an inversion of the truth.

In reality, it is always the inner content of facts which gives them their intelligibility. One can never arrive at a larger truth by analysing and reducing things into their component parts; this always leads down into greater materialism and into greater unintelligibility. It is only by inquiring to what higher, co-ordinating formative principle anything is a subject part that one can really make sense of it.

If we stand back a little from the developing course of events so as to see what has really happened and what is happening now, we can see that the scientific tradition of the past three centuries has been no more than a necessary diversion.

When we speak about restricted ideas, the limited horizons and localized beliefs of those who are shut off from the mainstream of thought and life we use the word 'provincial'. But Whitehead points out that it is possible to be provincial in time as well as in space and he suggests that the tradition of modern empirical science is an example of just such provincialism in time. It has been a backwater, astonishingly cut off from the great sweep of human thought, into which scientists have retreated for a while to repair the tools of their trade and to remedy some of the negligence of their immediate predecessors.

We know with what success their labours have been attended. Indeed, the very limitations they imposed upon themselves – or which were imposed upon them by their historical origins – have been the key to their remarkable success in the field of methodology. No one should belittle what is good in these achievements. But they have clearly been gained at a huge cost in the erosion of spiritual values, and not only in spiritual values as such, for all values are rooted in spiritual values.

However, all is not lost; the nadir, in some ways at least, is passed and the situation may yet be saved. If the overthrow of the old order at the time

45

of the Renaissance seemed in retrospect, remarkably swift, the collapse of the central concepts of modern science appears to be taking place far more swiftly; every decade now brings remarkable changes – almost every year.

There are two things which must be emphasized; the first is the supreme importance of the concept which lay at the heart of the old philosophy, of a hierarchy of principles, so that every higher cause is the origin of a multitude of effects on a lower plane, each of which expresses one aspect or function of the whole to which it is subordinated. From this we may understand that the originating idea or substance is not only the cause of its effects but is also, and remains, the organizing unity which gives coherence and intelligibility to their developments and activities, in time as well as in space.

The second thing to emphasize is that this concept has always been one of the essential truths of astrology, and astrology, conversely, has always been an integral and necessary part of the tradition of thought (the 'perennial philosophy') to which this doctrine is central.

As it is true that science is undergoing a transformation in its thinking about first principles, it is to this idea that we must expect it to revert and we may consider what signs are already visible that it is doing just this, and we may enquire how far it has progressed towards recognizing – even if only in a primitive form as yet – the involvement of the heavenly bodies and their motions in this new vision of scientific relationships.

What evidence is there that scientists are moving in the right direction? From symposia held to gather together groups of leading biologists, mathematicians and physicists to explore the possibilities of a 'firmly founded theoretical biology' come arguments along the same theme, and that theme is that the practice of taking things to pieces to unravel their secrets – the process of 'reductionism' as it is now called – does not appear to lead anywhere. The opposite hypothesis – that the nature, purpose and interrelationship of the parts must be considered as subordinate at each stage to their governing wholes – is the one which work in these fields now seems to require.

From the biological viewpoint:

Molecular biology assumes that the instructions for co-ordinating an animal's various parts, for directing it to its 'goals', are coded into the genetic blueprint. But copies of the blueprint sit inside each cell or an organism: how does one blueprint know what instructions all the others are issuing? How does one cell keep in step with another? How does each part 'know its place' in the organism as a whole?

A number of the scientists at Serbelloni emphasised that however this control is achieved, it must be involved with the hierarchical nature of living organisms; each organism consists of organs, which consist of tissues, which consist of cells, which consist of a variety of molecules, which consist of atoms, which consist of fundamental particles . . . At each level the parts serve a whole on the next higher level which somehow organises the parts of which it consists.

(John Davy, *The Observer* magazine, February, 1970.)

The 'reductionist' tradition of science assumes as a matter of course that a complex phenomenon must be explicable in terms of something simpler. The cells must explain the organ, the molecules must explain the cells, etc. Perhaps the most surprising event at Serbelloni was that this assumption was explicitly challenged by a physicist.

Professor David Bohm argued that 'the apparently chance behaviour of particles at one level reflects an orderly pattern at a higher level'. Bohm suggested that there is an analogous situation in biology and that rather than the parts of a living structure determining the whole, the whole may determine the parts. Perhaps 'hierarchies of order' are as fundamental a feature of the universe as 'particles'.

One aspect of the capacity of the dominant whole to organize its subordinate parts which impressed the Serbelloni group most is the self-organization of living things in time: 'At the heart of this problem is one central problem: the organization of living things – their capacity to arrange and maintain their cells and their organs as coherent wholes or "organisms". Again and again the suggestion was made that the answer would have to do with the peculiar relation of living things to time.' And again: 'Whatever ideas and experiments emerge out of this rich and complex endeavour, they are likely to centre on rhythmic processes in time.'

We see that, with suitable cries of astonishment, scientists are groping their way back to the idea of hierarchies of order, orders in which each unitive principle is the parent of a multiplicity of effects at a lower level.

The next step must be the realization that cosmic bodies are the primary unities of the manifested cosmos and that their motions and interrelationship are the primary determinants of the patterns in time – those 'rhythmic processes' – which characterize all natural processes of growth and unfoldment.

The scientific recognition of this should not take more than twenty years, but what prevents it from already being seen is the unmanageable diversity and superabundance of scientific information published today, allied to the natural reluctance and incapacity of scientists (one might say of men in general) to examine thoughtfully results, however scientifically sound, which cannot be readily assimilated with their present concepts and worldview.

The fact is that the past ten or fifteen years have seen a remarkable accumulation of scientific results which point clearly to the relationship between natural phenomena and cosmic forces. Let us consider some of these.

With a continuous programme of extensive and penetrating cycle analysis, the Foundation for the Study of Cycles, of Pittsburgh, Pennsylvania has built up a very large catalogue of well-authenticated cycles in the occurrence of human and natural phenomena in many different fields. Regular cycles of events continue to repeat decade after decade, and in many cases in century after century, in such social phenomena as economic and trade cycles and the occurrence of civil and international strife, not to mention cycles in biological, meteorological and medical phenomena, etc. All these presuppose some higher, unitive, regulating pattern or mechanism which the scientific fraternity has been loath to acknowledge.

In many of these fields scientists are content to observe cyclic phenomena without offering firm conculsions about the originating causes of their cycles, but there can be no doubt that the overwhelming, and growing, body of opinion now looks to extraterrestrial factors as the regulating mechanism. There are countless programmes of research proceeding all over the world into circadian and similar rhythms, very many of which are explicitly related to extraterrestrial causal factors.

An increasing variety of phenomena have been linked with sunspot cycles, which can be described very largely in terms of the harmonics of planetary periods: a discovery which might provide a sound scientific basis for some astrological predictions. 'The radiation from the sun is one of the prime hazards to manned space flight, so we find the curious anomaly that the dates of future space flights might be chosen using the textbook astrological techniques of Kepler to predict periods of low sun-spot activity.' (*The Times*, 5 December 1970.)

When we survey all these many developments in the world of orthodox scientific research, we shall find that the all-pervading concept is that of regular rhythms in the occurrence of natural and human phenomena.

If we turn to the world of astrological research, in all the leading examples of such work (and here I must include the work of Professor Gauquelin) the same concept is to be found; that of regularly recurring rhythms.

Only by seeing astrology in terms of the harmonics of cosmic periods can we begin the task of re-expressing our study in all its manifestations, in clear scientific – I mean really scientific – terms. In this respect, exactly the same principles underlie both astrology and all those subjects of inquiry which I have mentioned as now attracting the attention of orthodox science. There is no longer any dividing line, in principle, between them.

What we have in place of a dividing line is a graduated assortment of scientific results, some of which look like the familiar products of orthodox scientific inquiry, some of which seem to belong quite clearly to the field of astrology, and some of which could belong to either. To complicate matters, some of the first group have been produced by astrologers while some of the second have been produced by opponents of astrology. But they all embody the same principles and will ultimately be seen to belong to one science, the name of which is Astrology.

It is true that there are many astrologers who have misgivings about attempts to approach astrology through the methods of science. 'How do we know,' they say, 'that if we begin by adopting their methods we shall not end by adopting their philosophy?' This is not the position at all! How could scientists, as we have been accustomed to think of them, convert us to their way of thinking when they are no longer able to sustain their old beliefs themselves? We are not even in the position of a David pitting our strength against the Goliath of Modern Science. Science today – and I am speaking of the heart and core of the scientific worldview which has prevailed for the past 300-odd years – is not so much like a Goliath as like a great simpleton who is even now in the process of falling over his own boot-laces into the dust from which he will not rise again.

I hope indeed that we shall become more scientific in our methods, but we certainly need not fear their philosophy when they themselves are already deserting it in order to rejoin the road which we have never left. There is a difference between us and orthodox scientists and it is simply this: we have a clearer grasp of the principles towards which they are now turning.

Modern science has far greater resources than we have and their methods are better, but their thinking about scientific problems is behind ours. This is why I have taken the opportunity to set the present situation in its historical context, because unless we understand our position – our strengths and weaknesses *vis-à-vis* modern science – and shake off our timidity about it, we shall not have the confidence to take advantage of our basically strong position or the open-mindedness to move forward to that synthesis of the best elements in those two worldviews mentioned previously – thereby making use of the valuable methods developed by science to help us, where necessary, in clarifying and rethinking and re-expressing the principles of our science.

What then are the principles regarding which I believe we have a fresh opportunity to clarify and reformulate? Obviously they are manifold but there are certain key ideas which lie at the heart of our science, which we all tacitly recognize, which have the widest applicability for us, but which we have now come to see only in terms of rigid traditional concepts that have been drastically oversimplified. I would like to look closely at one of these ideas and show how a fresh approach could revitalize our thinking and our grasp of practical procedures.

Astrology belongs inherently to that tradition which sees the whole manifest cosmos as being brought forth by a hierarchy of principles, proceeding from unity to multiplicity by stages, stages in which each superior principle is the parent of a number of effects at a lower level, each one of which, in turn, has its own centre and unity from which still further effects proceed at a yet lower level.

In the procession from unity to diversity it is the character and properties of the successive formative principles which determine the number and variety of the subordinate effects and also the number of stages through which they pass in their unfolding. For this reason the symbolism of number is an integral part of astrology; it is embedded in all the rules of horoscopy and we use it, consciously or unconsciously, in every facet of our science.

Alongside this one may place the rediscovery of the fact, always implicit in the rules of astrology, that the symbolism of number is expressed primarily through the harmonic relationships of planets in the circle.

Pythagoras taught that there were only nine basic numbers and that all numbers beyond nine were repetitions. Our system of numeration exemplifies this, for we use only nine numbers plus a nought to indicate a return to unity and the beginning of a new cycle. (That is, when we reach nine we return to one with a nought after it.)

What is the explanation of this? It lies in the truth that all things, between their innermost unity and their outermost expression, pass through nine stages. There are those who believe that distinctions of this sort are merely arbitrary conceptions of the human mind which have no reality other than that given to them by our own thoughts. This is a heresy which has arisen as a by-product of an era of scientific materialism which cannot conceive of inner realities except in these terms.

The characteristic of the number nine of marking out the successive stages of unfolding of an idea is the reason why, in numerology, it is customary to add up the digits of any number in order to arrive at the root number from which it is dervied. What one is really doing, when one adds up the digits of any number, is finding out what is the root number in which a larger number had its origin in a series of ninefold progressions. Here we have a piece of occult lore which has seldom been clearly explained but which is now confirmable and explicable in scientific terms. This was brought home to me when we had the Sun-positions in all the available collections of data held by the Astrological Association subjected to harmonic analysis by computer. These included some 20,000 sets of birth data. From the collected data of 7,302 doctors of medicine the Sun's longitude was tabulated according to the total number of times it occupied each degree of the ecliptic. The distribution was then subjected to harmonic analysis in order to discover the rhythms present in the distribution. The harmonic which shows the highest amplitude of any of the 180 possible harmonics is the twelfth – which may be said to correspond to the traditional twelvefold division of the zodiac, showing the most vigorous presence of all rhythms governing the solar distribution. But the point with which we are here concerned is the procession by nines and their harmonics throughout the series, particularly those harmonics which fall at intervals of nine places from the 7th, that is the 16th, 25th, 34th, 43th, 52nd, and so on, all numbers of which the digits add up to seven. I call these successive subsistences of the number seven.

What it amounts to is that each one of these sets of birth data – doctors, artists, nonagenarians, etc. – are, when analysed in this way, just like different crystalline substances, each one characterized by a different numerical structure.

Over half a century ago D'Arcy Thompson, in his memorable book *On Growth and Form*, commented on the reluctance of morphologists (in contrast to, say, astronomers or chemists) to raise their study to a science by the proper employment of mathematics. It was as if they saw in the teeming forms of nature, in the lineaments of the growing plant or the convolutions of the snail's shell, mysteries too deep and too varied to lie within the scope of clear numerical expression. Yet Thompson and others have since shown how mathematical laws are at work in all the forms of nature.

Now science must learn that the lineaments of human character and convolutions of destiny, too, fall no less within the scope of number; for if it is true that God made 'every plant of the field before it was in the earth, and every herb of the field before it grew', it is no less true that He measured the ways of man before He was in the womb, and made Him an embodiment of ideal and divine numbers.

The principle described in my work is that the hierarchical arrangement of the principles in the human constitution gives the key to the descriptive harmonic relationship between the appropriate points in the horoscope. This is quite simply the 'quantum' principle expressed in terms of natural man. Intelligence is above nature, but Soul works on matter through nature. Once that is established we can immediately go much further.

All the characteristics of the physical body are determined by the genetic make-up, and are transmitted genetically from parent to child. But the body is what it is because man is what he is; all the parts of the body are an expression of the inner constitution of man. If the body is to be a true vehicle for the whole man then there must be an appropriate part or attribute of body corresponding to every one of his inner and higher attributes. The body is like a physical microcosm; its every detail is an expression of something in human nature as a whole.

For this reason, the harmonic relationships in the horoscope, immensely complex as they are, provide the basis of a complete genetic code and a total description of the genetic characteristics communicated from one generation to the next. I have chosen this particular application of the doctrine of harmonics because the science of genetics has been for some time a focus of interest in the scientific world.

The position is that geneticists now know or can deduce a great deal about the genetic transmission, its nature and processes. For this reason, and with the prospect dangling before us of being able to improve genetic strains and eliminate inherited disorders, there has been much talk about what is called genetic engineering – that is, the direct mechanical

51

interference with the genetic process to accomplish these apparently desirable objects.

In the accepted view of genetics, inherited traits are individually determined by genes by which there are conceived to be many thousands within each chromosome – forty-six chromosomes in the case of man. But R. C. Lewontin of the University of Chicago indicating that inherited traits do not normally appear singly but in associated groups determined by their chromosomal origin, declares that the new picture which is emerging is one in which genes entirely disappear, leaving only the chromosomes as whole.

This is another example of the assumption of parts with wholes and it is fully in accord with the astrological picture where groups of associated traits are regarded as springing from one astrological factor, and especially with the concept of harmonics where the same principle is brought into much sharper focus.

In this connection, one may ask if the time is not rapidly coming when geneticists, turning away from the laboratory approach, will gain far more enlightenment as to the nature and structure of the genetic inheritance from considering the statement of the Neoplatonic philosopher, Proclus, that there are in the soul 105,947 monads. A monad, in this context, being one centre or unit in the hierarchy of principles (called by Koestler, 'holons'), from each of which flows a range of subordinate effects at a lower level.

I have described in particular one application of the law concerning the harmonics of cosmic periods: that in relation to genetics. But its implications are vast and it can be applied throughout the whole field of science. The knowledge that the number of every substance is a submultiple of its originating substance (and I use the word substance in its philosophical sense as applying to spiritual as well as natural substances) will be one of the central pillars of the science of the future. It has already been acknowledged in one field in the form of the quantum theory of physics and, as we see, is becoming a source of interest in other respects. But this principle is of universal applicability and is the key as much to new forms of curative medicine as to the discovery of new forms of power based on the principle of resonance. It is, in fact, the key to all vibratory phenomena.

One result of these developments in the sphere of astrology will be a very great increase in the predictive potential of our science, and I am speaking now of the new and enlarged astrology which is also the true astrology.

Are we prepared for such an increase of predictive power? It has been said that humanity has already passed, in recent centuries, through three demoralizing experiences. The first was the realization, through the Copernican revolution in astronomy, that the earth was not at the centre of the universe and to many this had the effect of seeming to dwarf the significance of humanity. The second was the Darwinian contribution to science which, again, seemed to many to humble humanity still further. The third was the advent of modern psychology which showed just how far we are the puppet of unrecognized drives and pressures from the irrational side of our nature.

In so far as the construction placed upon these three discoveries by some was demeaning to humanity, it was a mistaken interpretation. Our true nature and dignity was really undiminished by any of them.

But a fourth and still more shattering experience lies just around the corner and its impact will be felt in the next twenty years. It is the revelation of just how far the ebb and flow of human events and activities take place in response to all the various pressures of cosmic forces.

The reaction to this discovery – which will be fortified by many different kinds of scientific evidence – may be severe and a wave of fatalism may sweep over humanity. Nevertheless, in the long run the experience will be a salutary and beneficial one, for post-Renaissance humanity has come to accept a totally false view of the nature of free will, and to believe that it consists in subjugating the environment to our own self-interest (usually a very narrow self-interest) in defiance not only of the natural order but, often, of the moral order too.

This is a totally false kind of freedom. True religion has always pointed humanity the way, and astrology has always been on the side of the true religion, for it is a God-centred science. But when the established church weakly turned its back upon astrology at the behest of a debased science, it lost its strongest ally. If it had upheld the right position of astrology as carefully as did, for example, Albertus Magnus and Aquinas, the story might have been different. As it is, it lost its grip on certain first principles and by degrees the allegiance of the people.

Taking the long view, we can see that it is not until man has been forced to the realization of just how far, and in what respect, he is not free, that he will be able to see clearly wherein his true dignity and liberty do consist, and that these, when they are realized, stand above nature and above all the fatal revolutions of the heavens.

Then indeed, if we are not in the meantime overtaken by Nemesis, we can begin, with safety and humility, to build a golden age. But I suspect, as the Duke of Wellington might have said, that it will be a damned close-run thing!

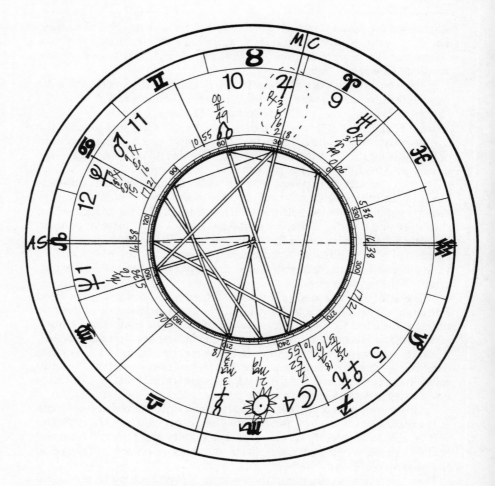

MICHEL GAUQUELIN

13 November 1928   10:20 pm GMT   Paris, France

Michel Gauquelin

Michel Gauquelin is probably the most controversial and celebrated researcher into astrology. He began his researches as a youth in the late 1940s and has spent his life assessing evidence for and against cosmic influences. To date he has gathered almost half a million birth-times of famous and ordinary people from Europe and the USA — all with birth certificates.

Michel studied psychology and statistics at the Sorbonne. His first book, *L'Influence des Astres, Etude Critique et Experimentale* (The Influence of the Stars, a critical and empirical study), published in 1955 in Paris, aroused considerable interest. In this book he first presented the 'Mars effect' of sports champions, and other relationships between birth-times, planets and careers. Later he demonstrated the strong links between planets and personality, and the role of heredity in them.

Since 1969, he has been the director of the Laboratoire d'Etude des Relations entre Rythmes Cosmiques et Psychophysiologiques (LERRCP), based in Paris. He is the author of more than twenty books about psychology and astrology, translated into several languages. He has also published, alone and in collaboration with his former wife, Françoise Schneider-Gauquelin, thirty scientific monographs and more than one hundred articles.

Michel Gauquelin has, since 1967, been editor of a series of books devoted to psychology, and since 1970 has been a scientific consultant for the French magazine *Psychologie*. He is a member of the: International Society of Chronobiology; International Society of Sport Psychology; International Society of Biometeorology; International Committee for the Study of Ambient Factors and the Society for Scientific Exploration formed for the Study of Anomalous Phenomena. In 1969, he was awarded a medal for psychological writings from the 16th Congress of Health, Ferrara, Italy. Gauquelin is currently working on planets at the birth of ordinary people and also in search of a possible 'causal' mechanism for explaining his discoveries.

Proponents and opponents to astrology agree about the importance of Michel Gauquelin's work — he was the first to use a sound methodology and the most hostile scientists did not find any error in the positive results he published. The significance of Gauquelin's claims is emphasized by

Arthur Mather, co-author with Geoffrey Dean of *Recent Advances in Natal Astrology*:

> Both those who are for and against astrology (in the broadest sense) as a serious field for study, recognize the importance of Gauquelin's work. It is probably not putting it too strongly to say everything (the evidence for any substantial kind of astrology) hangs on it.

Michel Gauquelin Bibliography

L'Influence des Astres (1955)
Les Hommes et les Astres (1960)
L'Heredite Planetaire (1966a)
The Cosmic Clocks (1973 and new edition 1982)
The Mars Effect and the Sports Champions: A New Replication, Series D, Volume 6 (1979)
Your Personality and the Planets (1980), and as *The Spheres of Destiny* (1981)
Zodiac and Character Traits (Statistical Tests of Zodiacal Influences), Series D, Volume 8 (1981)
Report on American Data, Series D, Volume 10 (1982a)
The Truth About Astrology (1983a), also as *Birthtimes* (1984)
Cosmic Influences on Human Behaviour (1983b); (new revised edn 1985)
2145 Physicians, Army Leaders, Top Executives (1984b)
1540 Authors, Actors, Politicians, Journalists (1984c)

With Françoise Schneider-Gauquelin:
Birth and Planetary Data Gathered Since 1949, 6 vols (1970)
Psychological Monographs, 4 vols (1973–77)
Statistical Tests on Zodiacal Influences. Part I: Profession and Heredity, Series D, Volume 3 (1978)

5

Neo-astrology: Forty Years of Research

MICHEL GAUQUELIN

'You shouldn't dismiss as incredible the possibility that a long enough search might reveal a golden grain of truth in astrological superstitition' was the advice of the great Renaissance astronomer Kepler. In all modesty I might claim to have proved Kepler right when I describe my work and the surprising results I have obtained. For I believe that I have shown a link between the positions of some planets at birth and human characteristics and career.

I started to verify the claims of astrology scientifically in the late 1940s, but the verdict of my statistical control was not often favourable to astrology. For instance, I found no confirmation of some main principles of the horoscope like the influence of the signs of the zodiac, the reality of the astrological aspects, the meaning of the houses or the prediction of the future. I also analysed in detail the statistical evidence proposed by the well-known astrologers Paul Choisnard, Karl E. Krafft and others. I was not able to replicate their findings and pointed out the lack of a sound methodology used by them. Through the years until recently, I have made several attempts to test again the validity of zodiacal signs or aspects between planets using more refined approaches and larger samples. However, I have still failed to get positive results.

Planetary Effects and Successful Professionals

But not all the results of my labours were negative. Beginning in 1951, I gathered the birth-times of successful French people of several professions and realized that the distribution of certain planetary positions diverged sharply from the norm. The results could not just be written off as chance – any statistician would have found them 'very significant'. L'Influence des Astres (1955) contains my observations together with the 6,000 birth data on which they were based. It was in this book – unfortunately not available in English translation as yet – that I described what has become known as the 'Mars effect' – the very strong tendency for champion athletes to be born when the planet Mars has just risen over the horizon in sector 1 or just

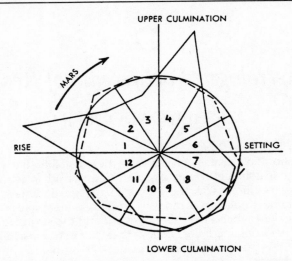

Figure 5.1 The Mars effect at the birth of well-known sports champions

The circle represents the expected frequencies.
Solid line: distribution of Mars in 12 sectors at the birth of 2,088 sports champions. They tend to be born more often after the rise of Mars (sector 1) and after its upper culmination (sector 4);
Dotted line: distribution of Mars at the birth of 717 ordinary sportmen. The peaks of births after the rise and the culmination of Mars have disappeared. The two curves were drawn at the same scale in order to allow the comparison.

(from Gauquelin, 1960 and 1983)

crossed its upper culmination in sector 4. The phenomenon is seen far more often at the birth of high-ranking athletes than for low-ranking athletes. Sectors 1 and 4 (Figure 5.1) roughly correspond to the twelfth and ninth astrological houses; they are often referred as 'key sectors' (Zelen, 1976) or as 'Gauquelin Plus Zones'.

As some readers may already know, the Mars effect has been under sceptical scrutiny by hostile scientists for several years. In many recent publications more details about this intense two decade-long controversy are given (Rawlins, 1981; Curry, 1982). Suffice to say here that American scientists involved in testing the validity of my claims, UCLA astronomer George Abell, SUNY-Buffalo philosopher Paul Kurtz and Harvard statistician Marvin Zelen eventually acknowledged the accuracy of my methodology in their own journal: 'Gauquelin adequately allowed for demographic and astronomical factors in predicting the expected distribution of Mars sectors for birth times in the general population' (Abell, Kurtz, Zelen, 1983).

Needless to say, the Mars effect at the birth of sports champions is just one among the many findings I observed. For instance, Jupiter was found

Table 5.1 Frequency of planets in sectors 1 and 4 for famous professionals

Group	Planet	Exp	Act	Computer results (rise/set sectors) Diff	Prob
2088 champions	Mars	358.5	435	+ 76.5	.00002
3647 scientists	Mars	626.2	703	+ 76.8	.001
	Jupiter	602.5	547	− 55.5	.05
	Saturn	598.0	685	+ 87.0	.0001
3438 soldiers	Mars	590.3	662	+ 71.7	.002
	Jupiter	575.1	686	+ 110.9	.000001
5100 artists	Mars	875.7	773	− 102.7	.0002
	Saturn	828.0	744	− 84.0	.003
1409 actors	Jupiter	234.0	273	+ 39.0	.01
1003 politicians	Jupiter	166.4	202	+ 35.6	.002
1352 writers	Moon	225.4	288	+ 62.6	.00001

Source Gauquelin, *Correlation*, May 1984.

to be linked with success in politics, cinema, theatre and journalism; Saturn with success in science; the Moon was found to be favourable for writers; Mars for military leaders, top executives and physicians. Significant clusters of planetary positions were found after the rise (sector 1) and after the upper culmination (sector 4) at the moment of birth of outstanding professionals.

Results found in France have been successfully replicated through the gathering and testing of 18,000 other European celebrities' birth data. These observations were published in my second book *Les Hommes et les Astres* (1960). In 1970, my laboratory undertook to publish, in six volumes, the birth and planetary data gathered since 1949, enabling all interested scientists to verify my material and conclusions. Table 5.1 gives the main results recently checked and re-evaluated by computer from these data.

In 1982, new replications using 1,400 eminent Americans and fresh samples of mostly French Europeans also produced positive results.

The Planetary Factors in Personality

Profession-planet relationships are not distributed randomly, but present an internal structure that must be taken into consideration in order to understand the results (Figure 5.2).

Moreover, there is the 'eminence effect'. When I tested low-ranking people of the same professions in 1955, the results showed new cluster groupings. Thus it was not the profession itself that showed a correspon-

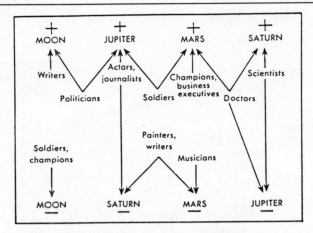

Figure 5.2 The Structure of the Results

The + sign means: high frequency of births after rise and culmination;
The − sign means: low frequency of births after rise and culmination.
The arrows indicate the significant bonds that have been observed between a profession and
a planet. These profession–planet relationships are not distributed randomly, but have an
internal structure that must be taken into consideration in order to understand the results.
(from Gauquelin, 1955 & 1983)

dence to cosmic factors but something more individual. I thought that
strength of character, and not merely good luck, provides a renowned
person with the capability to succeed at the highest level in his occupation.
Greek philosophers noted long ago that man's character makes his destiny. Accordingly, I suggested that the real correlation is not so much a link
between planets and success but between planets and personality factors.
Sports champions, for instance, are energetic and brave, and their times of
birth seem usually linked to Mars. Is there a relationship between the
planet Mars and the personality traits that go to make up a sports champion? One could extend this hypothesis for the other groups as well. What
all of these planetary oddities reveal is not luck or fate, but the working of
various personality factors associated with the planets and very probably,
of genetic origin.

In order to test this hypothesis in 1967 I devised a scientific technique
called the 'character traits method'. Helped by Françoise Schneider-
Gauquelin, I gathered character traits from thousands of biographical texts
about successful people. For the character trait material, we used the same
set of people as before, but collected their biographies. I based my procedure on the idea that there are permanent character traits such as those
defined by J. P. Chaplin in his *Dictionary of Psychology*, 'a relatively persist-
ent and consistent behaviour pattern manifested in a wide range of circumstances'. For each trait we opened a file, carrying on one side the subject's

name and on the other the position of the planetary factors at his birth. What we did for one subject, we repeated for other celebrities, using published accounts of their personality. This gave us files on more than 50,000 personality trait-units taken systematically from biographies of 2,000 subjects – sports champions, actors, men of science, and writers. Let us note that the use of biographies and personality descriptions in ordinary language is a classical approach employed or praised by the leading specialists in the field of the psychology of personality (Allport and Odbert, 1936; Bromley, 1977; Cattell, 1965; Eysenck, 1970).

Data were published by my laboratory in four 'Psychological Monographs'. The character-trait material demonstrates that the link between planetary positions at birth and personality traits is stronger than the correlation between these positions and professional success. Our research describes five planetary types: Jupiter, Saturn, Mars, Venus and the Moon. Despite our best efforts, nothing significant shows up for the Sun, Mercury or the planets beyond Saturn.

Table 5.2 provides a list of character traits that tend to belong to individuals born with Jupiter, Saturn, Mars, Venus or the Moon in the Gauqelin Plus Zones, i.e. in the astrological house placements described above. Two of my books explore the links between planets and temperament in detail (1980, 1983). In 1982, the results of a positive replication based upon a cata-

Table 5.2 Extract of twenty traits describing planetary types

Jupiter	Saturn	Mars	Venus	Moon
ambitious	cold	active	affable	amiable
authoritarian	concentrated	ardent	agreeable	disorganised
conceited	conscientious	belligerent	ambiguous	dreamer
gay (merry)	discreet	brave	attractive	easy-going
harsh	introvert	combative	beloved	fashionable
humorous	methodical	daring	benevolent	friendly
independent	meticulous	dynamic	charming	generous
ironical	modest	energetic	considerate	good company
lively	observer	fearless	courteous	good hearted
mocking	precise	fighter	elegant	helpful
prodigal	reserved	lively	flattering	imaginative
proud	sad	offensive	gallant	impressionable
show off	simple	reckless	gracious	impulsive
social climber	sombre	spontaneous	juvenile	merry
spendthrift	stiff	strong-willed	kind	nonchalant
talkative	taciturn	stormy	obliging	popular
warm	thoughtful	tireless	pleasant	socialite
well-off	timid	tough	poetic	spontaneous
witty	uncommunicative	valiant	polite	superficial
worldly	wise	vitality (full of)	seductive	tolerant

Source Gauquelin, *The Truth about Astrology*, 1983.

logue of 5,000 character trait-units collected from the biographies of well-known Americans were published.

Some modern personality research has proved very useful. Professor Hans Eysenck of the University of London, whose work on personality factors has been internationally recognized, was kind enough to express interest in my work several years ago. Eysenck and his wife Sybil described three fundamental personality dimensions – the E dimension on which you can range from introversion to extraversion; the N dimension on which you can range from emotional stability to instability; and the P dimension along which a person can be ranked from tough-minded to tender-minded. The Eysencks tested the hypothesis that there is a relationship between their personality dimensions and planetary temperaments. Jupiter and Mars, the planets of actors, politicians and soldiers, should be linked to introversion. The results of the experiment vindicated this hypothesis. The converging results of the Eysencks' work and our own have been published using the European data (Gauquelin, Gauquelin and Eysenck, 1979) then were replicated using the American data (Gauquelin, Gauquelin and Eysenck, 1981).

Gauquelin Plus Zones v. Astrological Houses

Astrologers need to know how to translate my scientific findings into the language of the horoscope. I will do my best to help them make this transition.

That the presence of Jupiter, Saturn, Mars, Venus or the Moon in a certain position at birth is related to our personality has important implications. It can help us to understand ourselves and other people better. Everyone can gain insight into their own character, given that they know where and when they were born.

The fundamental question becomes whether a planet is in a zone of high or weak intensity at the time of birth. According to my results there are four zones of high intensity, called 'Gauquelin Plus Zones': when a planet is rising; when it has crossed its upper culmination; when it is setting; and when it is at its lower culmination, the point midway between setting and rising. A person born with a planet in one of these four zones is likely to show the temperament associated with that planet. There is a distinction to be drawn between two sets of zones. The most powerful correlation between planetary position and character traits exists when a planet is either rising or at its upper culmination. The other two significant positions – when a planet is setting or at its lower culmination – are linked with personality, but in a less dramatic way. If a planet is neither rising, culminating, setting nor at its lower culmination, then it is in a zone of weak intensity. If a planet is in such a position when a person is born, it is unlikely that the individual will exhibit the personality traits I have found associated

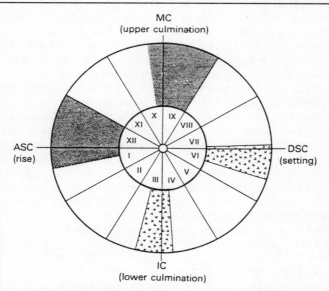

Figure 5.3   Gauquelin Plus Zones v. Horoscope Houses

(for explanation see text)

with that planet. But what do these terms 'rise, culmination', and 'setting' mean astrologically speaking? If you know your birth chart you can immediately see which planet(s) are in Gauquelin Plus Zones without extra astronomical calculations. (It is preferable to use the Placidus house system which is astronomically closest to the rising/setting division I have used in my research.)

In Figure 5.3, the Gauquelin Plus Zones are superimposed on the twelve astrological houses (I,II, . . .XII). If the Moon or one of the planets is situated in one of the shaded areas, then it is in one of the Gauquelin Plus Zones. The rising zone corresponds to the XIIth house and the third of the Ist house which is closest to the ascendant (ASC); the culmination zone corresponds to the IXth house and the third of the Xth house which is closest to the Midheaven (MC). If the Moon or one of the planets is situated in one of the stippled areas, it is in a high intensity zone; but not as high in intensity as the shaded areas. This is the case when the planet is at the descendant or in that part of the VIth house which is closest to the descendant or when the planet is at the Imum Coelii (IC) or in that part of the IIIrd house which is closest to the IC.

Gauquelin's Findings and Astrological Tradition

Having translated my observations into astrological language, to what extent can one see these results as a confirmation of the doctrine of astrology? In astrology's favour my work has demonstrated a fundamental assumption – the role played by planetary influences at the moment of birth. Believers in astrology may also point out that the Gauquelin Plus Zones seem to vindicate an important astrological claim i.e. that the 'angles' of the horoscope – mainly the Ascendant and the Midheaven – are prominent. A (rising) planet is in conjunction to the Ascendant; a culminating planet is in conjunction to the Midheaven. But the fact that the Gauquelin Plus Zones are on the side of the 'cadent houses' (XII and IX) rather than on the side of the 'angular houses' (I and X) must puzzle many astrologers: according to astrology a planet situated in a 'cadent house' at birth acts at its weakest. The shift in emphasis to cadent houses demonstrated by my observations raises some very serious interpretative problems for the practice of astrology and cannot be dismissed, because they are based upon thousands of observations.

More favourable to the astrological doctrine is the traditional symbolism attributed to the planets. Since my first positive results, it has been evident that there may be something true – but only partly true – in planetary symbolism. Planetary symbolism is firmly anchored in our minds, and our everyday language has preserved the astrological meanings of the planets. Consider these dictionary definitions (from Webster):

Saturnine: born under the influence of the planet Saturn, which tends to make people morose; of a gloomy temper; heavy; grave.
Martial: from Mars, the God of War; military; warlike.
Jovial: the planet Jupiter was believed to make those born under it of a jovial temperament; merry; joyous; jolly.

Likewise, the words 'mercurial, moony, lunatic and venereal' are part of our everyday vocabulary. There has been a surprising similarity between the descriptions of planetary influences attributed to the Moon, Jupiter, Saturn, Mars and Venus since the origin of astrology.

My statistical studies could lead to a partial restoration of the very old planetary symbolism which has been transmitted from one astrologer to another over the centuries. Investigations in recent years demonstrate the reality of such a restoration.

It is also true that my findings do not vindicate some of the major claims of astrology. For instance, the results with zodiac signs and with aspects are still negative. Even my positive observations cannot be interpreted as a verification of orthodox astrology, but rather as heterodox effects. But West and Toonder in *The Case for Astrology* (1973) do not hesitate to write: 'Gauquelin's work proves once and for all and incontestably that there is something to astrology. . . Gauquelin has given quantitative expression to an ancient qualitative belief: i.e. that the planets are meaningful.'

If I am right, and I hope I am, that the planets are 'meaningful', I would hope to see an increasing number of astrologers accept the importance of the Gauquelin work, even if it means taking a new look at astrology – perhaps especially if it means taking a new look at astrology.

Neo-Astrology: In Search of an Explanation

Astrological or not, planetary influences are difficult to explain. Is a child's personality determined by astral rays which mark it with an indelible stamp? A child comes into the world fully formed with all potential elements inherited from its parents. We cannot accept that the planets have an effect on the chromosome structure of the child's cells and that it can change and redistribute these to bring about a change in the personality. The planet would not be able to add anything that the child did not already have. The effect of the planets would seem to be more acceptable if their role could be associated with heredity.

The work of biologists and psychologists, E. Kretchmer of the University of Tubingen and W. Sheldon of Harvard University in particular, shows us that there is a hereditary basis for the predispositions of temperament. This area is also touched on by H. J. Eysenck in his work *The Biological Basis of Personality*. We even hear about a so-called biochemistry of behaviour linked to the genetic make-up since the publication of research work by the Michigan Institute and the University of Edinburgh on the uric acid content of the blood in relation to certain kinds of social behaviour. As the position of astral bodies is an indicator of character tendencies, these tendencies must be inherited. Children must come into the world under the same planetary conditions as their parents.

I have been able to confirm this hypothesis with an experiment using 30,000 births of children and their parents, selected from civil registers. Children tend to be born when a planet has just risen or passed its point of culmination if the same planet was in the same part of the sky when one of the parents was born. The planetary effect in heredity is weak, but in the light of the large number of births considered, the probability of chance is in the range of one in 500,000. The effect is doubled at the birth of a child if both parents were born at the rising or culmination of the same planet. Nevertheless, the tendency is only significant with the planets that are either near to the Earth (the Moon, Venus and Mars) or large (Jupiter and Saturn), all of which are clearly visible to the naked eye. No hereditary similarity is observed for distant planets such as Uranus, Neptune or Pluto, or for Mercury, the smallest planet in our solar system.

A child seems to be endowed with a 'planetary sensitivity' which brings about his moment of birth at a certain time in the diurnal course of a planet. The planet does not modify the organism of the child, but rather acts as a trigger to his birth and its position in the sky is a witness to the psycho-biologicál temperament of the new-born child. But we have not solved all problems at this stage. How can we justify the planetary effect in heredity? There is a biological problem and also an astronomical one – which we will now consider.

The Unknown Biological Aspect and the Unknown Astronomical Aspect

First we will look at the unknown biological aspect of the problem. We know that in medicine it can take nothing at all to trigger off the birth of a baby, when it is due. This 'nothing' could be linked to certain subtle cosmic factors. The child could react to a cosmic 'indication' that his particular hereditary type demonstrates more clearly than any other. This hypothesis has the merit of being in accordance with the most recent medical observations. The work carried out by G. C. Liggins of the Women's Hospital of the University of Auckland, New Zealand, established without any doubt that it is the foetus that acts first when the moment of birth has arrived. The very complex mechanism would appear to be of a hormonal nature. Observations by Liggins and his successors have been the subject of recent international symposia.

What happens when a doctor interferes with the normal process of birth, either through surgery (Caesarian section) or by induction by means of a chemical compound? Our controls show that in such cases the planetary influence in heredity disappears. Medical interference destroys the influence of the cosmic indication. The position of the planet at the time of birth is no longer relevant to the type of personality.

There remains the unknown astronomical aspect of the problem. How does a planet influence the start of the birth process? It would seem to have the function of a catalyst or a screen in the solar field. A recent experiment established that the planetary effect in heredity was twice as marked in children born on a day of strong solar activity than children born on days with less solar activity.

For more than twenty years technological progress has enabled us to record a number of effects on our globe from the planets apart from their simple reflection of light from the Sun: radio-electric emissions, gravitational disturbances, modulation of the Earth's magnetism, etc. Such planetary effects could also have certain biological consequences, namely to affect the very delicate hormonal balances that are created during the birth process. A demonstration of the result of these biological planetary effects has yet to be carried out.

The future will tell us if we can accomplish such a demonstration. Specialists agree that the biological and psychological rhythms of humanity are tied by invisible strings to different clocks in the cosmos. The ancients already knew all this intuitively, and I wonder about it in the pages of my latest book, *Cosmic Influences on Human Behaviour* (1985):

The observation of planetary effects at birth would demonstrate that the age-old, good-for-nothing, fossilized astrology was not pure legend after all. And that is the source of scientific opposition to my work – the fear that an 'astrological' Copernican revolution would destroy a particular vision of the universe and shatter belief in a scientific creed which has excluded 'neo-astrology', just as it ignored the intuition of the Chaldean priest.

Bibliographical References

Abell, G., Kurtz, P. and Zelen, M. 1983: *The Skeptical Inquirer*

Allport, G. W. and Odbert, H. S. 1936. 'Trait-Names: A Psycholexical Study', *Psychological Review,* vol. 47, no. 1

Bromley, D. B. 1977: *Personality Description in Ordinary Language*

Cattell, R. B. 1965: *The Scientific Analysis of Personality*

Chaplin, J. P. 1968: *Dictionary of Psychology*

Curry, P. 1982. 'Research on the Mars Effect', *Zetetic Scholar,* no. 9

Eysenck, H. J. 1970: *The Structure of Human Personality*

Gauquelin, M., Gauquelin, F. and Eysenck, S. B. G. 1979: 'Personality and Position of the Planets at Birth: an empirical study', *British Journal of Social and Clinical Psychology,* vol. 18

Gauquelin, M., Gauquelin, F. and Eysenck, S. B. G. 1981: 'Eysenck's Personality Analysis and Position of the Planets at Birth: a replication on American subjects', *Person. Individ. Diff.,* vol. 2

Rawlins, D. 1981: 'Starbaby', *Fate,* October

West, J. A. and Toonder, J. C. 1973: *The Case for Astrology*

Zelen, M. 1976: 'Astrology and Statistics, a challenge', *Humanist,* vol. 36, no. 1

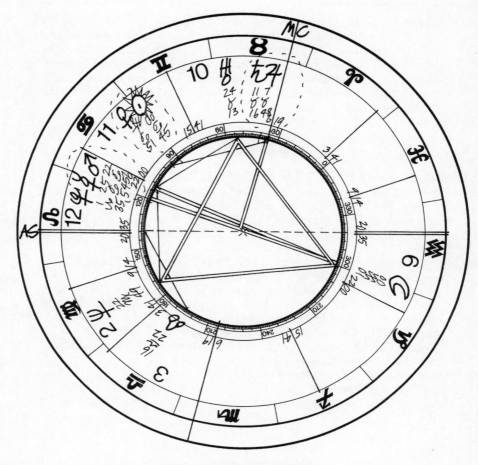

CHARLES HARVEY

22 June 1940   9:16 am BWT   Little Bookham, Surrey

Charles Harvey

Charles Harvey was interested in astrology and numerology and other 'fringe' subjects from an early age and has been a full-time consultant astrologer, teacher, lecturer and writer since 1966. He has always been interested in all aspects of both the science and the art of astrology, from its history and organization to education, research and consulting, and has been involved in organizing the Astrological Association's annual conferences since 1969 and its special research conferences since 1979. His special areas of interest have been in harmonics, on which he worked closely with John Addey until his death in 1982, in promoting and developing the Ebertins' work in cosmobiology, in mundane astrology with Michael Baigent and Nick Campion, and in the area of financial astrology working with Michael Harding. He is married to fellow astrologer and consultant Suzanne Lilley and they have two sons.

Harvey began his formal studies with the Faculty of Astrological Studies in 1963 and gained his Diploma (DFAstroS) in 1966 and joined the FAS Council the same year. He was FAS Vice-President from 1977 to 1986 and is still closely connected with the FAS education programme, teaching in their London Schools programme, and for their summer schools and special seminars. He joined the Astrological Association in 1963 and worked closely with its co-founder and president, John Addey, on the development and teaching of harmonics. He became Records Officer of the AA in 1965, General Secretary in 1968 and succeeded John Addey as President of the AA in 1973, a position he still holds. In 1970, he became a founder trustee of the Urania Trust, a registered educational charity dedicated to the advancement of education by the teaching of the relationship between man's knowledge and beliefs about the heavens and every aspect of his art, science, philosophy and religion. He has been Chairman of the Trust since John Addey's death. In 1971, he was co-founder with John Addey and Dr James Williamsen of the Cambridge Circle, a group dedicated to the development of harmonic astrology. In 1980, along with Michael Baigent and Nick Campion he founded the Institute for the Study of Cycles in World Affairs (ISCWA) for the promotion of the serious study of mundane astrology.

Charles Harvey Bibliography

Translated the supplement of Reinhold Ebertin's *Combination of Stellar Influences* (1969)
Collaborated on *Recent Advances in Natal Astrology* (1975)
Editorial consultant to the *Larousse Encyclopedia of Astrology* (1980)
Consulting editor to the journal *Correlation* (1981)
With Baigent and Campion, *Mundane Astrology* (1984)
The International Astrological Handbook (in progress)
Dictionary of Astrological Biography (in progress)
The Urania Trust, 58 Harrowdene Road, Bristol BS4 2JJ

6

Ideal Astrology

CHARLES HARVEY

Imagine that you are at a wine tasting. The experts have been sniffing and snorting and gargling over their glasses and identifying, with almost uncanny accuracy, the precise year and locality of each vintage presented to them. Now your host steps forward and calls for quiet. As the hubbub subsides a French astrologer is introduced. He calmly announces that he is himself a student of *human* vintages and that from his evening's observations he will now tell each of you present your exact year, month, day and time of day of your births. And, with more accuracy than discretion, he proceeds to do so. Impossible? In fact, not only possible but a logical consequence of astrology's claims. And although he is no longer alive, you can read the tragi-comic biography of just such a connoisseur of time in Henry Miller's hilarious book *A Devil in Paradise*. It is a true story of Henri Moricand, a highly colourful astrologer, artist and bohemian who clearly had each line of the ephemeris and each nuance of the ever-changing planetary dance of creation etched upon his memory. Moricand's virtuoso performance, though very rare, reflects the fact that each one of us literally 'speaks our chart' in every aspect of our life from our physical appearance, dress, gesture, and voice, to our opinions, attitudes, aspirations and actions.

However, such delicacy of astrological perception is at present extremely rare. In the future we can predict that such 'perfect pitch' as regards the imprint of the music of the spheres will be something which will be cultivated to a far greater extent by all students of astrology. If at present even the finest astrological schools in the West offer all too little training in working from astrological effects to causes, this will certainly change. With appropriate study and training, the student who forecasts the likely effects that will arise from a particular cause, such as Mars rising at the moment of a birth or event, should be able to deduce the likely causes from the visible and manifest effects, a skill which, after all, our wine buffs regularly demonstrate as a matter of course. Indeed the basic essentials of such a skill are waiting to be put together, and are, to a limited extent, already being used effectively by some.

Many students can recognize certain Sun-sign characteristics, especially of their own sign. Prominent planets can likewise often be spotted by the trained eye. In 1970, I witnessed Michel Gauquelin, then supposedly in an anti-astrology phase, predict with the confidence born of years of his specialist study on angular planets (and an angular Jupiter of his own), that the ebullient Roger Elliot, whom he had only recently met, 'must have an angular Jupiter'. (Now you know it could you doubt it, but could you do it?) In similar vein, the late lamented Jim ten Hove often recalled how the great Dutch astrologer Theo J. J. Ram could accurately identify a client's Moon sign and house position simply by observing the way he or she entered and walked across a room and sat down. Even more strikingly, Charles Jayne reports that Professor B. V. Raman, the highly distinguished editor of *The Astrological Magazine*, was able to tell him his time of birth simply from an examination of the palm of Jayne's hand, a skill that it is alleged is fairly common in India. On a less dramatic note, I have myself witnessed a group of a dozen or so final year Diploma students at the Faculty of Astrological Studies' London School put together, over a couple of hours of discussion and group work, a commendably accurate, consensus picture of the main features of the chart of an unknown person, working only from published biographical details. As well as being of obvious value in rectification, the mere possibility of developing such skills has dramatic implications for the future credibility of astrology.

I have begun with these observations about what may seem like 'party-trick' astrology because I believe our future art-science will be, within the next century, one in which the quantitative and qualitative aspects of all things are studied as complementary expressions of the same archetypal, formative Ideas and principles of Creation. In such a philosophical climate the average practitioners of astrology will be as comfortable working from effects to causes as from theoretical formal causes to effects as at present.

The reason that our future astrologers will work with such increased confidence will be threefold. Firstly, because the growth of interest in astrological education, through the work of such bodies as the Urania Trust, will lead to greatly improved educational facilities and very much more thorough and intense training of astrologers. Secondly, because as the result of greatly improved systematic observation and experiment, the astrologer will know and understand much more fully and rigorously the laws by which the archetypal Ideas of Creation manifest themselves. Thirdly, because of a major cultural shift in outlook, brought about in great part by the proven realities of astrology, which will place consciousness, rather than matter, at the centre of our daily life.

The student who consciously knows with demonstrable certainty that the whole manifested cosmos is a purposeful, meaningful, living body of Ideas, who takes it as given that Time is indeed the flowing image of

Eternity, who consciously perceives that the heavenly bodies are indeed the first-born thoughts of God, and that the planets do indeed unfold creation, that student will the more eagerly savour each moment of the music of the spheres, and each corresponding manifestation in consciousness and matter. Our future students, knowing with inward certainty that each moment, and each product of each moment, is, in terms of itself, an expression of the Eternal, will be the more eager to train themselves to see and to know the potentials of each cycle, of each phase, of each subtle interaction of the Gods. Such students will hear the Mozart, see the Michelangelo, understand the Shakespeare and perceive the Plotinus in each milli-arc of the Earth's rotation.

Yet well before astrology is woven into the fabric of our lives, indeed in the fairly near future, when full-time astrology courses begin to appear in universities and at specialized schools, we can expect that the serious would-be astrologer will expect to have to study and practise their science and art with as much dedication and discipline as a topflight pianist or conductor. The student's 'scores' will still be charts, but charts technically analysed and presented by computer in such a way that the different 'themes' and harmonies and the parts of the different 'instruments' in the chart are immediately apparent. For study purposes, such charts will be integrated with video astro-portraits of individuals from every walk of life, with profiles of the pattern of their life and work. Banks of material on the widest range of individuals and their charts and case histories will be available on compact disc for study and comparison. Such material will allow detailed study of simple and complex chart patterns and symmetries. Ever-growing libraries of videos, mainly compiled by the students themselves from around the world, will provide in-depth interviews, and analyses of the lives of time-twins, of historical characters, and studies which relate works of creative art to their creators. Through such means students will constantly be adding new dimensions and perspectives to the available repertoire of studies of Time.

With such aids and the active study of their own and fellow students' lives, the budding astrologer will come to an increasingly deeper understanding of the countless ways in which individuals can give outward expression to 'the ideas of the time'. In conjunction with such studies, similar approaches will help the student appreciate the way in which the creative ideas which produce and shape the cosmos unfold through other kinds of entities such as companies, countries, societies and organizations, and are reflected in every aspect of life from specific mundane and political events to the broadest sweeps of history. Indeed the profits of prophecy when applied to mundane affairs will probably mean that applied economic and political astrology will rapidly overtake individual astrology as a career for the budding astrologer. The rewards that will come from being able to predict weather patterns, and from making forecasts for businesses, nations, and international matters, will undoubtedly rapidly attract the

73

more ambitious students and demand far greater emphasis on these areas in our educational programme.

Such technical advances in astrological education are already beginning to happen. Needless to say, techniques alone are not enough. For the student to encompass a discipline which deals with the archetypal potentialities of all manifested things and their unfolding, an area which has as its subject matter both Eternity and Time, must demand that, ideally, the astrologer of the future be himself more consciously universal in outlook. Ideally we can expect that the future student will receive an education and training which will include the fullest development alike of Heart, Mind, Will, and the higher Intuition. It will likewise demand that the student has a real grasp of psychology, philosophy and theology as well as a good grounding in all the sciences and arts from the most pragmatic to the most abstract. To begin to discuss in any detail such an education, at once scientific and artistic, theoretic and practical, left-brain and right-brain, would require many essays and must be left for another occasion. That such a kind of training will demand that our universities do indeed become truly universal once again goes without saying!

Sublime vistas! Meanwhile, for the present, it has to be faced that for astrology to begin to approach its ultimate future of being reunited with astronomy as a single, integral, cosmological science and art-embracing quantity and quality, many more astrologers will need to dedicate themselves, at the full stretch of their skills, imagination and understanding, to real astrological research. Whilst we can be certain that it will indeed require a 'New Science' to accommodate astrology, we cannot evade the need for demonstrable, quantifiable evidence for astrological effects. No amount of rhetoric about quantum physics, indeterminacy and so on will replace imaginative, rigorously individual, collective and mundane astrology. The future of astrology depends on us facing up to the reality that astrological effects occur in the phenomenal world, even if they are rooted in the noumenal world. Such effects can be measured. Astrology works according to laws and principles, and much of the building of the larger future of astrology will depend upon the demonstration of these laws and principles in clear, unambiguous and often quantifiable terms.

Such laws and principles may have much more to do with consciousness and Plato's Ideas and archetypes than they have to do with reductionist particle physics, but laws will certainly be found to exist. Indeed the daily experience of our tradition by every active astrologer and the work of such diverse pioneers as Addey, Gauquelin and Rudhyar, Barbault and Ebertin, reveals that there are such laws, and that these laws speak of the cycle and number, and the processes and sequences involved in the unfolding of the creative processes of time. As we uncover the deeper realities behind astrology we will find laws which will make an integral sense of our traditional knowledge and which at the same time will point to a larger, more all-inclusive vision of a living, spirit-informed universe. It will point to the development of what I like to think will in the future be known as 'Ideal Astrology'.

An ideal is an Idea to be realized. We can call such a future integral astrology based on clear first principles 'ideal' in the sense that Platonic and Neoplatonic philosophy is described as 'ideal' philosophy, i.e. it is the philosophy which considers the manifested cosmos as a living body of Divine Ideas in the Mind of the Creator. The implications for the ideal astrologer are that if life is an expression of this interweaving symphony of formative ideas, in the guise of planetary archetypes, then the chart is not only a basis for pragmatic interpretation and forecasting, but it is also a map of what this moment could be, a map of the 'ideal' fullness of that moment. In this sense the planets and their interrelations in an individual's chart represent the ultimate ideas to be consciously attained and realized within the depth of that soul.

With this approach the astrologer considering the Sun square Mars in a chart will be attempting to come to some root understanding of the real Ideas, formative principles, and functions represented by the Sun, Mars and the number four. Such an astrologer will not only be forecasting how a square of these bodies might manifest in a particular person in particular circumstances, but he will also be suggesting how such principles could 'ideally' be manifest at the different levels within and around that individual or entity from the environmental and physical levels through to the emotional, volitional, intellectual and intuitional.

The fact that the same pattern of astrological ideas will express itself in different ways at different times and in different circumstances, according to the level of consciousness of the expressing being, is perhaps self-evident to the astrologer, yet all too often the significance of this fact is overlooked. We tend to translate our birth-charts according to our own and others' experience. Faced with a Sun square Mars we can find from Charles Carter's superb compendium of observations, that there will be, inter alia 'restlessness', 'a desire to contradict', and 'to fight *something*', and to 'lead crusades' and from Ebertin's indispensable Combination of Stellar Influences, 'the inclination to quarrel', 'the desire to exercise power', 'advancement in life through one's own efforts', and 'overstrain'. That these and many other analogous *effects* have been observed is certainly true. That such effects may manifest in our particular case is also certainly likely. But we would like to think that for the future ideal astrologer, noting such particular effects will only be the beginning. His real job will be to attempt to deduce from the client something of the deeper more ideal meaning of Sun square Mars by beginning to reach back to the formal causes of things, to the universal 'ideas' behind these specifics. Through such exploration we can begin to glimpse something of the deeper 'why' of a situation, and of how it might be more ideally expressed. Such an astrology, already beginning to be practised by some, offers a real path to individual transformation and regeneration. When the same principles begin to be consciously applied by individuals and world leaders to the future possibilities for national and international affairs, there begins to emerge the possibility of a far deeper level of collective consciousness. The first seeds of such collective focus on particular times can already be seen to be happening through such events as 'Band Aid', 'Live Aid' and '60 Seconds for Peace'.

At an individual level, the remedial value of such a deeper more ideal appreciation of astrological principles can be seen in the experience of the Churchill Sailing Schooner Scheme for delinquent adolescents. That organization has noted that the more violent and tearaway the past history of the trainees placed on the scheme, the more likely they are to rise to the challenge of crewing a sailing schooner. It is the worst delinquents who most often become the hero of the hour when it comes to braving and battling the elements. This is an ideal that astrology would predict. The bored but energetic teenager with Sun square Mars, whose life is being lived out at an almost entirely physical level, may readily get into brawls (Mars) seeking (Sun) to manifest (square) excitement (Mars) to prove (square) and assert (Mars) his own virility (Mars) and individuality (Sun). The same individual, as part of a crew faced with having to get their boat across the Atlantic, will be purposefully (Sun) tested and challenged (square) by dangers (Mars) demanding determination and resistance (square Mars), and will be likely in the process to manifest (square) powers of courageous leadership (Sun) when confronted (square) by the real life dangers (Mars) of a force 10 gale (Mars) and the general challenges (square) of such an adventure (Mars) which gives him the opportunity to shine (Sun).

Such an approach to chart potential will demand that the astrologer make and seek suggestions based on an intelligent understanding of the past and present expressions of the birth-chart under consideration. The astrologer will be able to see ways in which the chart's energies may be made increasingly conscious and more constructively directed. Thus the Mars-Saturn type who gives up hunting for conscientious reasons and then develops acute arthritis and depression, is going to need to be pointed in the direction of forceful and demanding activities which can give creative expression to these energies. He might also be told by the astrologer, using Astro-Carto-Graphy techniques, of places on the earth where he might go to become more conscious of the issues indicated. That most people in future years will certainly have learned at least some basic astrology in school, will greatly assist in encouraging individuals and groups to work more consciously with the higher, and increasingly more ideal, manifestations of their patterns.

Computers obviously have a potentially powerful part to play here, especially in finding illustrations of alternative expressions of particular chart patterns. Cumulative data banks can be used to identify other individuals who share the same specific chart patterns so that their case histories can be used to suggest alternative approaches to a planetary picture. Even more powerfully, we would envisage that in due course an individual will be able to explore the possibilities of their moment of birth by logging on to a data bank and arranging a discussion with one or several close time-twins. Indeed one can visualize that communicating with time-twins will in the future become a very common occurrence, albeit one that will appeal to some chart patterns more than others! Equally, historical data banks made up of news reports and so on, chronologically arranged, will no doubt become available. From these it will be readily possible to construct what Arthur Koestler called, in his autobiography *Arrow in the Blue*, the 'secular horoscope', enabling us to see how the birth ideas that an individual is working out over a lifetime were expressing themselves in the world during the period of birth itself.

The foregoing conjectures may perhaps not seem so radically different from the work that a good astrologer might be attempting at the present time. However, in one highly important area I think we can expect to see some major advances, in fact we *must* make some major advances, if astrology is to realize its full potential for describing the unfolding of events. These essential advances involve the creation of *models* which can enable astrologers to present and discuss their findings in a coherent and un-ambiguous way. Scientifically and philosophically mankind will soon be obliged to develop a conceptual model of reality which embraces astrology. Within this there will need to be an adequate model of the human psyche itself, and a model of the individual and collective human psyche's relationship to the larger whole.

As long as we lack these models, and especially an adequate model of the psyche, the language we use to describe an individual's character, individuality, predispositions, nature, motivations, etc. and their relationship to their environment and their future possibilities can all too rapidly descend into universally applicable generalities which befog rather than illuminate. It is this lack of a coherent model of the human psyche that seems to be the downfall of all attempts to date at generating really convincing computerized analyses. With the exception of Terry Dwyer's 'Starword' trait-centred model and Liz Greene's 'Astro-Intelligence' program, the first based on artificial intelligence principles, most computer analyses pour forth an amorphous assortment of contradictory character descriptions, many of which could be applied in some sense to most of us.

This criticism could, of course, be applied with equal force to personally prepared analyses. The problem that both astrologer and client face is not that the birth-chart contains contradictory information, we are all full of contradictions and paradoxes, but rather that as yet there is no commonly agreed model or way of describing a person's psyche so that we are in a position to recognize unequivocally its characteristic qualities, dynamics or contradictions in a relatively objective way. (Relatively objective in that the observer is within what is being observed.) Thus whilst we can readily describe a person's *body* and its parts in a relatively unambiguous way, this is not true of a person's *psyche*. If someone describes me or a friend as 'tallish, skinny, thinning fair hair, small mouth, large nose, bluish grey eyes, long legs, large hands, nervous quick movements, etc.', I can assess fairly objectively in what respect this description does or does not describe me or my friend. However, when it comes to describing the psychology of an individual there is hardly any agreement even on the 'parts' of the psyche, let alone how we go about describing those parts.

This is not to say that a valuable picture of an individual psyche is an impossibility at the present. A good novelist, dramatist or biographer may in fact be able to convey a picture of a unique human being so that we really begin to know something of that person. A gifted writer, or indeed actor, can convey something of the deepest aspirations, motivations, contradictions, hopes and fears within a person, their strengths and weaknesses, their relationship to others, their impact upon the world and so on. But equally, two biographers, one friendly and one hostile, may attribute very different significance and motivation to the same pattern of events. We may say that someone is 'strong willed' or 'soft hearted' or 'hard headed' and know what we mean, but does anyone else? You are 'firm and a person of strong principles' but he is 'stubborn, indeed pig-headed'. And even agreed that these are two different views of the same trait, what in fact is that trait describing? The future of astrology depends upon our grappling with these problems and coming up with adequate models to accommodate our insights.

Traditionally man is tripartite: Body, Soul/Mind and Spirit. Likewise the Soul's gnostic faculties have been described under the classifications of Heart, Mind, Will and Intuition or the Mystical faculty. Such dimensions to the human condition are certainly much richer than the flat-land uni-dimensional picture conjured up by contemporary academic psychology. But how many people today could even begin to define these terms in an unambiguous way or recognize a description of themselves couched in these terms?

As astrologers, believing that 'as above, so below', our own natural model is that of the solar system. We say that the Sun and Moon at our birth reflect the relationship between our own inner Sun and Moon. The orientation of the meridian and horizon at birth and their relationship to the other bodies and the heavens are seen to reflect an analogous inner relationship. So far so good. But when we describe the Solar and Lunar principles and the MC and AS in the chart of a client, to what part of that individual are we in fact referring and how can they unequivocally identify it? If one of these chart factors is closely configured by Mars, the astrologer confidently starts talking or writing about 'self-assertive' qualities, of possible 'impatience', of martial interests and affinities generally. But is this good enough? Clearly not. We need to know much more precisely that area of the psyche which will have these character attributes and motivations.

Put another way, if someone wants to uncover the reason for particular pain, the doctor needs to know where the pain is. Is it in the head, the tooth, the heart, the stomach, the toe? Yet, because of our current lack of a coherent psychological model, astrologers may be content to describe someone as 'impatient, forceful and something of a fighter', without attempting in any way to locate the aspect of that individual to which these attributes are supposed to apply. Is this 'impatience and fighting spirit' characteristic of their spontaneous reaction to life, is it central to the kind of career they have chosen, or is it part of an outward approach to the world, or does it just come out in close relationships?

The future development of astrology will need to allow us to be much clearer and more specific about what it is we are describing. Given a chart of an individual with Sun square Mars we need to be able to specify in what area and aspect of life and consciousness these qualities will manifest. We need to be able to define with clarity the function within the human psyche of the Sun and how our reader or listener is to identify and understand this aspect in themselves and in others. Likewise with the function of Mars. Once we can unequivocally define these analogous functions within the human psyche, and presumably they must have identical functions in every psyche, just as the heart and muscular systems have identical functions to play in the body, we can begin to describe a *specific* and, at least theoretically, identifiable 'function' within an individual which will have certain characteristics.

The pressing need for such a model is highlighted in a recent textbook by a fine and influential astrological writer and teacher, which, with the best intentions, gives an excellent list of quotations from famous people 'to illustrate the meaning of each Moon sign . . . and help us to experience more deeply our intrinsic Moon energies'. Unfortunately more often than not the individual quoted does not have the Moon in the sign that the quote is supposed to illustrate. Thus under Moon in Aries the writer quotes Harry S. Truman as saying, 'I am going to fight hard. I'm going to give them hell'. Certainly this is a martial statement but is it a lunar statement? Does anyone *from a lunar level* announce the *future intentions* of their 'I'? Surely such a statement is much too purposeful, categorical and decisive to relate to the Moon in any sign? Is this not much more a statement which must be coming from somewhere near Truman's centre, from his Sun or MC perhaps?

To check on how characteristic of the man such a statement might be, we can inspect a biography. Truman's short, potted biographical entry in *The Macmillan Dictionary of Biography* reveals, inter alia, that 'despite bad eyesight, which prevented his entry into West Point Military Academy, he served in the First World War', then a failed business venture cost him fifteen years of effort to pay his creditors, that on becoming a US senator he became well known through his chairmanship of the Committee for Investigation of the Defence programme, that he had to order the dropping of the atomic bombs on Japan, that he took the decision that initiated the Korean War and showed great courage in dismissing General Macarthur, that he encouraged the formation of NATO, and was responsible for the Truman Doctrine, a policy of economic and military aid to counter Soviet influence and expansion in Europe. By contrast with all this martial activity, we find his home policy, aimed to promote racial harmony and help the underprivileged, was summarized by the term 'Fair Deal'.

Much more detail might be required by an Henri Moricand, or a Dennis Elwell for that matter, to make categorical deductions from such a biographical picture, but turning to Truman's chart they would not be surprised to find that he has Sun conjunct Neptune in close square to Mars, as befits a man, the very centre and focus of whose life was spent grappling with martial things. Truman's Moon was in fact in Scorpio, another martial sign, but closely trine the Ascendant ruler Venus, just past the MC in Cancer! Does that sound like his home policy and the 'Fair Deal'? It does – after the event – but we still need a clear model that will enable us to identify in unambiguous terms the kind of ways and areas in which such natal paradoxes will work out, in advance.

Much work is obviously needed, but, once we have cleared back the jungle and scraped off the moss, the stone that the builders have rejected for so long will indeed become one of the corners of the Temple; of that there can be little doubt. But to be worthy, to 'Assume an almost central role in scientific thought', as John Addey affirms it will, we astrologers must be prepared to set ever higher standards in astrological education. We must be prepared to investigate our tradition with rigour and imagination, and we must begin to develop and work with a far deeper and more disciplined understanding of the human Soul and its relation to the Cosmos and the Creator. It can only be such a living, inquiring, creative, intelligent, ideal astrology that can fulfil the prophetic insight of the Vatican's Professor Cunibert Mohlberg and be 'destined to lead all the other branches of knowledge out of the blind alley of unspiritual rationalism and materialism . . . in order to effect the reconciliation that Science so ardently desires with Belief'. Such an astrology is worthy of the deepest dedication, for it contains not only the future of astrology but much of the hope for the future of mankind.

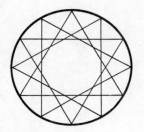

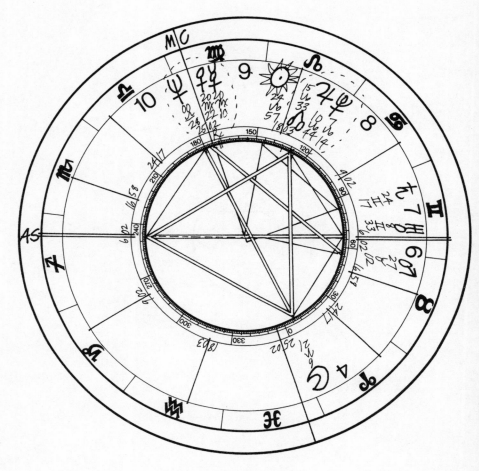

A. T. MANN

18 August 1943   3:05 pm EWT   Auburn, New York

A. T. Mann

Tad Mann was raised in New York and graduated from the architecture school at Cornell University in 1966. He worked as an architect in New York City and Rome, during which time he designed many buildings including world's fair pavilions and private houses in New York City and the Middle East.

After 1969 he travelled extensively and lived in Europe, North Africa, Central Asia and India, in the process meeting astrologers, holy men and others questing after the truth. On his return to the USA in 1972, his daughter Ptolemy was born and he began learning astrology and tarot.

He moved to England and co-founded Phenomenon Publications with Giuseppe Sesti, Mary Flanagan and Painton Cowen and produced, illustrated and wrote the series of Phenomenon Books of Calendars from 1974 to 1980 which were almanacs integrating many calendar systems from different cultures, published in many languages.

The Round Art: The Astrology of Time and Space (1979) was an adaptation of the idea of a logarithmic time scale derived from Gurdjieff and Ouspensky and applied to astrology. The following years were spent lecturing and giving workshops all over the world.

Upon his return from India in 1972, he painted a deck of tarot cards which are based on astrology, recently repainted for publication as *The Mandala Astrological Tarot* (1987). A return to architectural ideas transformed into a deep study of sacred architecture, about which a book is in preparation. A book on the mantic arts as inner process with the rune-master Ralph Blum is also forthcoming.

An interest in dowsing led to a study of the healing arts of radionics and homoeopathy in 1975, and in addition to developing Astro★Radionics, a technique for diagnosis and treatment through the horoscope, he is a theorist and has lectured for the Radionics Association on many occasions. Presently he is a co-director of The Well Centre, an international healing organization based on astrology and energy medicine as an organizing principle of complementary therapies.

On a less serious note, he is a low-handicap golfer, raises bonzai trees and is a practitioner of many national and regional styles of cooking to be presented in *Cosmic Cuisine: Alchemy in the Kitchen* (1988). He lives in an ancient cottage in deepest Kent and lectures worldwide.

A. T. Mann Bibliography

KALA astrological calendar (1972) with Peter and Mary Barton
Phenomenon Book of Calendars (1974–80) with Giuseppe Sesti, Mary Flanagan and Painton Cowen
The Round Art: The Astrology of Time and Space (1979)
Life ★ Time Astrology (1984)
The Divine Plot: Astrology, Reincarnation, Cosmology and History (1986)
The Mandala Astrological Tarot (1987)
The Future of Astrology (1987)
Cosmic Cuisine (1988)

7

Life ★ Time Astrology

A. T. MANN

When I began studying astrology it struck me that while the ancient art and science of astrology was very mysterious and powerful, it needed to be transformed for use in the twentieth century.

Astrological principles have been utilized by almost all cultures since the dawn of time, in many different ways. The structure of the horoscope has remained the same, but there have been numerous, often contradictory, ways to interpret it, usually dependent upon the demands of the time. At present there are two different pressures on astrology. First, it is important to demonstrate that the basic principles of astrology contain rather than contradict the new relativistic models of the physical sciences. Second, astrology needs to become a more effective tool for the integration of the spiritual and psychological realm with the physical.

Most astrologers accept one or the other of these issues: either they wish astrology to mate with science, or they wish to use astrology as a symbolic, psychological tool. The two types rarely integrate because there is no clear crossover between them. One task I set myself was to find such a bridge. Astrology contains an integral set of principles which are in alignment with ancient ideas, as well as new paradigms of the world and the psyche which are relativistic and vital.

The starting point for my work was two ideas presented in the book by Rodney Collin, *The Theory of Celestial Influence*. The first is that the solar system travels through time in a spiral pattern with the Sun as a central filament, as a 'step-down transformer' of cosmic energies, and that from the form and mathematics of that movement all physical laws arise. I recognized immediately that the pattern of the spiralling pattern of the solar system through time was similar to the double helix shape of genetic code, DNA, which creates and regulates form in living organisms (Figure 7.1). Astrology is a way to interpret the meaning of the pattern of planets moving through time to an individual. The spiral of planets in the outer world (the macrocosm) resonates with the spiral genetic code within every

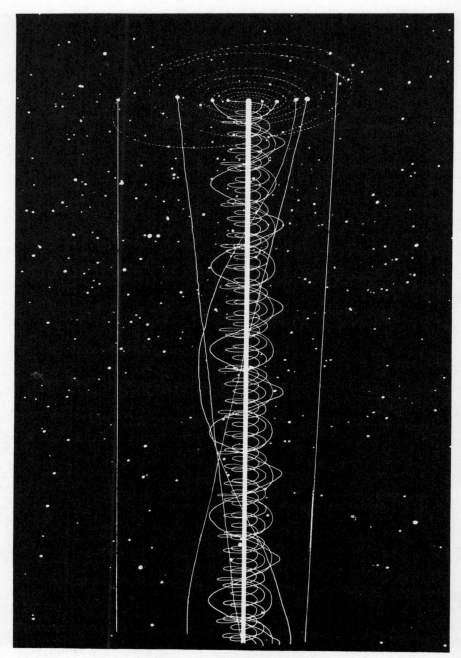

Figure 7.1 The Spiral Solar System

The central filament is the Sun travelling through space, round which the planetary paths spiral in their order from the Sun.

living cell in the inner world (the microcosm). There is a simultaneous transmission of information always going on. In this context astrology is much more than a symbolic system − it reflects the physical laws of the universe as well. Astrology is a way of decoding biology. Recent scientific research is supporting this hypothesis (the work of both Prof. P. A. H. Seymour and Maurice M. Cotterell on astro-genetic theory).

The second idea was *'biological time'*, that time-perception is relative to the size, metabolism and lifespan of all beings in the universe, and that time-sense changes throughout life. Atoms, molecules, cells, humans, planets, suns, solar systems, galaxies and the universe are organisms in their own right, as well as being components of larger systems with longer lifetimes and containing smaller systems with shorter lifetimes. Time is perceived as relative to each level of being, so that smaller organisms like cells, despite the fact that their lifetimes are very short, experience the passage of time relative to their lifespan in the same way that human beings experience a life of months and years.

The passage of time is measured with a logarithmic scale by all beings. The rate at which time seems to pass changes as the metabolic rate of respiration and digestion slows down as one ages − in youth metabolism is fast and time passes slowly, but in old age metabolism is slow and time passes quickly. When graded logarithmically, every organism has three developmental *octaves* in its lifetime, each octave being ten times longer than its predecessor, but carrying the same amount of information. These are Gestation, when the physical body is created, Childhood, when the emotional body of personality is created, and Maturity, when the mental body is created and all possibilities are expressed in the world.

When the model of three octaves (and bodies) is superimposed on an astrological horoscope, the result is a symbolic picture of a lifetime which is also a biological model for the human life process. The fact that the time-scale works both symbolically and biologically is a quantum leap for astrology as it is a working model for the hypothesis that psychological states parallel physical events. Events and psychology are not separate but integral, and can be seen to be so.

An important implication of the logarithmic time-scale is that gestation is the first third of the lifetime, during which time the developing foetus repeats the entire evolutionary process within the womb, confirming the importance of that time (the collective history of all humanity) in the work of genetic scientists as well as psychologists such as Jung and Dr Stanislas Grof. Contemporary astrologers present the horoscope as a set of characteristics starting at and determined by the birth moment, a personal profile which remains in effect throughout life. In *Life★Time Astrology* it is clear that from conception, when the divine spark of soul animates the fertilized ovum carrying a cosmic-genetic pattern, every quality a person contains unfolds into being at a particular time, either in Gestation through heredity modified by the mother's behaviour, during Childhood within the home and family system, or during Maturity in the outside world, with one's partners or society. Behavioural patterns do not just appear, they are created by the interaction of the human soul with inner and outer forces. There is a continuous manifestation of soul and spirit. Life★Time Astrology is the only astrological system to present a human lifetime as a process in time from conception to death.

In this model, gestation is the creation of the body and also a prototype of the pattern of the development of a higher transpersonal body which extends beyond the physical.

The periphery of the circle records the process of life in time, whereas the centre of the circle is the timeless centre of the psyche where unity resides, and which is available at all ages through life. A central aim of Life★Time Astrology is to gain access to the soul and its purpose through higher and more central energies – transformation lies within.

In Life★Time Astrology the horoscope is a model of the life process. Each planet registers and releases its energy at specific ages and manifests psychological mechanisms attached to events. When Uranus registers and indicates a sudden, dramatic change in life at 17 years and 6 months old, it is immediately clear whether or not such an event happened. Actual experiences may be compared with the astrological pattern; the symbolic related to the real. The value of such correlations is that when a specific behaviour pattern is identified with a planet, subsequent movements of the planet are determinate, and when the planet is reactivated again, another experience related to the initial registration may be expected, with the hope that each time successively higher and more well integrated responses ensue. Events may be predicted to a quite high degree of certainty, and their accuracy checked. The original and subsequent events in life, which create psychological behavioural patterns or blockages, may be identified as a prelude to psychotherapeutic experiential work.

This view of astrology raises many important issues. It implies that every human carries the entire biological and spiritual history of life within. During gestation we experience the entire grand creation of humanity at an accelerated rate and retain traces in our soul, body and mind of the early stages of biological development, and the deepest and most primal instincts, urges and myths, a collective unconscious from which we draw in being in the world. During childhood we repeat the evolution of consciousness within the family, stage by stage, until we reach the present moment. Life★Time Astrology is unique in presenting the process of life in the horoscope as a mirror of the development of consciousness.

Instead of feeling, with many astrologers, that astrology must be adapted to the conditions of science, I feel that scientists undervalue the importance of time, particularly relative, biological concepts of time, and they can learn much about the world by investigating and testing the astrological worldview. The foundation of astrology is a valid view of the world, particularly in relation to the most modern paradigms of the new physics or biology.

The current world of patriarchal values is not working, and the inadequacy of Sun-sign astrology is a reflection of that. The logarithmic scale is mathematically generated by integrating the masculine solar year with the feminine lunar month, which leads to a balance of male-female, yang-yin and conscious-unconscious on which balance in the world depends. The alchemists used the conjunction of the king and queen as a symbol of integration, and this is a mathematical manifestation of the sublime Key.

The Proof of Astrology

Proving Life★Time Astrology is a twofold issue. During fourteen years of astrological practice, I have found the level of accuracy to be astonishing, but at present I have only subjective verification. A great drawback is that most feedback has been sporadic or haphazard in quality. When valuable feedback has been received, it has been difficult to process it systematically. When hypotheses presented for confirmation in a reading include all events in a person's life, it is hard to organize and process the sheer volume of information. In many cases people do not have accurate records of their own lives – while outer events such as accidents, surgery, births, marriages and deaths can be dated precisely, much of the fabric of life is composed of inner psychological or spiritual events which are not as easy to define or date. Who can remember when they decided to become a doctor or marry, in distinction to the date of graduation from medical school or the wedding day? Our outer life is easier to verify in a way that will never be the case for our inner life. The 'next stage' of Life★Time Astrology is to remedy this state of affairs.

Life★Time Astrology is relative, rather than static like traditional astrology, and carries a biological structure in addition to psychological, emotional and spiritual levels of reality. Once a format for comparing which planetary combinations manifest as particular outer events is established, the next stage is to determine whether the times when they manifest are accurately shown in the horoscope.

The problem with proving astrology is similar to that which has confronted scientists: in order to analyse or define an event or state statistically, it seems necessary to isolate a part from the whole. Most astrological research to date has been done by analysing single elements, such as planets, of the horoscope. For example, the position of Saturn may be determined in the horoscopes of many medical doctors, as has been done by Michel Gauquelin, and its meaning evaluated statistically. While the correlations are provable, the issue becomes: What is the next step? and How valuable is the proof? But, the same problems arise as those which faced physicists who attempted to discover the elementary particles of which the universe is made. Particles cannot be isolated from their context, and if they are, they change character. Removing one planet from the whole does not take its relatedness into account in any way. If Venus is 'relationship', it matters greatly whether Saturn, which tends to restrict, is near it. In any event, whatever 'proof' is obtained has a limited relevance for the mass of astrologers because they do not interpret planets out of context, but as part of the whole.

A fruitful future for astrological research lies in creating an approach which benefits astrologers and leads to tools, techniques and facts which allow greater understanding and personal growth. A more 'holistic' research structure would lead astrology into a totally new and much more relevant domain.

A principle of the new physics is to investigate processes rather than particles. Existing astrological research into single planets could be upgraded to include groups of planets which act together. The geometrical 'web of relationships' of planets in every horoscope is the core of its vitality, rather than the static positions of the planets in signs or houses. Physicists use bubble chambers to see the patterns made by colliding subatomic particles, and these are analysed to see the overall pattern of interactions. The horoscope aspect pattern is a similar model which allows interactions between planets to be catalogued and their outer effects correlated. The German school of Cosmobiology has already described the triplets of planets, together with their psychological, biological and sociological correspondences and probable manifestations. The degree of precision of interpretation increases as the number of planets in the configuration increases. Such triple combinations of planets is an essential part of Life★Time Astrology.

Astrological Expert Systems

There are at present many computer interpretation programs which take minutes to generate an individual printed report of up to twenty pages of text. The main problem with such programs is that their method of organization is 'cookbook' style, that is, each part, such as Mars in Aries and Mars in the 3rd House, and Mars sextile Jupiter, is represented by a paragraph of text which is printed for everyone who has that combination. The number of permutations for most such services are the ten planets in each sign ($10 \times 12 = 120$) and in each house ($10 \times 12 = 120$) plus each planet aspected to every other planet (seventy-eight combinations). The use of three-planet combinations would increase aspect varieties to $12 \times 12 \times 12 = 1728$, in addition to the planets in each sign and house, a tenfold increase in standard paragraphs. The resultant structure would be much more accurate in more ways than one.

The advantages to using such a system would be twofold. In the context of Life★Time Astrology, the planets and their aspect harmonics occur in sequence around the entire periphery of the horoscope, from conception to old age. The sequence of Moon-Mars-Jupiter would show a dynamic situation where a feeling seeking expression (Moon) leads to the desire to change (Mars) and the outcome is an expansive improvement (Jupiter). If the order were different, the process and the outcome would be also different. The focus is on the dynamics of combinations of planets. Dating the times in life when the planets register leads to the determination of exactly what events correspond to which combinations. Each combination then retains the last two planets, which are qualified by another new agency, so that the previous triplet would become Mars-Jupiter-Pluto, etc.

What is required is an astrological 'artificial intelligence' program which would not only generate information determined by an individual's horoscope, but also would have the ability to process and integrate corrections and alterations in a feedback loop. If every individual, upon receiving and evaluating their computer horoscope dating events and psychological mechanisms in their lives, was to evaluate the information, and provide data which described exactly what 'did' happen, through time the computer could collect a fund of actual manifestations for every triplet of planets. The accepted interpretation for the combination could then be compared to the actual feedback received, and if conclusive evidence for a particular mechanism or type of event is produced, the interpretation could be changed to accommodate it. In time the system would become an *'astrological brain'* capable of becoming more and more accurate and relevant.

In traditional astrology, the process would be more difficult because planets are not associated with specific times of registration in life, but with Life★Time Astrology they are. Therefore, if Mars represents the potential for accidents or surgery, at the times in life when Mars is in difficult aspect, one would expect to have accidents or surgery. If that were not often the case, then the association of Mars with accidents or surgery would be unjustified.

An example of possible research along these lines concerns the one very important event in life which is easily evaluated – the birth process. The Ascendant or Rising Sign indicates birth in traditional astrology. When there is surgical intervention at birth, the planets Mars or Uranus should be either near the ASC or in geometrical aspect to it. Similarly, in induced births or births where anaesthetics are used one would expect to find either Neptune or the Moon present. I believe that the research will lead to a definitive proof of the correlation of events in life with astrological patterns, and lay a foundation upon which a more systemic research may be used.

Shared Information

The time is already approaching when interpretative information and research data will be available to astrologers through common computer banks, accessible through telephone modems or on laser disks. Archives will allow a furthering of collective astrological knowledge. Such an effort is essential in order to bring astrology to greater relevance in the world.

An important area in the future is medical astrology. The association of astrology with medicine is ancient, and is being revived now. Each planetary combination has equivalent events and psychological mechanisms, but also biological and medical correspondences. For example, the aspect combination of Venus/Saturn is interpreted as 'inhibitions in love-life, suffering through love, or control of the emotions'. Venus rules hormonal balance and Saturn is the process of hardening or crystallization, therefore the biological correspondence for Venus/Saturn is 'malfunctioning of the internal glandular secretions, glandular atrophy, or pulmonary emphysema' (Ebertin, *Combination of Stellar Influences*, 1940). Every psychological mechanism has its equivalent biological mechanism, and doctors and healers with astrological knowledge are better able to 'cure' by encouraging healthier behavioural patterns on emotional, mental and spiritual levels in addition to the physical, and establishing balance from level to level. It is accepted that psychosomatic afflictions caused by psychological stresses cause physical disease, but in future a *holistic astrological medicine* will emerge. The research project envisioned would therefore include complete biological and medical correspondences so that the correspondent emotional and mental behavioural patterns may be diagnosed and brought into equilibrium.

The advantages of such research for humanity is great. One important effect would be that it would be possible to identify in new-born infants astrological tendencies to carry diseases or psychological patterns which are pathological or dangerous, and steps could be taken to prevent their manifestations, in the belief that 'an ounce of prevention is worth a pound of cure'.

A primary function of medical astrology will be in the domain of what I call the *Ultimate Alternative*. Alternative therapies abound today, and there is a danger that as they proliferate the public will become overwhelmed by their variety and seeming foreignness. A person needing such therapies often has no idea where to start. To complicate matters, many holistic therapies claim to be capable of treating any and all afflictions. In reality, most modern individuals require a combination of therapies in the course of life, including physical exercise, diet, stress relaxation, meditation, psychotherapy and others. Astrology has the potential to be used as a guiding mechanism for alternative therapies. Each zodiac sign, planet and aspect combination corresponds to body parts, organs, biological systems, acupuncture meridians, chakras and by extension, therapeutic activities. For example, Virgo has domain over the intestines and health in general, so prominent Virgo in a horoscope would indicate sensitivity to diet and a tendency to afflictions of the intestinal tract. In a general way the Earth-signs relate to physical therapies, air signs to mentally identified or talking therapies, water signs to emotionally oriented therapies and fire signs to energy medicine such as acupuncture or radionics.

In The Well Centre in London, of which I am a co-director, we have attempted just such a healing synthesis of astrology and the complementary therapies. Through astrology it is possible to direct each individual to those therapies, exercise programmes, medicines, and healers which are appropriate, and at the times when they are called for. The advantage of using astrology is that the timing of such information can be taken into consideration.

Astrological Education

Astrologers need to advance their professional attitude and training. Since the turn of the century there have been great developments in astrology, but they have never been taken seriously by the public, and astrology has not become a part of the educational process as it should.

During the Renaissance, astrology was one of the arts and sciences which all educated individuals studied. It provided a link between the celestial universe and human experience which was central to humanist ideals. At the present time astrology is a subject in which many people are interested, but few have the opportunity or possibility to study seriously.

Astrology should be a part of education through all levels of school, as indeed should psychology. The training of astrologers should not be split off from university curricula. When the study of how we relate to the cosmos and to each other is an acceptable part of early education, humanity will begin to balance itself.

An essential realization of the new physics is that the results of an experiment change by the presence (and consciousness) of an observer – the observer cannot be divorced from the observed. This idea needs integration in astrological practice as well. The astrologer changes a client through the process of interpreting the horoscope, a responsibility which must be understood in all its implications. The degree of awareness, understanding and spiritual evolution of the astrologer is directly related to the ability to encourage personal growth and understanding in clients. At present the transference is a misunderstood if not unknown aspect of the process. Work on oneself and a sense of responsibility on the part of astrologers is essential in the future.

Although much of the energy in astrology is directed to areas of concern which are obvious and natural, such as research, computers, prediction or psychotherapy, there is an older approach to astrology which warrants attention. The Renaissance humanists understood astrology as a 'celestial science', a way for organizing the psyche. The spiritual aspect has been overshadowed in our materialistic age, but is a primary and essential part of astrology.

Celestial astrology is not very highly valued at present, but is potentially a central focus. Beyond an astrological reading about the patterns of life, the dates when events register, their psychological implications, and the experiential directions which may bring increased actualization, better relationships and growth, there are higher levels at which astrology acts. The mere description of a life related rhythmically to the cosmos prepares a map for potential wholeness towards which the psyche will naturally be attracted. Physical, emotional and mental life become channels through which soul energies manifest to irradiate earthly life. When the ultimate aim of astrology is recognized and accepted, humanity will benefit from its oldest science and art.

Man exists and consequently must abandon himself to Life, bowing to its law in order to justify his high predestination which, according to Pythagoras, requires him to 'ascend through the radiant ether to be among the Immortals, himself a God'.

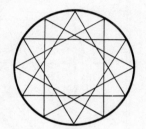

DENNIS ELWELL

16 February 1930   11:43 pm GMT   Stourbridge, West Midlands

Dennis Elwell

In over forty years of astrological activity, Dennis Elwell established an international reputation through articles and lectures. Born in the industrial heartland of England, he remains grateful for this no-nonsense background. He attended a venerable grammar school which treasured the carved initials of the youthful Samuel Johnson, but caned boys for doing likewise. Leaving no lasting mark himself, he was comforted by the subsequent discovery that not only was he a late developer and divergent thinker, but an autodidact to boot. The latter was some advantage when he became interested in astrology in the 1940s, because at that time there were no courses and few books.

During his teens he had agonized over eternal verities to the detriment of his irregular verbs, and at 19, *Prediction* magazine published his first article, on reincarnation. The editor of the local weekly took it as evidence of a rudimentary ability – 'but we have to restrain our imagination here' – and hired him. It could be said he drifted into journalism by the blindest chance, having applied for the job as buyer at the bookshop owned by the same editor across the road. But in time he perceived the hand of destiny: the paper was a unique institution, a haven for colourful characters, and its relaxed style did not impede such serious activities as coffee shop politics, crosswords, snooker – and horoscopes. So congenial was the atmosphere to the pursuit of his major obsession that he stayed, under various pretexts, for a third of a century.

In 1953 Dennis Elwell began to contribute to *American Astrology*, the magazine that put astrology on the news stands, and was a platform for such names as Dane Rudhyar and Garth Allen. The association continued for twenty years. But living miles from London, he had little contact with the British astrological community until his first talk to the Astrological Association in 1963. He had joined the Association in 1959, the year after it was founded.

His early lectures, with such titles as 'Virgo-Pisces in Man and Nature', and 'Perils of the Goat-Fish', had an occult flavour acquired through immersion in the writings of such enigmatic figures as Rudolf Steiner and Gurdjieff, plus some first-hand psychical research which convinced him there was far more to life than met the eye. His inclination has been to explore any byway that might throw light on the astrological.

Turning to full-time counselling and teaching in 1983, he developed a problem-solving approach. But a major concern has been to help in the rehabilitation of astrology by defending it against trivialization, the equally damaging reductionist approach of scientism, and a too-close identification with psychotherapy, while at the same time trying to convey the awesome challenge of the astrological viewpoint.

He has been a guest speaker at all three World Congresses in Switzerland (1981, 1984 and 1987), international congresses in Berkeley, California (1983 and 1984), Berlin (1986), and many other venues in Britain and abroad. Recent lectures have been translated into German and Dutch for republication.

Dennis Elwell has been twice married and has four children.

Dennis Elwell Bibliography

The Cosmic Loom (1987)

8

Here's the Answer, Now What's the Question?

DENNIS ELWELL

Astrologers are agreed that the squiggles called a horoscope contain some sort of message to be decoded, but there has never been enough discussion on what the message is about.

In fact different kinds of information can be extracted from it, depending on what is uppermost in your mind. That situation is not peculiar to astrology. In this world (as all pollsters know) the answers you get very much depend on what questions you ask. An unsuspected range of options is open to us; we are free to take hold of our reality by an assortment of different handles, and which handle we choose decides the outcome. So if answers defy you, change the question! The reason we don't do this routinely is because we have been brought up to believe asking questions is easy, and that answering them is what is difficult. After all, anybody can ask questions! Yes, but asking the *right* question is another matter.

In astrology it is important to be aware that whenever we embark on interpretation we are interrogating the heavens. We are throwing questions at the birth-chart. The usual question posed is: 'What is this person like?' Many astrologers, and almost all the public, seem convinced that this is the only question possible. Indeed, the question usually implies something even more specific, and amounts to a demand for the chart to yield up an assortment of adjectives applicable to this person, as if knowing what an individual 'is like' involved nothing more sophisticated than sticking a few handy labels on him. Even if the labels were accurate – which can be far from the case – we should not be deceived into thinking that this is the only approach, nor that describing is the same as understanding.

It may come as a surprise to those raised on the average textbook, but the question 'What is this person like?' is probably the least fruitful of all the questions available to us. Every question contains built-in assumptions, and if we imagine a birth chart exists to spew out a list of labels, computer fashion, we are assuming that the only or best way to know human nature

is in terms of traits. Not even psychologists would subscribe to that dictum!

Another assumption hidden in this question is exposed when we change it to: 'What *should* this person be like?' The alteration of one word gives us a completely different slant on what the chart means, because the implication of our new question is that the person may not automatically become what the chart suggests. Here we are recognizing that few people are fortunate enough to grow up in optimum conditions for self-development, and that the potential inherent in the birth moment may be frustrated for a number of reasons, ranging from brain injury, nutritional deficiencies, a hostile environment, and lack of educational opportunity, to less dramatic inhibitions like unimaginative parents and the social pressures that make for conformity. Or if not frustrated, perhaps delayed until a more facile stage of life: people do change with the passing years, within their horoscope pattern, and so of course do their circumstances, so they may be able to give better expression to their chart at 50 than 15. Or vice versa!

It also has to be realized that even given optimum conditions for self-development, no one can ever express the full potential of the birth moment, because astrological influences can never, in their very nature, pour out their richness of meaning to the last drop. By definition 'cosmic' signifies qualities above and beyond the limitations of terrestrial existence and the finite scope of human nature. When astrology claims that we have a cosmic dimension, in addition to all our other dimensions, it means we are embedded in a transcendent reality, in which weave tendencies so widely diffused, so multifaceted and comprehensive, that they cannot be compressed into any single instance, any one personality or any one life. Our cup is never big enough to receive the cosmic in its totality.

According to this model a person is in a process of becoming, and can never be quite 'become'. We can never be so developed that no further progress along the lines indicated in the chart is possible. After all, the same set of planets and signs has to serve for infants and adults, for cavemen and modern city dwellers, for twentieth-century man and those humans – possibly evolved out of all recognition – who hopefully will be around 3,000 years hence. So the upward potentialities of the chart may be infinite. At any rate they are unlikely to be exhausted in the modest span of our lifetime!

How you feel about this formulation will depend on what kind of universe you imagine astrology describes. We can think of the planets and signs as simple tropisms, like the tendency of roots to seek the Earth, or of the sunflower daily to follow the Sun. Or we might think of them, as many do, as energies which have to be directed into positive channels. Personally I would say that since the planets and zodiac can be understood so lucidly as overarching principles or ideals, then that is what they must be. From which it follows that the birth-chart itself can be defined as a certain configuration of principles or ideals which the individual makes his own.

From the standpoint of practical interpretation, this approach means that no criticism can be made on the basis of the chart alone ('Mercury opposition Mars means you're irritable') only according to how far the individual has strayed from the cosmic intent – how far the reality approximates to nature's blueprints – which in the case of Mercury opposition Mars might be for the creation of a formidable debater, or one who combines muscle and agility in some activity.

Other questions may be put to the chart. Since whatever it signifies is obviously present at birth only as an agenda, we might beneficially ask: 'What must I do to develop myself as far as I can, and attain everything that is possible for me?' Looked at from this angle, the chart can be treated as a road map rather than a gazetteer of destinations. Or, to change the metaphor, as well as being the picture on the seed packet, the chart contains hints on cultivation! It shows what ingredients must be present to ensure optimum development, what conditions must be satisfied as prerequisites for the flowering of the personality. Every zodiacal sign thus becomes a set of imperatives to be obeyed. Every configuration can be interpreted as a symbol of those activities, problems, projects, aspirations, issues, questions, and so forth, which themselves will become the catalysts for development if the person engages wholeheartedly in them. In this context a positive programme could be worked out for Mercury opposition Mars.

However, it is a quaint conceit of contemporary Western astrologers that their clients are obsessed with anything so abstract as self-development! Many people come to the astrologer with a question, perhaps unspoken, which could not be more down to earth, namely, 'How can the stars help me to be successful and prosperous?'

Curiously, this is the easiest question of all to answer. If you are in a hurry to make a name as an astrologer here's how! All you have to do is issue the Gypsy's Warning.

This is ridiculously simple, because actually most people are motivated by the self-same desires, drawn to the same goals. If you want to know what those goals are, watch the TV commercials! There you see the images of worldly success and comfort, of perfect marriage, ecstatic love, wise parenting, secure old age, fragrant armpits, and all the rest. Moreover, it has to be admitted that the route towards these beckoning images is well signposted, and the reason more of us don't arrive is that the demands and quirks of our own personality are apt to get in the way.

The Gypsy's Warning hits clients where they are most vulnerable. It takes very little experience in astrology to guess from the chart the characteristics that might stop the person achieving those socially desirable goals. As we all know, criticism is child's play compared with the art of giving constructive advice. Negative statements have more impact than positive, bad news gets more coverage. So you have a lot going for you.

Start every sentence with 'Don't . . .' or 'Be careful that . . .' If Uranus is fiercely aspected you say don't be so independent, people will not like you. If Saturn dominates you say don't be so serious, be more fun. If there is an Air sign emphasis you say don't waste time with fine ideas at the expense of practicalities. If there is a lot in Fixed signs, you say don't be so stubborn, it will upset your boss. Early in her career actress Joan Collins was told by an American astrologer that she was trying to pursue two objectives at once, and if she wanted to succeed she must drop one of them and go all out for the other. That sounds suspiciously like the astrologer's stock advice to Sun-Geminis!

This is undeniably a legitimate use for astrology, and the average chart interpretation flirts nervously with it, afraid to go all the way because the client may not be robust enough for so methodical a demolition of his personality.

We should be clear what is happening here. By effectively asking the question 'What might prevent my success in life?' the birth-chart is being discounted, the cosmos overruled. The objective is to become an acceptable clone. Those who want to explore this cloning phenomenon in depth might profitably start with a study of Management Man.

One of the little recognized problems facing the astrologer is that humans do seem able to defect from the blueprint of the cosmos for them, so that they by no means always appear to be like their horoscopes. They can suppress a large part of their charts. No longer authentically themselves, like actors they choose to live life as they have seen others live it. I say they are a problem for the astrologer, but of course to disavow their true nature can also become a problem for them, because eventually something inside may rebel. When that happens they may turn to astrology for help, asking to be reminded who and what they really are, asking to be shown the picture on the seed packet.

This requires a psychotherapy of a sort. Instead of taking over the values and ideals of the TV commercials, the aim now has to be to recognize that every sign of the zodiac, every planet, is itself an ideal to be pursued and cultivated, and if possible brought to near perfect expression, turned into something approaching an art form. Thus the resistance to one-pointed concentration that is a feature of Gemini is not to be deplored, because many-sidedness can be valuable. It is a plus to be able to kill at least two birds with one stone, to run activities in tandem, turn the hand to many things, to have dexterity, the skill of the juggler. After all, many everyday activities, from cooking a meal to driving a car, require that we do things simultaneously, dividing our attention between them.

Of another Gemini actor, Laurence Olivier, it was said he wanted 'to dazzle with his versatility'. Everything in the chart has positive value. There is no aspect so horrendous that it cannot be capitalized, and indeed the worse a configuration looks the more likely it is to be a springboard for success. If you complain that some planetary position or aspect has been an impediment, I guarantee to produce cases where that same aspect has become the key to achievement. If any factor in the chart is proving trouble-some, a liability, it means we have yet to exploit its potential. Frogs can become princes!

So 'How can I get out of this mess?' is another question which can be put to the birth-chart. However, this does not mean astrology is all about psychotherapy, as is sometimes assumed nowadays, and least of all that it should be relegated to the role of handmaiden to some recognized form of psychotherapy, hoping to gain respectability by association. If Jungian analysts, or the followers of Assagioli, find astrology useful then that can only be to the good – just as it would only be to the good if market analysts, criminologists, politicians, spymasters, mountaineers, business execu-tives and so on, found it useful. What must be deplored is any suggestion that this is all astrology is.

Nor is it immediately self-evident that any of the existing brands of psychotherapy faithfully represent the astrological viewpoint. It is all right to ask 'How might this chart be interpreted in the Jungian terms?' if that is where you are coming from. But as an exercise, why not look at the same chart from the Freudian, Alderian, behaviourist (and what have you) standpoints as well. Or if that is too academic, you could successively interpret the one chart in the context of a Mickey Mouse cartoon, a Superman adventure, and a kitchen sink saga. I am quite serious – the cosmic stuff inherent in any one moment is plastic and indeterminate enough that it can be poured into many different moulds without losing its essential compositions.

We should never lose sight of the fact that when we examine your chart or mine there is always an implied question, namely; 'How might this chart be expressed in a *human* context?' The cosmic conditioning of any moment is not written in specifically human terms, and the chart could equally apply to every other kind of creature, and not only to living organisms but inanimate objects as well. Nothing in the chart itself tells us whether we are dealing with a living being, the launching of a ship, the foundation of a nation, the registration of a business, or the birth of an idea. If the chart is not even human, it is difficult to believe it must be written in terms of some particular theory of human nature.

There are many schools of psychology, by no means compatible with each other. The cosmos is wide enough to embrace them all, or at any rate those parts of them that express a fragment of its truth. But the vision of the human being as an embodied universe is so radical, and so at variance with any other, that ultimately only a therapy generated out of astrology itself can meet the need for psychological help based on its insights.

Several approaches might be proposed for a genuine astrotherapy, but the following will also serve to indicate one way to break out of the sterile straitjacket of trait psychology.

Here you envisage the planets as a kind of checklist of functions, organs of the psyche which – like the organs of the body also associated with them

– need to be kept in good repair. The functions of the luminaries and planets can be extracted from any textbook, and in great detail. For psycho-therapeutic purposes, however, it is necessary to ask how each adds to the effective functioning of the whole.

Above them all in importance is perhaps the Sun, which stands for the hunger for appreciation, the need for self-esteem, the desire to feel you count, rather than be a worthless cipher. Everybody has to shine a little! Saturn's contribution includes a disciplined lifestyle, undeviating concentration on objectives, and the ability to establish an organized framework that lends structure to the activities. Of course Saturn especially favours the organizing of his own element, your *time*. Or consider Uranus, the organ of independent or unilateral action, giving the power to stand on your own feet, live by your own rules. Then there is Venus, which on the contrary operates in association, collaboration and unity. And so on.

Now suppose that life has gone sour, and the person is at a loss to know how to begin to put things right.

It is possible to offer advice, friendly or professional, with no horoscope before you. Psychologists, not to mention family and acquaintances, do it all the time. Thus the vital function associated with the luminaries and planets could be used as a basis for inquiring into whether the right ingredients for happiness are present. Going systematically through the checklist, we can ask if all these functions are working as they should. Are there adequate occasions for nurturing the self-esteem? How organized is this person? Is there a proper degree of independence, or is the life being dictated by others?

But with the chart to guide you the unique value of astrology becomes immediately apparent. By looking at the condition of each planet in turn – like a doctor examining now the heart, now the liver, now the kidneys – you know what elements are essential to the health of each, and what needs to be done if they are deficient. For instance if Saturn is powerfully aspected by Uranus, the discipline must be a *self*-discipline, autonomously chosen and imposed by the person himself, and indeed one dictated by some outside authority might only produce rebelliousness. If Saturn is aspected by Mars the discipline, self-imposed or otherwise, needs to be tough; if aspected by Neptune it might beneficially be harnessed to achieving some perfect and far-off goal. If Saturn is in Scorpio it needs to be a little masochistic; if in Sagittarius it needs to become a Puritan ethic.

Or maybe the trouble is not with Saturn but Jupiter. We could all do with a tonic for our Jupiter! We say Jupiter means expansion. Well, just as the body resists being crushed by atmospheric pressure by pushing outwards against it with the same force – remember how the tin can in the physics lesson crumpled pathetically when all the air was sucked out? – so the psyche has to maintain its inner space by pushing against the pressure of events. Call it morale, buoyancy, staying on top, keeping your bounce, being cheerful. Havelock Ellis writes that 'even the momentary expansion of the soul in laughter is, to however slight an extent, a religious exercise' — and indeed we need plenty of such exercise if we are not to sink under the sheer weight of physical existence.

Considering that Jupiter can give a sorely needed lift, we ought to be sure we know from our own chart where and how it works best for us, examining its sign, house and aspects more minutely than is the rule in interpretation, and remembering that astrology can symbolize concrete details, like the activities, people and places, that could facilitate the expression of each planet. We are then in a position to initiate the appropriate action, or place ourself in the right circumstances, favourable to its manifestation.

Thus it is possible to boost or regulate the effects of each planet more or less at will, depending on what seems desirable at this stage of life. Of course, students of progressions and other methods of timing will wish to take their cue from what the planets themselves are underlining as currently important.

The realization that a variety of questions can be posed to the chart is of fundamental importance to the development of astrology, because it highlights the crucial issue of the nature of the link between the heavens and the earth. Of all the questions that can be asked, some must be more fruitful than others because they reflect more closely the how and why of the cosmic penetration into earthly life.

Usually insufficient weight is given to the testimony of those questions that astrologers have slowly recognized cannot be asked at all, because the chart simply does not contain that type of information. The chart does not indicate the sex, the race or nationality, the level of intelligence, the level of morality, or whether the person will be rich or poor, a success or failure, good looking or ugly. Why should it, when we cannot even guess if it is for a human being! I have discussed these seeming limitations, and the explanation, at length in the *The Cosmic Loom*.

Frankly acknowledging that the birth-chart does not contain everything there is to know about the person, the task is to discover what specialized information *is* encoded there, and what sort of language it is written in, recognizing that the language may be different from what we expect. If the chart cannot answer all our human questions, perhaps it contains answers to questions we have not yet had the wit to ask?

There is a forgivable human tendency to project our human preconceptions, desires and obsessions on to the horoscope. But the neglected question is what it represents, in itself, without any interference or dilution from us. Tigers can jump through hoops, bears can ride bicycles, seals can juggle, but a visit to the circus is not the best way to understand animals — to do that you have to leave them alone and study them in their natural habitat. Forgetting what tricks we would like stars to do, what is our relationship with them really about? What is the cosmos of which we are a part itself up to? The problem is not unlike that of 'hacking' into a large computer to clandestinely extract vital facts.

The hallmark of an authentic astrology is a readiness to be instructed by the cosmos, which means we must expect the astrologer to surprise us with what we do not know already, both about ourselves and life in general.

With these considerations in mind, I would describe the approach I have quarried out, over the forty years I have been watching astrology at work, as first and foremost *cosmocentric*. By this I mean I try not to push a distorting screen of my own making between me and the heavens. In particular, instead of noisily firing questions at them about what to me seems important, I try to listen hard to catch whatever they may be whispering. Almost all astrology today is homocentric, in that we insist that the heavens work in our parameters rather than theirs. We continually want the cosmos to toe some line we have drawn. Homocentrically we expect instant understanding, but from the cosmocentric standpoint we accept that we may not immediately be able to grasp what is being conveyed, but may first need to stretch our concepts, or acquire a new vocabulary.

To the newcomer to this subject nothing seems easier than to prove the existence of the astrological by collecting the birth data of several thousand clergymen, soldiers, doctors and so on, or a similar number of sufferers from polio or dyslexia, and analyse the charts to find out what each group has in common. Interesting results may certainly be obtained that way, but there will also be many failures, and the reason is that the cosmos seldom operates in the categories which seem important to us. It has categories of its own, which cut across ours, and clearly there must be some value for the understanding of our reality to discover what they are.

A scientific approach, surely, to let nature speak for itself! There is an oft-repeated criticism that science may not be so much discovering truth as manufacturing it. Scientists are adept at setting up experiments to confirm their preconceptions. It worried Eddington, who asks: 'When Lord Rutherford showed us the atomic nucleus, did he *find* it or did he *make* it?' Reminding us how Procrustes stretched or chopped down his guests to fit the bed he had constructed, Eddington adds: '. . . perhaps you have not heard the rest of the story. He measured them up before they left the next morning, and wrote a learned paper *On the Uniformity of Stature of Travellers* for the Anthropological Society of Attica.'

Astrologers are no more immune to such errors than their orthodox brethren, and much interpretation – and almost all of what is termed serious astrological research – bears the thumbprint of Procrustes! If we accept that depth psychology has got it right, and the individual is ruled by unconscious impulses, we interpret the chart as a map of the unconscious. (How absurd that the cosmos working in man should be dubbed the 'unconscious'!) Or if we follow the conventional wisdom and look on personality as a bundle of characteristics, what more logical than to expect the heavens to provide a handy list of such characteristics.

Again, many practitioners start out with the conviction that their role is closer to that of the portrait artist than the doctor or pathologist. So in practical interpretation students are routinely taught to produce a 'synthesis' of all the separate factors in the chart, attempting to blend them into a plausible picture which will be immediately recognizable. There are many objections to this procedure. One trouble with synthesis is that it tends to blur the contradictions and paradoxes that are present in everyone, and which often tell us more than the consistencies. Fusing all the factors into ·a single image is a bit like taking a snapshot of a hospital patient instead of an X-ray. No matter how superlative the snapshot you cannot dispense with internal examinations, laboratory tests, and all the rest.

Instead of mixing all the ingredients into an indigestible stew the cosmocentric viewpoint insists on keeping separate what the cosmos separates, only uniting what the cosmos itself unites. It respects the way the heavens themselves describe and divide human nature. For example, if astrology is to be useful it is necessary to separate out the solar configuration from the rest of the chart, because this is the symbol of what the individual must develop as the creative centre of his life, the basis of his sense of significance within the totality of existence. This is often in need of remedial attention, because so many people live almost exclusively in their robotic lunar self that it has become atrophied. The lunar configuration needs to be analysed separately, and so does the ascendant, especially because this Aries-like point shows where the leverage is, what the person's approach should be − the best line of attack − if he is to wrest the initiative from a world that might otherwise enslave him.

Indeed, every configuration in the chart requires careful analysis in its own terms.

But to grasp the revolutionary significance of the cosmocentric approach we must consider what I call the cosmic process. There is only one cosmic process, and it accounts for all the effects that comprise astrology. It is the process whereby the actual and tangible becomes manifest out of the invisible ocean of infinite potential· in which everything is immersed, much as a crystal is precipitated from its solution. The process is going on every minute of every hour without interruption, a continual coming to birth in which each entity shares the characteristics of its birth moment with all other entities born at that time, each expressing those characteristics according to its capacity as a vehicle.

To maintain an unceasing awareness of this process, responding to its promptings, would come close to what for the old Chinese was 'living with the Tao'.

Humans belong to this creative thrust like everything else. We too embody the purpose of the All at one moment of its existence. Sadly it is often the superficial, accidental by-products of that purpose stirring within us that are called our character or personality, although they may not be indispensable or unchangeable features. Astrology provides a different, and more fundamental, concept of personality than any current today. Instead of a sum of more or less static attributes, this picture is dynamic, but the dynamics do not so much belong to the individual as to the cosmos as a whole. You are the personal expression of something suprapersonal. When you create you are not originating ideas in the privacy between your ears, but rather voicing what in some sense already exists. You are an experiment in which the cosmos that brought you into being is attempting to work something out, and your role in the transaction is either an unconscious (and perhaps on that account sketchy) compliance or an aware and eager participation.

It means that every individual must be viewed as a cosmic deed, directed to some end; through you something unique is intended to enter the stream of world-becoming. The psyche is thus a stage on which a drama of cosmic dimensions is enacted, well or badly. Human personality is written in a language of strivings, struggles and wrestlings, pinnacles to be climbed, battles to be won, contributions to be made. Why do I say that so confidently? Because when you interpret planetary configurations in this way, *seeking to discern in them a life task*, interpretation becomes that much easier, that much more accurate, and that much more helpful.

As an illustration, let's take the James brothers – not outlaws Jesse and Frank, but philosopher William and novelist Henry.

William James was born under a conjunction of Jupiter and Saturn in Capricorn, and anyone who understands the dynamics of these planets will be able to accept that contacts between them must symbolize a struggle between spiritual buoyancy on the one hand and the downdrag of physical existence on the other. Here faith defies unyielding fact! The life is (or ideally should become) a battleground in which optimism fights with depression.

It is central to my understanding of astrology that the outcome of such a conflict is not determined in advance, but that through it the individual can gain something for himself, and by so doing even win a bridgehead for the evolution of the race. I also believe not everybody will take up the challenge as vigorously as William James, and that some individuals seem better fitted to serve as representatives or examplars of the issues involved.

William was well aware of physical reality, Saturn's kingdom. His academic career began with medical training, and he went on to teach anatomy and physiology at Harvard. His pioneering work in psychology placed it on a firm physiological foundation. Later, as a philosopher, he was a leading pragmatist, asserting that beliefs do not work because they are true, they are true because they work. And when he came to write sympathetically about religion as a human phenomenon his taste for concreteness showed in the emphasis he gave to direct experience rather than metaphysics. Confronting the final Saturn reality as a psychical researcher, he was ever (true to this conjunction) the cautious explorer.

With Jupiter-Saturn the balloon tugs at the mooring ropes, but never quite gets free. William went through periods of illness and depression, dark nights of the soul. Yet even after long physical and nervous prostration he could summon an elasticity and even gaiety of spirit, lifting himself by his own bootlaces. In his youth he had resolved to overcome depression by using his free will to believe in free will! He once wrote: 'Faith is one of the forces by which men live, and the total absence of it means collapse.'

Jupiter-Saturn, then, was an important axis. And what are we to make of the fact that Venus also conjoined these planets? Regardless of what character traits, what labels, we might associate with this configuration, in terms of a life task it must mean that a relationship, or relationships, would be inseparable from the Jupiter-Saturn struggle.

And so it was. A new life began for William with his marriage: there was a redoubled zest for work, and the disappearance of the neuroses that had dogged his early years. Says a biographer: 'It was as if some deeper level of his being had been tapped: his life as an originative thinker began in earnest.' On the death of his father, a remarkable man with deep concern for religious and moral problems, William wrote touchingly to his wife: 'You have one new function hereafter . . . you must not leave me till I understand a little more of the value and meaning of religion in Father's sense, in the mental life and destiny of man . . . I must learn to interpret it aright as I have never done, and you must help me.'

The outcome was that influential classic *The Varieties of Religious Experience*.

However, the heavens exercise a certain neutrality, and I believe Venus's involvement meant only that close relationships had a power decisively to affect, one way or the other, the Jupiter-Saturn struggle to overcome the doubts and oppressions of the physical world – so it was lucky for William and posterity that he was fortunate in his marriage.

A Jupiter conjunction is a feature of the chart of Henry James, but here the planet is with Neptune in Aquarius. In discerning life tasks it is as well to jump straight in and try to seize the essence of a configuration. What does it mean, basically? At the risk of sounding high-flown, this Aquarian conjunction immediately suggests that there lived in Henry James an aspiration towards the boundless brotherhood of man.

If our textbooks have any credibility at all, Jupiter-Neptune must signify the kind of expansion that dissolves and goes beyond existing boundaries, and in Aquarius it must indicate a transcendence of social and cultural horizons, perhaps through a merging of different groups. Is there not an overwhelmingly global feeling about this configuration? Equally we might say it stands for the imaginative (Neptune) exploration (Jupiter) of society – its structure, classes, ideologies, roles, morals and mores – especially as the conjunction is exactly sextile the probing Pluto.

Henry James, born in New York, became a naturalized British citizen, and both he and his work repudiated everything provincial. Many of his novels deal with the collision between American and European cultures. Extolling Henry's crusading internationalism, Ezra Pound wrote of his 'unending endeavour to provide a common language, an idiom of manners and meanings for the three nations, England, America, France'.

He delighted to write in such a way that it was impossible for an outsider to say whether an American was writing about England, or an Englishman was writing about America, regarding such ambiguity as a civilized sign.

It is consonant with the Aquarius conjunction that Henry's emotions seemed to be in affinity with society at large, and never focused in marriage. A kind, friendly, even gregarious man, he liked his human contacts to be impersonal and carefully avoided 'involvement'. One ingredient here was Venus in Pisces, and hence linked with Jupiter and Pisces by rulership.

Intellectually too he remained sensitively extended. Whereas his pragmatic brother William looked to experience to provide the certainties he sought, for Henry the stuff of life remained congenially elusive and diffuse. He wrote: 'Experience is never limited, and it is never complete; it has an immense sensibility, a kind of huge spider-web of the finest silken threads suspended in the chamber of consciousness, and catching every air-borne particle in its tissue.' Accordingly he insisted that nothing he said could ever be his last word about anything! Jupiter-Neptune wants to keep everything permanently opened out, and full of possibilities for transformations.

In this way configurations can be interpreted in terms of life purpose. They may never be articulated or understood by the person himself – and of course that is what astrology is for! Nor may these purposes manifest with equal force in every individual born under them, although it must be emphasized about, in whatever corner of the world we are placed, no life is of so small account that it cannot take up the planetary theme. Beethoven can be played on a penny whistle!

To interrogate the chart on this basis we have to keep asking: 'What does the universe that brought me into being require of me? What is my nature fashioned to mediate into the great stream of life? What *difference* am I intended to make?'

If you think we humans live unto ourselves alone, rather than as an integral part of the advance of cosmic and human evolution, such questions will seem strange. Yet I believe that here we come close to the uniquely astrological revelation of human nature. The horoscope is indeed a code and (to repeat a favourite metaphor) can be likened to sealed orders from High Command, to be opened and acted on with all speed!

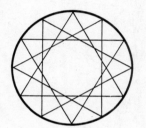

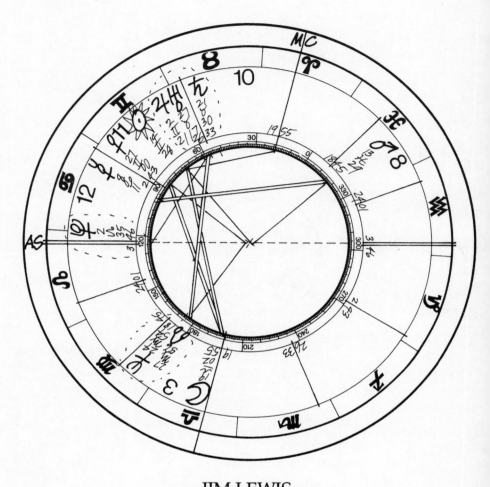

JIM LEWIS

5 June 1941   9:15 am EDT   New York City

Jim Lewis

After high school Jim Lewis set out on what turned out to be almost a decade of travel, which took him to some forty countries, with brief stops to work at various professions, and to absorb ideas and life experience. He attended three colleges during this period, and studied several languages in situ.

Travel periods shortened, and rest periods lengthened, as he integrated himself into the small but very stimulating society surrounding the psychological renaissance then emerging at the Esalen Institute in Big Sur, California, whose atmosphere of psychological inquiry and intellectual liberality fit well with his own consolidating consciousness. Working as a labourer at the Institute during the day, and watching the sky at night, it was inevitable that a link was perceived between the highly charged and the very self-conscious social microcosm at Big Sur and the journey of the planets through the stars.

An unplanned trip to Tucson, Arizona (his Mars Midheaven line), radically changed his life direction, as he befriended astrologers there who encouraged him to study astrology formally. He began his professional career in 1969 as a personal service astrologer for *American Astrology* magazine, then under the guidance of the late Donald A. Bradley. In 1972, he moved to San Francisco, where he has served a large clientele, taught classes, and appeared on radio and TV programmes. In 1975, he began work on *Astro★Carto★Graphy*, and has since devoted most of his time to popularizing the concepts of locational astrology.

His work with *Astro★Carto★Graphy* earned him the Marc Edmund Jones Award for the outstanding contribution to astrology at the 1978 National Astrological Society Convention, and since then, he has appeared on the faculties of almost every important North American astrological conference; he was one of five Americans selected to attend the First and Second World Conferences in Switzerland in 1981 and 1984. His lecturing credits now include twelve nations and twenty states and Canadian provinces.

In 1982, he completed work on *Cyclo★Carto★Graphy*, an important adjunct to *Astro★Carto★Graphy*, for which he was awarded a US patent. As well as contributing frequent articles on many aspects of astrology to the popular press, he publishes annually the *Source Book of Mundane Maps*. He has been very active in AFAN, a professional organization serving the astrological community, since 1982.

Jim Lewis Bibliography

Astro★Carto★Graphy: A Guidebook for the Interpretation of Astro★Carto★ Graphy Maps (1976)
Cyclo★Carto★Graphy: A Guidebook for the Interpretation of Cyclo★Carto★ Graphy Overlays (1982)
Mundane Source Books (every year from 1979 to 1987)

9

'And the Future Will Be Nothing Less Than the Flowering of Our Inwardness'

RAINER MARIA RILKE

JIM LEWIS

Anticipating the future of astrology should be easy – after all, aren't we in the business of analysing trends and cyclic phenomena and projecting the future on the basis of such cycles? And doesn't astrology have an incredibly long and rich history from which to draw? The problem is, most astrologers are committed to their craft – we have an emotional investment in the worldview it represents, and can no more be expected to be objective about its future than we could about the future of our children or parents. Until presented with the concept for this book, I cannot remember seeing or hearing much concrete, informed speculation on the topic.

The 'future of astrology' must needs be treated from two points of view: from one that looks at astrology itself, and from another that views its organizations, structures, and interactions with society at large, in which it constitutes a definite minority point of view. As an astrologer, who came to the profession largely because it permitted me the expression of a worldview I had already developed, it is impossible to be objective about the subject, and equally impossible to discuss it without referring to astrological data. It must therefore be assumed that the astrological hypothesis is accepted for the purpose of this essay – that the relative locations of the planets are analogous and referrable to social and personal events in the human universe. Given this assumption, certain planets' positions in the remaining years of the century will be taken as the prime indications of astrology's development during that time. In this context, the predominant influence is that of Capricorn: Saturn, Uranus and Neptune will transit the sign, focusing immense collective energies into its practical, political and ambitious nature. How this will influence astrology, both organizationally and as a craft or science will be what we examine in the remainder of this essay.

115

How the 'Age of Aquarius' Turned Out To Be the Age of Sagittarius

Since the discovery of Uranus in 1781, astrology has seemingly become increasingly identified with this 'new' planet of ideas and revolution. Classically, astrology was ruled by Saturn (we might presume appropriately, in an age when it would take hours of wrestling with an astrolabe and protractor to derive approximate planetary positions, and in which even logarithms were as yet undreamt of). Myth tells us that Saturn, the dour god of time and earth, was unfriendly to his airy father, Uranus, a sky god so antipathetical to materiality that he condemned Saturn and his other children to Tartarus, because of their (to him) loathsome physicality and earthiness. Uranus seems to symbolize the masculine principle freed from earthly attachment – a sort of detached animus closely aligned with the *Puer Aeternus*, and an eternal antagonist of the ordinary, the practical, as well as the fecund, mothering, moist, and nurturing impulses associated with water. As such, it seems a fitting symbol for astrology's identity in the modern world, an identity untrammelled by attachment to physical science – unorthodox, yet sure of itself. If the concept of the planet Uranus is closely aligned with astrology, its cycles in the solar system, the signs it occupies and aspects it makes to other planets must be taken as indications for the future of the craft.

Neptune as well has a strong relationship to astrology; the planet of intuition, cultural aspirations, and spirituality adds to astrology the ethical, mystical and religious dimensions that make it so abhorrent to 'pure' scientists, yet which give it its depth, spirituality and personal relevance. The astrological theory of transits suggests that should both these planets of astrology occupy signs of cultural significance, that astrology will undergo analogous change, evolution, and alteration in its social presentation. Whatever the theory, this has certainly proved to be the case over the last decade, during which time, both Neptune and Uranus have been in the outgoing, culturally oriented, and philosophically inclined sign Sagittarius.

The Sagittarian period, which began as early as 1971, and reached a peak in 1983 and 1984, was marked by three developments which have unalterably changed the face of our craft: a resurgence of spirituality, astrological politics, and computers. The spiritual astrology of the 1970s reiterated themes that emerged in the last great Sagittarian period, 1890 to 1905, when, with the exception of Neptune's position in Gemini instead of Sagittarius, a similar planetary alignment occurred. As in the 1890 to 1905 period, practical, event-oriented astrology was disowned in the early 1970s. Largely under the influence of Rudhyar and his followers, 'person-centred' astrology became the mainstream, not unlike the strongly Theosophical astrology and blossomed in the early years of this century, wherein the soul's evolution towards wholeness was the object of astrological inquiry. There was a religious cast to the whole process, and, in its extremity, there were even those who asserted that it was inappropriate for astrologers to take payment for their services — presumably, like yogis, they ought to have transcended such mundane needs as nutrition, clothing and shelter.

The spiritual movement probably reached fullest flower in the early 1980s, with the brilliant and profound work of Liz Greene, astrology's most recent 'superstar'. While it is impossible to gauge the effects of any one person's contribution to our craft so early in the game, there can be no doubt that Ms Greene's rise to unprecedented fame in our field reflected astrology's willingness to embrace her singular adaptation of Jung's abstract and highly psychological worldview. Suddenly astrology acquired a new spiritual perspective, one that also had as its object the wholeness of the person, and it acquired an authoritative philosophical basis as well, the teachings of Carl Jung. The prediction of events was still seen as irrelevant at best, except when they were guides to the fulfilment of personal wholeness under a semi-medical, psychiatric model. Liz Greene has actually become an accredited Jungian analyst, perhaps so symbolizing the 'marriage' of astrology and psychotherapy.

In the mainstream culture at this time, a parallel spiritual awakening was occurring, with the early 1970s marked by the 'Age of the Guru', which evolved into the fundamentalist doctrines of the 1980s. In both the mainstream society and the astrological community, the Sagittarian influences are striking. They are made all the more so by contrasting this to the aforementioned similar period in the 1890s — for in that case the opposition of Neptune and Pluto to Uranus's position in Sagittarius militated that the spiritual awakening come from external sources — the Far East — while in our own era, Neptune's conjunction in Sagittarius suggests the sources to be closer to home: Jesus and Carl Jung. It is geographically appropriate that in the earlier period the ideal gurus should have come from the other side of the world (opposition), while in our own era they have been generated from within our own culture.

In such periods of Sagittarian evolution, it might be argued, astrology and similar cultural institutions work towards a spiritual ideal of wholeness and unity, and do so somewhat within a 'medical model' — one that presupposes a problematical (diseased) state of unwholeness in the individual which is mitigated by the ministrations of a professional of some sort — a priest, Jesus, a shaman, doctor, or astrologer. In the early 1980s, his social tendency at times reached almost ludicrous proportions in certain suburban centres, where almost everyone was simultaneously learning new healing techniques, working to heal others, and being intensely therapized themselves. Still, it added valuable psychological depth and perspective to what have most often been hide-bound and rigid cultural institutions.

Mark Lerner, an Oregon astrologer, in early 1986 suggested demarcating the end of the 'Age of the Guru' by Bhagwan Shree Rashneesh's rather undignified flight from the USA in mid-November 1985, with federal authorities in hot pursuit. Moreover, both Rudhyar and Krishnamurti died during this period. Lerner observed that this was the time when Saturn, having recently entered Sagittarius, again the sign of religion and culture, attained the very degrees at which Jupiter and Neptune had conjoined in 1971, a conjunction which he characterized as the beginning of the 'Guru' period. In 1972, Saturn and Neptune also opposed in this degree area (0 – 4 Sagittarius). So Saturn, old father time, rung down the curtain on the inflated pursuit of spirituality that characterized the excesses of the 1970s, and initiated a period where its more conservative, practical and pragmatic influence is apt to become a cultural norm.

The Sky God Visits the House of Saturn

In February 1988, Uranus, planetary symbol of astrology, will enter Capricorn, the sign of his hated son, Saturn. Neptune entered Capricorn in 1984, signalling the beginning of the end of the mini Age of Sagittarius described above. Saturn itself will also occupy Capricorn in the late 1980s, so that 1989 and 1990 see a peak of Capricorn activation, which will tend to lessen gradually until 1998, when all three planets will have left the sign. Given the astrological hypothesis, the future of astrology (and of our society as a whole) will reflect this change of emphasis from Sagittarius to Capricorn, which deserves some detailed analysis.

As is so often the case, the Greek myth provides us with some answer, in its conceptualization of the relationship between Uranus and Saturn.

We have already discussed how Uranus, scarcely anyone's idea of 'parent of the year', confined his children to Tartarus because of their earthy materiality. One of these unfortunate progeny was Saturn, or Chronos, who, when Uranus was unaware, rose up with the others, slew his father, and took over the universe. As is so often the case, maltreatment in childhood produced a less-than-nurturing parent, as Saturn himself then proceeded to repeat the pattern, but to make doubly certain that his reign would be untroubled he ate his children as soon as they were born. Jupiter, one of these children, managed to escape and, in turn, overthrew Saturn.

The important concept in this myth is Saturn's intolerance of change, growth, and evolution, suggesting that the fears of inadequacy and the natural diminishment of power that come with age are projected onto youth in the sign of winter and privation. Ideally, there is a gradual process by which a new generation overcomes an older one, being gradually initiated to power and trained in its use. But modern society (perhaps forced by demographics – too few children in the 1930s, then too many in the 1940s) has no such process. For the most part, every sector of society from politics and religion to astrology and industry, leadership is becoming increasingly concentrated in a gerontocracy, whose only true interests lie in the perpetuation of their power. This concentration is exacerbated by a stagnation in the growth of economics, limitations imposed by shrinking resources and overseas competition, and increasing populations. Absolute control is sought and any force that resists it is seen as evil. Youth, always rebellious, is underemployed and rigidly repressed. The upcoming mini Age of Capricorn then, if this myth has relevance to the situation, is apt to be one of analogous polarization of age and youth, and competition between them for resources.

The sociological results of this could range anywhere from the slight increase in the conservatism of the last few years to a more radical and frightening psycho-social upheaval. If the symbol of Saturn proves appropriate, it seems likely that conservatism, retrospection, and rigidity are apt to accelerate and continue for at least a decade more in the social mainstream.

Capricorn owes its rather lugubrious reputation to the season of the year for which it is a symbol – the darkest, coldest months of winter, when one must rely upon what one has stored from the past, and when the present is at best unpleasant. In such times of natural privation, authority may not be questioned, and deviations from norms can be less tolerated. Regimentation and conservatism seem necessary and, as James Hillman wrote about the *Senex*, 'fixations upon literalisms and materialized abstractions' become the intellectual standards. Political conservatism and a cultural sense of retrospection follow from this *Weltanschauung*, as forms become more important than content and the pronouncements of authority are taken as absolute truth.

As must be obvious, in such a climate of fixed ideas and retrospection, science itself becomes more conservative, materially oriented and intolerant. This process seems already well established, at least in the popular press, where self-proclaimed 'scientists' (usually otherwise undistinguished in their fields) can achieve a ready-made reputation and unlimited media exposure simply by making unfounded pronouncements against 'superstitious and unscientific' thought – usually astrology or some allied field. More objective writers such as Paul Feyerabend have observed that such unquestioned dogmatism makes it impossible reasonably to explore the fields so circumscribed, and as well establishes doctrines based on authority and coercion, rather than on objective truth and experimentation. This is paradoxical, as science at present has encountered, as it always will, metaphysics on the cutting edge of any of its disciplines. Discrete, material, non-interactive realities simply do not exist, and seem to be mythic holdovers from the nineteenth-century's stress on materialism and physical science.

But, instead of seeing the impossibility to quantify absolutes as a challenge and invitation to reach into more profound and universal territory, too many scientists instead project this failure onto scapegoats like astrology – imputing to it some mystical power to corrupt minds and bring down civilization. As is often the case with projection, such scientists are usually guilty of the very sins they project, as it is rare that even lip service is given to scientific method in their unconditional and dogmatic denials that astrological effects could even exist. It is possible that in the increase of Capricornian influence for the rest of this century, such attitudes may increase in currency, and scientific dogmatism may discourage truly needed inquiry from proceeding beyond the threshold of materially explicable reality. In a sense, this tendency must be seen as necessary reaction to some of the excesses of the Sagittarian decade, but one should neither throw one's babies out with the bathwater, nor eat them when they ask impertinent questions.

Astrology itself certainly qualifies as an authoritative tradition, so the Capricornian period of the late 1980s could ironically see a sort of retrospective respect for astrology develop in some non-scientific circles, but, from the point of view of a holistic or 'person-centred' astrology, the respect would be for all the wrong reasons, as such traditionalists would seek in astrology authoritative answers to impossibly complex questions, a tendency which is already evident in several recent trends which underline the increasing requirement that astrology have some practical, pragmatic, and material application. Financial and investment astrology is now a field of considerable interest, reflecting a perception that where in the 1970s personal growth and wholeness were objects of astrological analysis, in the 1980s the growth of the bank account seems more relevant.

There is also a firm movement towards attempting to quantify astrological phenomena – despite the obvious difficulties inherent in such undertakings. Michel Gauquelin, Françoise Schneider-Gauquelin and Hans Eysenck are only among the more well-known names labouring toward this end and, while their modest successes hardly 'prove' astrology, they certainly demand a more rigorous examination of our principles and requestioning of our techniques and processes of thought.

My own contribution – *Astro★Carto★Graphy* – reflects this trend as well – a computer-assisted application of relocation astrology, it symbolically 'brings astrology down to Earth', redrawing the traditional horoscope on a map of the world, distributing planets' energies not through abstract houses, as in a traditional chart, but over the geographical surface of the Earth itself. This specialty perhaps reflects my own natal Uranus and Saturn conjunction in Earth sign Taurus, and as well offers some practical insights – identifying different locations at which various parts of the potential and personality are more apt to manifest.

The trend should be obvious – investment astrology, Earth-centred computer horoscopes, attempts to quantify astrological effects, and increasing antipathy, usually based on unfounded dogma, from mainstream science. These trends are apt to be amplified and developed in the next decade or so by Capricorn's inclination towards the concrete, the authoritarian, and the dogmatic.

As mentioned above, in medieval times astrology was ascribed to the planet Saturn. This makes sense when one realizes that in addition to the enormous discipline required to calculate a horoscope without the benefit of modern astronomical and computational tools, kings and medieval politicians were not at all interested in personal growth towards wholeness, but rather in practical information such as auspicious times to wage wars or to attempt to usurp enemies' authority. The medieval worldview was somewhat more fatalistic than the *hubris* of modern technological scientism, and rulers were probably more willing to accept that for everything there is a season, themselves included. Moreover, ancient astrology changed little over the millennia: the astrology that Rudhyar reformed with his 'person-centred' holistic astrology was remarkably similar to that written by Ptolemy in the Hellenistic era. The authoritarianism of the time was reflected in a blind obeisance to an ideal of classicalism that permeated astrology as well – if the Greeks had done it, it must be right, and few were intellectually courageous enough to even add to their classical heritage.

How then is the new, psychologically mature astrology apt to react to the mini Age of Capricorn that its own cycles must predict? Some insight into this can be gained by looking at a theoretical chart of astrology itself.

Clearly it is not possible to derive a horoscope for the craft or science of astrology – no birth-date could ever be established. However, modern astrologers generally agree that astrology is associated with the sign Aquarius (even the Broadway musical agreed on that), and that sign's opinionativeness, intellectualism, and airy nature seem in keeping with its individualistic, subjective, and anti-authoritarian nature.

Capricorn exists in a particular relationship to Aquarius – if the latter sign of astrology is placed in the first house (identity) on the theoretical chart, Capricorn would fall in the twelfth house of the same chart, and from this relationship may be inferred how astrology itself might perceive a period of time dominated by Capricornian values and social structures.

In traditional astrology, the twelfth house rules the unconscious mind, dreams, imprisonment, illness, and self-undoing, among various other related ideas. As the unconscious mind it conjures up concepts of the shadow and projection – while easy to admit that authoritarian science sees in astrology its own projected failings, the same could be said to be true of astrology, in reverse. The dogmatism of material science stands for an earlier stage of evolution for astrology, one that it would rather not look back on, and which it would tend to regard with considerable antipathy. The dogmatism of intolerant scientists who follow materialism as a religion reflects astrology's own unaccepted past, and yet it is this very materialism that demands astrological inquiry. For all its metaphysics, astrology requires a physical universe, and its pronouncements affect people, that is, those extraordinary interoperations of physical and spiritual laws.

So many planets, including astrology's ruler, Uranus, in Scorpio, the sign of conservatism and politics, throughout the late 1980s hint at increased relevance of the 'astrology versus science' argument, as both factions may tend to polarize opinions and retreat into inflexible and intellectually defensive positions. Astrologers, for their part, while tolerant, are seldom adequately informed on matters of astronomy, statistics, physics or other hard sciences. The decade to come presents an opportunity to correct these insufficiencies, and the leaders of the astrological field will probably continue to do so. Philosophically, astrology may become preoccupied with its historical past and its physical origins. It should proceed to look less like a religion and means to self-fulfilment and more like an objective science, adapting wave theory, gravitation, statistics, or some probably yet unnamed branch of psychology to justify itself to an increasingly rigid and intolerant academic establishment.

Astrological Politics

If Capricorn represents astrology's twelfth house, then Sagittarius, the period that drew to a close in 1986, must represent its eleventh. This traditional astrological house symbolizes social organizations based on common ideals, unions, mutual benefit societies, and the like, and it cannot be denied that the 1970s and early 1980s saw unprecedented activity in these areas. Up to 1980 or so, astrological organizations were content to issue journals, sponsor conventions, and sell books; some tried to encourage a little research among their members. But, in keeping with the Uranian and Neptunian nature of astrology (and, thus, astrologers), practical and political matters were not given much priority. Anyone familiar with astrology has many recollections of astrological groups torn with internal dissension, totally incapable of handling the most elementary practical exigencies of running a group, while at the same time proclaiming a New Age of Eternal Cooperation and Enlightenment. Saturn, Capricorn, and their concepts of responsibility to monetary and practical exigencies comprise astrology's own shadow – so it is not surprising that neglect of the political and practical resulted in astrological organizations that all too often simply accrued power to their leaders or dissipated energy in petty, internecine conflicts. Edmund Burke's assertion that 'all that is necessary for evil to triumph is for good men to do nothing' was all too often proved true in astrological politics.

Still, astrological organizations grew and expanded throughout the 1970s, even with their limitations. And this growth was substantially stimulated by the social and political realities of the 1980s after Uranus entered Sagittarius. New groups (particularly AFAN, which has worked for legal reform and networking among astrologers) sprang up, often from within older, less responsive groups, or older groups reasserted their idealistic origins and undertook new efforts on behalf of the astrological community. And, none too soon, it might be added, as fundamentalist Christianity and other conservative social forces in the USA simultaneously mounted a concerted attack on astrology, backed up by the 'scientific' authorities alluded to above. Partly in response to such attacks, and also as part of a natural process of growth as Neptune entered Capricorn, several astrological groups show signs of political and economic maturity, this perhaps a harbinger of further consolidations as Uranus joins Neptune in Capricorn, which would be astrological organizations' second house of finances. For now, the ideals are more concrete and practical; the future should see astrology and its organizations better able to operate on the physical plane, and to acquire the substance and power necessary to defend its ideas.

Yet such material maturity carries with it great risks: power and money mix very badly with idealism and committed, individualistic vision, and, as has been the case often in the past, financial success may prove to be a critical trial for astrological organizations. Means have a way of becoming ends in themselves, particularly when the ends are ideas that are, and probably will remain, rather heterodox and unpopular. But these ideas are of great importance to our civilization, and will be all the more needed in the scientistic era of the late 1980s.

Astrology has moved from becoming a worldview with relevance only to its practitioners, to an important focus of social and intellectual energy; it, along with other similar minority points of view, stands for the entire concept of intellectual freedom. Increased networking and political organization is always the result of oppression, and, as has been the case in racial, political, ethnic, and sexual minorities, unreasoned majoritarian attacks on astrology have resulted only in a greater internal cohesiveness and a more tightly knit community. Since Neptune entered Sagittarius in 1971, astrology has grown from a belief, practised in private by a few, mostly unrelated individuals who held in common only that belief, to a true community, with recognized authorities, ethics and, above all, the means of inter-communication and organization. New ideas and discoveries, news of attempts at social coercion or oppression, scientific advances, and so forth are now communicated rapidly to thousands of astrologers worldwide.

As the emphasis on Sagittarius wanes and Capricorn takes its place, this tendency to expand our community may seem to stall or even reverse itself. Militancy (which has hardly ever existed in astrology at any time) will give way to a more subtle, practical networking, as the mainstream of society pursues its authoritarian fantasies and materialistic dogma, in one more attempt to resurrect an age in which values and standards stand still. The astrological community may itself seem to rigidify again, as a new echelon of authorities and leaders could emerge to replace the older generation, of whom so few now remain. Astrology may seem to lose influence, perhaps abetted by some of its practitioners who will be all too willing to act out whatever role the producers want them to in exchange for a spot on prime-time TV. Astrologers may find themselves forced to choose between selling out to mainstream expectation, or losing power and influence in the larger society, which may seem to many like failure.

Westerners tend to see implementation of the will as success – the illusion of extraverted power can be maintained as long as one's desires are realized, and one's worldview justified and accepted. Astrologers often fall into this trap as well, unquestioningly believing that if only The Leader would express a belief in astrology, then those millions of followers of whom society is largely comprised would embrace the truth, and the millennium would arrive.

But the planets do not revolve in their orbits to assure mere humans the gratification of seeing their worldview on prime-time TV. Astrology has a different message for the world than to state that it is 'right' and those who don't accept it are 'wrong'. Christianity's truth was not much advanced when, at last, the Roman emperor embraced it, and one could make a case for asserting that it was irrevocably compromised; any astrology that can play to the masses will not be very astrological. So long as Westerners feel that exercise of their ego and will constitutes success (rather than integrating with nature and the universe), astrology is not apt to be very successful. The networks and organizations may prove to have a purpose different from an evangelistic 'conversion' of our society to a belief in astrology, a purpose more in keeping with a twelfth-house Capricorn epoch that lies in the immediate future.

Computers and the Electronic Monastery

Undoubtedly, the most important technical advance to change astrology is the development and increased accessibility of the computer. This outward materialization of humankind's capacity for intelligence will affect astrology in at least two major ways, technical and social. While the social ramifications of the creation of a computer network are perhaps ultimately the most significant, the technical aspects will far sooner have revolutionary effects on the art of astrology. It seems symbolically appropriate for Uranus in Capricorn that computer technology will make it possible within a few years to encode vast amounts of interactive astrological knowledge on a chip, or synthetic crystal. (Crystals have traditionally been associated with Capricorn and its planetary symbol, Saturn.) While it is impossible to foresee all the implications of such an extraordinary technical achievement, a few consequences are inescapable.

The programming of chips, their marketing, and distribution all require capital, and while it will soon be technically possible to embed most astrological knowledge on an inexpensive chip, economic pressures will demand that only the 'best' – that is, most orthodox – knowledge be so distributed. This mineralization of knowledge may well tend to create an astrological orthodoxy and as well remove the individual factor from astrology. This latter possibility is already evident in the various programs available in the USA and Europe, which, even with primitive capacity for synthesis, are successful enough to reduce the astrologers who use them to mere distributors of preconceived categorizations. Just as the god Uranus would not be very comfortable in this situation, even when increased computing capacity allows for some measure of synthesis and variation, and even though the mass production aspects of the whole process mean wider distribution of astrological ideas to the public.

Computers do not think – they just store and retrieve data very efficiently. They are more like an automated library than a brain, and as such, astrologers who use preprogrammed chart analyses will always be librarians, or information delivery persons, rather than astrologers. While it is at present very difficult to define what makes astrology anything more than the sum of the knowledge of its traditions, it becomes very obvious that it is more than that sum when one peruses a computer-generated horoscope delineation. It seems inescapable to conclude, painful as it may be, that just as one must cross the threshold into metaphysics when one discusses why a living human is different from a dead one, one must do the same when one compares the potential efficiency of all possible astrological knowledge on a chip, to a living astrologer. Whatever the difference, this Capricornian epoch should make it 'crystal' clear, though possibly only after a lot of resources have been spent on trying to find some way around the dilemma. The nineteenth-century materialistic science pilloried above has already acknowledged (grudgingly) that the whole is often more than the sum of its parts; astrology may have to realize the same, in the near future. Whatever the problems of the time to come, this necessary realization that information is not the only factor involved in knowledge, is bound to be an exciting and stressful one.

Perhaps as important as the problem outlined above is the capacity afforded by computers to change the astrological community itself. Computers, along with the already existent telephone network, make possible a new type of social organization – a network that exists within the larger society made up of highly specialized and particularly non-majority-believing individuals. Hitherto, the only way that people, believing in a worldview at odds with the prevailing one could work together was by actually creating a ghetto – such as the Amish, Quakers, hippies, homosexuals, and any number of other variant groups have always done in the past. Such communities afforded mutual protection, support, and the opportunity to develop one's own lifestyle apart from the mainstream.

Computers make possible a new type of community, one not based in geographical location, but in communality of ideas, for no matter how small your minority, they can all be inexpensively linked together, at least on intellectual planes, by a computer-telephone network. Selection of mailing lists, modems, and automatic data-transmission and recording capacities make intervening distances between individuals irrelevant.

The 'Electronic Monastery' may serve to shelter astrology in the period to come when, as noted above, tolerance, intellectual freedom, and unbiased inquiry may become somewhat rarer. Just as monasteries in the Middle Ages acted to preserve classical traditions in a world in which social order had largely disintegrated apart from authoritarian social institutions, computer networks can preserve astrological (and other variant) worldviews if times of trouble are ahead. The training astrologers have undergone in the past few years in political and social organization will stand them in good stead when, in the perhaps less enlightened age that lies immediately in the future, a rigorous and persevering dedication is required.

Astrology represents a worldview quite in opposition to that which is apt to become more current by the end of the decade of the 1980s. When Capricorn seeks control, and the containment or destruction of what cannot be controlled, astrology sees a cyclic universe, polytheistic, eternal, and somewhat more fatalistic. Those who believe in power cannot acknowledge fatalism, and both points of view balance each other out: controlling technocracy and absolute patriarchy ultimately destroys all life itself (the Pluto-in-Capricorn of the USA's birth-chart, and its fearful implication of atomic destruction), while the fatalistic humanism of matriarchy has little motivation to advance beyond the hunter-gatherer stage of social evolution. Astrology fits clearly with the latter, while the times may tend to the former.

As of this writing (mid-1986), there are about two and a half years left of the partially Sagittarian period described above. Until late 1988, astrology, and especially its organizations and networks, will seem to grow and flourish, encouraging many of us to believe that we may have the power and opportunity to contribute to the future. The latter years of this decade are apt to see climatological (Capricorn suggests cold), economic, political, or natural events, in keeping with Pluto in Scorpio, that require radical realignments of society's objectives; astrology may find itself retrenching, consolidating its community and belief systems, and waiting for the spring which must perforce follow winter. Its knowledge will be encoded on crystals, not unlike the seeds of a plant, which bear within themselves the genetic heritage and future of their species. And, just as seeds can wait indefinitely for an environment that encourages the expression of their potential, the highly individualistic worldview of astrology may need to wait through this period, with its computerized blind alleys and scientific dogmatism, to see a true flowering in a future time.

In the most abstract context, astrology will always exist as a repository for an anti-purposeful worldview to temper the wilfulness of the Judaeo-

Christian-Moslem tendency to patriarchy and control. When Western civilization has once again defied the gods with its eternal hubris, and been stretched on the rack of those gods' indifference, astrology will be there to assure those who would listen that it is all part of a pattern, perceptible to those who look for it, but unconcerned with human aspirations and delusions of immortality.

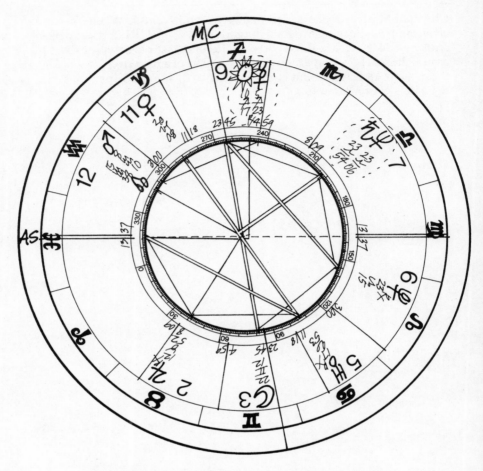

KAREN HAMAKER-ZONDAG
2 December 1952   1:30 pm CET   Schiedam, Holland

Karen Martina Hamaker-Zondag

After finishing high school, Karen Hamaker went to Amsterdam and received a degree in Social Geography from the University of Amsterdam in 1975 and in Environmental Engineering in 1978. She had an interest in astrology and parapsychology since her early school days in 1968, but did not really believe that they worked. She started studying with the intention of convincing herself that it did not work and ended up becoming an astrologer.

In 1970 she became interested in the psychology of Jung, and for several years studied the connections between Jungian psychology and astrology, aided by a series of dreams in which she 'saw' their connection. In 1976 she left her job as a teacher and researcher at the university and began work as an astrological counseller, with the intention of starting a school in which people could learn all aspects of astrology.

In 1977 she started the first of a series of books on astrological interpretation based on Jungian psychology which formed the basis of the four-year course in astrological theory and practice at her school *Stichting Achernar* (Achernar being a fixed star near her Ascendant). As of 1987 there are 250 students and the school is still expanding.

Besides writing, teaching and counselling, she gives lectures in Holland and abroad, and raises her two children. She owes much to her husband Hans who critically analyses all her books. She is currently writing a book on the *Twelfth House* and intends in the future to publish books on such subjects as The Progressed Horoscope, Synastry, The Moon's Nodes and the Yod Figure.

Karen Hamaker-Zondag Bibliography

Psyche en astrologisch symbool (Astro-Psychology) (1977)
Elementen en kruizen als basis van de horoscoop (Elements and Crosses) (1979)
Wezen en werking van planeten (Planetary Symbolism in the Horoscope) (1984)
Aard en achtergrond van de huizen (1984)
Analyse van aspecten (1985)
Huisheren en huizenverbanden (1985)
Handbook voor de uurhoekastrologie (A Handbook of Horary Astrology) (1986)
Oude europese voorspelkunst (1986)
Wat is toch astrologie? (1987)

10

The Future Casts Its Shadow Ahead

A Jungian View of the Near Future of Astrology

DR KAREN M. HAMAKER-ZONDAG

If it is true that astrology is principally concerned with prediction, then it would not be so difficult for an astrologer to predict the future of astrology itself. However, most astrologers know better. It is tempting to delineate the future by the simple interpretation of planetary combinations or cycles on which there is at least some general agreement.

But there are many snakes in the grass.

First of all, prediction is not really the most advanced part of astrology, and furthermore the value of prediction is relative. There is great disagreement about the techniques used and their validity. No one has yet been able to find the ultimate, all-embracing method. Even with existing techniques, there are many possibilities in prediction, although not for the prediction of events in great detail.

Secondly, in the interpretation of the horoscope and future trends, called transits and progressions, the psyche of the astrologer plays a very important role. The basic material is the patterns of the heavens as interpreted by man. The personal fears and expectations, hopes and desires of the astrologer appear to be of some importance to the interpretation. No matter how hard we try to deny this and attempt to justify our interpretation by invoking techniques and rules, there is no way to ignore the unconscious. It always finds a way of breaking through. How else is it possible that while we pursue objectivity, we end up being subjective? What part does the subconscious play? Carl Gustav Jung has proposed several approaches to this problem which may give us insight. He distinguished between a conscious and an unconscious part of the psyche. In the unconscious he made a distinction between personal and collective layers.

Our personal unconscious contains the repressed contents of which we have not yet become aware, but could at some future time. As long as they remain in the realm of our unconscious, we tend to project them onto other people, objects or situations outside ourselves. This mechanism of projection enables us to become aware of contents in the outer world which actually come from within our own unconscious psyche. For instance, if a man has a hidden, repressed hunger for power, he tends to suspect that people around him to be power hungry. In anticipation he becomes defensive, while, in reality, possibly none of these people yearns for this supposed power. This person has projected a content of his own unconscious onto the outside world and has attributed to it characteristics which are his own. This means that we continuously confront our unconscious through contact with the outside world. The extent to which we feel affected by people and events tells us something about the importance of the unconscious contents involved.

Just imagine that an astrologer is afraid of some destructive traits within himself, and has repressed that dark side. He doesn't recognize that side of himself any longer and refuses to face it. These contents are projected automatically onto the outside world. A possible result is that he will become annoyed at even the tiniest reflection of his own dark, hidden traits in others and in particular in his clients. Therefore his fears can result in exaggerating possible destructive tendencies in the horoscopes of others, and also in interpreting a client's behaviour in a way which applies instead to himself. His own repression has become a blind spot which influences his interpretation.

By this mechanism we interpret everything we come up against in the world so that our subjective premises are reinforced. This becomes a negative spiral. Another example is an astrologer who unconsciously fears the future because of a repressed inferiority complex. He will tend to predict a future that is gloomier than necessary, all in good faith. He doesn't realize that he and other people become victims of his projections. However, we should keep in mind that in contrast to such negative projections there may be just as many glorifying, extolling and wishful projections. What is relevant is that our interpretations have a subjective hue as a result of personal projections.

When we look into the future of astrology, the ideas we form are arrived at through the interplay of technical skill and our psyche. We can suggest possibilities by extrapolating trends of the past. We can investigate how the slower planets, symbolizing collective tendencies and attitudes, were related to each other in the past and which signs they transited, and compare it with what happened at that time. Studying history in the light of these planets is really fascinating. What happened then could enable us to make our conclusions about what might happen in the future, although we still have to take human limitations into account.

How can we ever foresee something not yet incorporated into our view of the world and which cannot possibly be derived from extrapolation of existing patterns? Perhaps through extrasensory perception, but that is not astrology. Perhaps we must take into account these limitations when extrapolating trends in the future. Nevertheless, realizing that personal factors are inevitably involved, I will now try to give a view of the future of astrology on the basis of extrapolation.

In order to get a better understanding of the nature of collective principles, we must look into Jungian psychology, in particular that which concerns the archetypes and the collective unconscious. Deep in our unconscious is a layer which binds us to everything and everyone. It is not individual but universal. It has contents and modes of behaviour that are more or less the same in all individuals everywhere. It is a layer wherein time and space do not exist and which contains all psychological reactions and experiences of humanity from the very beginning of its existence. Jung has named this layer the collective unconscious, the source of all human motives and urges. The collective unconscious contains 'archetypes', ideas that exist before material takes form. Jung used the image of the axial system of a crystal which preforms the crystalline structure in the mother liquid, although it has no material existence of its own. The archetype itself has no form but has the possibility of a priori representation. Archetypes are ideas which reflect the common patterns of human reaction which precede and underlie all human behaviour. We can learn about archetypes through their expression in psychic images and in actions. Although we all carry the same archetypes deep inside, we all react differently to them.

But what has this got to do with astrology?

A great deal. For example, we all have the instinct for self-preservation which enables us to fight for ourselves. It does not matter whether it manifests in a constructive or destructive way. The impulse is in our unconscious and how we perceive it in our unconscious is what is expressed in or outside ourselves.

The archetypes express themselves differently through all cultures and times, but their basic principle stays the same. We find them represented in all expressions of life, for example, in art, music, mythology, etc. The Greeks symbolized this impulse for self-preservation in their god Ares, the Romans in Mars, the god of war and strife. He had a place amidst a host of gods, a greater grouping in which he had to function. The other gods reflected other urges and traits of the human unconscious. Man projects materially as well as spiritually in all he creates the contents which are deeply hidden inside himself. Even though the form is personal, they all have an archetypal basis.

Projection is the mechanism by which we learn to recognize archetypal contents in ourselves, and as a result understand ourselves. All original urges from within our psyche try to express themselves separately or in combination with each other. This means that they can either support or be in conflict with each other.

Astrologically, we recognize the projection of an archetypal reaction of self-preservation in the symbolism of Mars. These two different projections, the mythological and the astrological, have the same origin deep within the human psyche. Astrology has not chosen a number of gods from Olympus arbitrarily – the source lies deeper in man himself.

The planets symbolize the archetypal reaction patterns of man. They are reflected in every horoscope in different ways, for example, through the signs, houses and aspects, etc. In every one of us the same archetype can manifest itself in a diversity of images and situations.

For many centuries we have realized that it is particularly meaningful to work within the conceptual framework of astrology. We continuously re-define the meanings of planets, signs, houses, aspects, and we use other interpretive tools. In the course of the centuries, mankind has also developed further. As archetypes lie in the collective unconscious of man, where all the experiences and psychological reactions of mankind are stored, the development of man will also mean a manifestation of increasingly differentiated archetypes. Apparently new situations can be traced back to existing archetypes time and again.

Using the slow moving planets as an example of taking this image further, when we look at their mutual configurations and the signs they transit, they show certain expressions which can be traced back to an archetypal idea or pattern. The collective of humanity vibrates in accordance with the slow moving planets. Thus the historical images, patterns and facts reflecting the archetypal pattern find expression. Studying the past with this in mind can give us a useful indication of the future. But there is more. When a certain tendency, conceived in the slow moving planets, shows up at some time in history, it is suddenly picked up by individuals all over the world. Through their behaviour, their wishes, their desires and ideals they give it form. Such an archetype is expressed collectively as well as individually. Those who are sensitive to the characteristics of that tendency will lead the way, but they will seldom or never be aware of the process, because it is subliminal. The role of the individual will not become clear until many years later.

Thus the collective and the individual cannot be separated. We can look at what happened in the past when the planet Pluto, the symbol of transformation, went through its own sign Scorpio. By looking at what happened in the past we might be able to understand what is happening now because Pluto is transiting the sign Scorpio again. Extrapolation can give us a general view, and we can try to fit astrology into it.

Pluto transited Scorpio between 1492 and 1502, between 1738 and 1750 and in 1984 entered Scorpio again until 1996. In 1492, Columbus discovered America. No one at that time could possibly know that this event was to mark the end of the Middle Ages, yet historians have pointed out that this period was the beginning of a new era. In many ways, the discovery of America did usher in a completely new view of the world and the universe, for Western man. His horizon was broadened in ways he could never have dreamt of before. Not only did his view of the world and the universe change, but his view of everything else in society, in art, in science, etc. Columbus's discovery was the beginning of a transformation and renaissance in the way European man conceived and experienced life.

The subtle but irreversible changes associated with configurations of Pluto are not always linked with major world events such as the discovery of America. When Pluto returned to Scorpio again in 1738, the shockwave was much smaller, yet there was an event that marked the beginning of a radical transformation process. In England, the 'high speed' shuttle, which made weaving much faster, came into use. Its success stimulated further improvements, and within a few decades the first seeds of industrialization can be discerned. First the 'Spinning Jenny', then spinning machines driven by water power and then the steam engine was introduced. In about 1750, England, which was a farmers' nation, began an industrial revolution. The social consequences were enormous.

Adam Smith, the founder of modern economics, lived in the same period. This change was to concern the whole Western world. Matter and outer appearance became emphasized and a wave of iconoclasm flooded libraries and scientific establishments, purifying them of books on 'astrology, superstition, fortune-telling and other ridiculous nonsense'. Within a short time, astrology, a respected branch on the tree of knowledge and connected with the development of science since the beginning of history, became the outcast and shadow of science.

These few examples depict an undercurrent which moves in a new direction, quickly followed by the main flow of development of new approaches to the world, to nature, to mankind and to society. The same is likely to happen now. However, it is difficult for contemporary man to catch sight of precisely what is happening and how far reaching the consequences will be. In our time, we can hardly imagine that we are now in an unbelievable period of acceleration, which, within a couple of decades, may force us to radically change our conception of life and our role in the universe. The process is already going on. If the signs do not deceive us, the general public will become aware of new scientific discoveries relating to the fundamentals of the universe. We need only to point out the many recent publications about the new physics or about holography. The ideas were already there but now they are becoming public property.

In contrast to the discovery of America, which helped man to extend his knowledge of the outside world, it now looks as if we are being helped to expand our knowledge of ourselves and matter. It is as if over the previous centuries, the tangible and consciousness have become more and more refined, brought to greater depths through transformation processes and culminating in a science based on objectivity alone. On the borders of objectivity man finds himself confronted with his very subjectivity, the same that originally created the idea of objectivity. It seems as if the new transformation is trying to bring this more into balance. The values associated with the feminine are becoming more appreciated and the irrational is gradually being valued again. The occult is being examined through different eyes and many people no longer see it as strange, impossible or unscientific. It looks as if what science had come to see as its shadow has to be absorbed by it and assimilated by it in order to keep functioning properly. The shadow is the irrational part of the rational, the feeling part of reason, the unexplainable part of the irrefutable explanation.

The integration of the shadow, rehabilitation of the outcast, is a plutonic process. The more fierce we grow on the one side, the stronger the process of integration will be on the other dark side. For centuries, astrology has been the shadow of science. Honourable scientists have projected evil and superstition on the shadow which is also part of their psyche as well. Now the very same shadow is knocking at the doors of the scientific establishment to be let in and to be recognized. Seen in this light there will be an increased interest in astrology, as well as growth in the number of practitioners. This will be a more rapid increase than previously, considering the accelerating effect of the period during which Pluto transits Scorpio.

But astrology also struggles with its own shadow. Some astrologers disdain or reject the scientific establishment which treats astrology as an outdated superstition. In their eyes, science has no value. However, the astrologers who take on this attitude will also be confronted with their shadow, namely a science that grudgingly retraces its steps so that it can be rebalanced. These two processes can lead to a schism on the astrological front between the anti-scientific 'believers' and the astrologers who stand for the scientific approach, with a large group of people in between.

Everywhere in society are processes which bring to light the shadow in ourselves, which can lead to tensions or projections being foisted onto others when we do not want to see them. Then one can observe that while opposing positions are becoming fixed, at the same time they are being unmistakably driven towards each other beneath the surface. Each fanatical point of view has its roots in the unconscious and leads to projection. Stubbornly adhering to a strict scientific approach to astrology is just as much a question of projection as stubbornly hammering on the unassailable character of astrology. As always, the truth lies in the middle. Therefore, it is senseless being obsessed by either one point of view or the other. When we keep our minds open to signs of what is happening under the surface, we shall see that astrology may very well establish a place for itself as a result of science and astrology subtly growing towards each other.

So what is actually going on?

In recent years there has been an ongoing, important discussion within and also outside the scientific world. Ken Wilber remarked that: 'Its topic: perhaps the first serious and sustained look at the interface of "real science" (e.g. physics and physiology) and "real religion" (e.g. mysticism and transcendence), a topic that more than one scholar has termed "epochal".'

The pioneering neurosurgeon Karl Pribram has compared the working brain to a hologram. Suppose we make a three-dimensional holographic photo and the plate falls and shatters. Each fragment, however, contains the total image, and thus we can reproduce the original image through the smaller fragment, although the smaller the fragment, the more blurred the image will be. So in a hologram, every part has access to a greater whole.

This led Pribram to the idea that if the brain functions like a hologram, it might have access to a larger whole called the 'holistic frequency realm'. This larger whole transcends the boundaries of time and space. In the opinion of Pribram, this realm is likely to be similar to that referred to by mystics through all ages.

The English physicist, David Bohm, who was a friend of Krishnamurti, came to a conclusion through his work in physics that has a splendid connection with the ideas of Pribram. From his research into the field of subatomic physics, he concluded that physical entities which seemed to be separate in space and time are in fact linked or unified in an implicit or underlying fashion. He conceived of the physical universe as a gigantic hologram, in which the whole is present in every part and every part in the whole.

From these two ideas the 'holographic' model originated. The brain is a hologram which is itself part of the holographic universe. What things or events are separate in time and space, called by Bohm the manifest realm or the explicate order, are undivided beneath the surface in the implicate or frequency realm. In that realm, space and time do not exist and all things are one.

What are the implications of this new scientific model for astrology? It will mean that astrology can regain its accepted place in science. When everything is mutually linked beneath the surface, then people, events and planets are also linked up with each other. In the holistic frequency realm they are one, while in the perceptual world they appear to be discrete. We need not concern ourselves with proving astrology statistically. Statistics are used as a quantitative research tool which is inappropriate for understanding the quality-oriented, holistic approach of astrology. Moreover, statistics and astrology belong to two different conceptions of reality. Does this mean that there should be no further research into astrology? The answer should be in favour of research. However, I plead for methods and forms of research which do not violate the principles of astrology and which recognize the holographic view of reality.

The search for a causal link between planets and people can lead to research into interconnections of a different nature, which also applies to parapsychology. At the end of the 1960s, Eugene Dolgoff tried many times without success to show a transfer of energy in cases of psi-occurrence. He came to the conclusion that a transfer of energy is not necessary and said that: 'Nothing needed to go from here to there, because in that realm there isn't any "there".'

If causality can no longer claim exclusive rights as an explanatory mechanism, we arrive automatically at the principle of synchronicity, an explanatory principle developed by Carl Jung as a complement to the principle of causality. Synchronicity starts from a non-causal but meaningful connection of events, and we can distinguish two aspects of it:

(a) an objective aspect: events are non-causally arranged in relative simultaneity.
(b) a subjective aspect: man experiences the events as meaningful instead of senseless coincidences.

We are concerned with order and meaning. Jung has taken this further. According to him, synchronistic phenomena, the meaningful coincidence of events which need not have caused each other, are manifestations of an all-pervading, latent meaning of existence.

The meaningful coincidence of planetary combinations in the heavens and the psyche of the person who is born at that moment on Earth is a possibility when seen from the synchronistic point of view. Jung's postulated latent meaning bears a resemblance to the 'holistic frequency realm' of Pribram or the 'implicate order' of Bohm. Jung stated that synchronistic phenomena involve archetypes of the collective unconscious. In these phenomena a meaningful order becomes manifest, of which the subjective and objective manifestations form parts of one and the same archetypal content. This means that events (the outer aspects) and the psyche of the individual (the inner aspects) are linked together in a meaningful way by means of synchronistic phenomena which are 'too coincidental to be coincidence'. The archetypes appear as arranging factors although they do not themselves cause the phenomena. Jung's view also clearly corresponds to the view that results from the new model of a holographic world-view in which, beneath the surface, matter and spirit are one.

Synchronicity is acceptable and understandable in a holographic universe. The astrologer who has always seen astrology as a synchronistic phenomenon will welcome the holographic model.

What can be the meaning of this for the future of astrology? Let us examine the implications for the astrological profession and for the relation of astrology to the public. Within the field of astrology there are many streams and schools with ancient and modern directions. During the times in which the collectively expressed shadow tries to unite with that which casts that shadow, there is a danger that all these different schools will project their shadow on each other, especially the more extreme factions among them. This may add to the danger of schisms, above all between those who glorify science and try to adapt astrology to this and those who reject science because they feel it can never understand the exalted and the spiritual nature of astrology. This rejection is no less than an expression of projection of this glorification. Astrology as a whole is more vulnerable to attacks from without, although fear of such criticisms can be more devastating than the actuality. The emotions generated by Shawn

Carlson's investigation show that there is still much left to be desired.

Despite such internal problems, the main body of astrologers will accomplish fruitful astrological research and certain new links will be discovered and rediscovered. Specialized branches such as medical astrology and political astrology will make more rapid progress than in previous years. Pluto in Scorpio favours the clarification of the basis of power conflicts and undercurrents in the world, as well as the mysterious connection between body and mind. In a Jungian context, the projection mechanism produces effects not only in the individual, but also in collectives such as countries and races. There are countries which clearly represent the shadow of other countries. No matter how difficult it is to secure the horoscopes of countries, research into such relationships is worthwhile. It will not be the first time in history that astrology will have been useful in politics.

Astrology can also expand further for individual psychological purposes and for the helping professions through the use of Jungian insights on the projection mechanism. Previously, we have seen that the general understanding of interpretation is changing more and more rapidly. A horoscope is no longer used to saddle us with an inescapable and fatalistic destiny, but identifies our individual pattern which has a potential that we can express in many ways.

If we see the horoscope only as a blueprint of our destiny that reflects what will happen in our lives, then we will fail to see the link between the inside and outside of ourselves. The principles of synchronicity, the holographic model and the collective unconscious presuppose that there is such a connection. When we see the principles of a horoscope as a set of partly conscious, partly unconscious fears and expectations, we can see that our experiences of the world are meaningfully connected with us and related to our psyche. It is then no longer the environment that makes or breaks us, but our projections that elicit both pleasant as well as unpleasant reactions from the environment, which are referable to ourselves.

Insight into and understanding of these mechanisms are keys to a creative life. Astrology in general and the horoscope in particular can become tools which deprive us of the opportunity to point out the culprits outside ourselves, and that can help us on the way towards integration of our hidden sides. It can assist us to hold our conscious and unconscious in a lively working interaction so that it can lead the way towards our true Self. We can then see projections in a clearer light. A projection is neither good nor bad. The projection mechanism may be the only mechanism through which man can learn to know himself and to give shape to his destiny.

Concerning the relation of astrology then to the outside world, as the holographic model, although still in its infancy, gains further acceptance in the scientific world and science will no longer be able to ignore paranormal phenomena or astrology. There is a good chance that during the following decades, astrology will re-enter the gates of the universities and science will re-embrace her former companion. But science itself will obstruct the course of its own shadow, just as astrology does. There are also currents of opposition which will clash with each other. Due to the new developments in science, one side leans towards the irrational which is now suddenly more understandable, while the other side resists more strongly this inclination.

Wherever the shadow shows itself, both in the individual as well as in society, we can expect fears, confrontation and overt struggles. Out of these conflicts there will certainly emerge something new within astrology itself, as well as a new relationship to the outside world. Where astrology is concerned, we are in a paradoxical and penetrating age which might be a time of preparation for a complete shift, socially and conceptually, regarding the place of mankind in the universe, like the pattern of previous periods.

If we had considered the trends of the other slow moving planets, there would be much more to tell. Already the return of Pluto to Scorpio warrants the possibility that in the near future science, parapsychology, Jungian psychology and astrology will come closer to each other and work in close cooperation. One can feel it already beneath the surface. The future will show if it becomes reality.

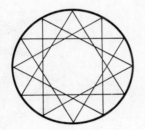

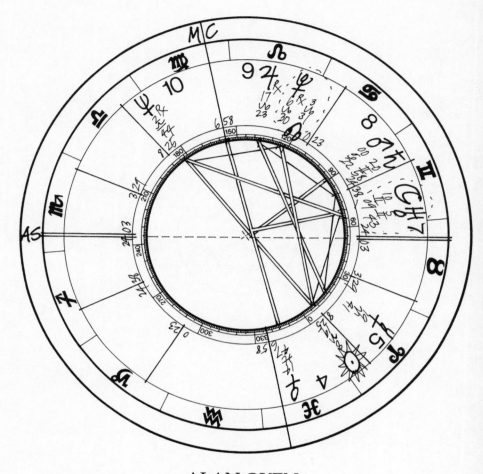

ALAN OKEN

28 March 1944   11:05 pm EWT   New York City

Alan Oken

Alan Oken has been a student, practitioner, teacher and lecturer of meta-physics and astrology since 1967. His published writings consist of over 200 articles and five books. He is a world traveller and linguist who speaks and writes in seven languages. He has given presentations for groups in Mexico, Canada, Great Britain, South America and throughout the United States. He has often appeared on television and has had his own radio programme in Santa Fe, New Mexico, where he also makes his home. Alan is a student of the works and teachings of the Tibetan Master, D. K., and is a member of the New Group of World Servers.

Alan Oken Bibliography

As Above, So Below
The Horoscope, the Road and its Travellers
Evolution and Revolution
Star: An Astrological Guide to Living in the Age of Aquarius
Alan Oken's Complete Astrology
Soul-centred Astrology: A Key to Your Expanding Self. To be published by
    Bantam Books in 1988.

11

A Soul-centred Approach to the Future of Astrology

ALAN OKEN

> Matter is the vehicle for the manifestation of soul on his plane of existence, and soul is the vehicle on a higher plane for the manifestation of spirit, and these three are a trinity synthesized by Life which pervades them all. *The Secret Doctrine*

> It is intuitive astrology which must eventually supersede what is today called astrology, thus bringing about a return to the knowledge of that ancient science which related the constellations and our solar system, drew attention to the nature of the zodiac and informed humanity as to the basic interrelations which govern and control the phenomenal and subjective worlds. *Esoteric Astrology*

Astrology is not a static science. Its methods, techniques and applications constantly develop and evolve. Astrology must possess such elastic and mutable qualities in order to be a successful interpretation of the Universal Consciousness as it moves through and affects the human condition. The planet, signs and houses in any case are not the causal elements of human events. They are the reflections of a transcendental synchronicity manifesting through the movements and timing of a cosmic clock.

The current 'ticking' of this clock is revealing a quantum transmutation of human consciousness. We are, as one humanity, in the midst of an incredible reorientation of consciousness, one which is affecting everyone both individually and collectively. This is indicated by the movement from one world age (Pisces) to another (Aquarius) within the unit of time known as a Great Year (25,920 years). This apex point in the universal rhythm for our planet creates a life of vastly increased tension as well as great opportunities in both our inner and outer lives. If astrology is to remain a useful tool for healing and service in the present as well as in the future, certain

145

techniques must be developed to answer the special needs of these times. There must be a system and an approach to astrology which can be utilized to perceive the quality and meaning of these evolving crises of transformation in our daily lives. Such a system must also possess a framework for delineation and counselling which can and will meet the challenging problems (as well as the special joys and victories) inherent in our individual and collective destinies. Most importantly, there has to be an evolved group of astrologers equal to the task of creating, developing and applying such a system.

The astrologer for the New Age must be thoroughly trained and intellectually centred in his/her science to be able to measure and interpret celestial movements. But he/she must be equally heart-centred and intuitively focused to be able to apply the results of the assessment of such data to the level of consciousness through which others are functioning. This will require of, and give the opportunity to, the astrologer great personal, mental and spiritual growth. Fortunately, both the seeds for this kind of astrology and the presence of this initial group of astrologers already exists.

A new focus of human expression is being born in the lives of a growing multitude of people. This is the developing vision of the physical world and the physical body as vehicles for the expression of a transcendental existence, one in which the orientation and exigencies of the inner life of the Soul is a predominating theme. What has been the major focus of life for the few down through the ages will shortly become an integrated fact of life for many. The waters of the Man with the Urn are indeed being distributed and Aquarius is most certainly the ruler of astrology and its practitioners!

The quality of human consciousness as expressed through astrology is conditioned by two primary factors: on a collective level, it is the historical age and generation into which one is born and raised; individually, it is the degree of personal evolution. The astrology of the European Middle Ages for example, was filled with dire predictions of gloom and negativity. It focused on a fated and sin-filled reality, one of little hope (except for the redemption of a preferably martyred physical death) and very little if any degree of free will. The astrology of Classical Greece was 'cleaner', more orderly and logical in its presentation, while that of the ancient Chaldeans and Hebrews was steeped in metaphysics and interpretations of cosmic law. Like the minute subdivisions of its caste system and the abundantly populated heavens of its religion, Hindu astrology is a vast, complex, labyrinthine system of rulers, sub-rulers and sub-sub-rulers, expressing themselves in a Capricornian structure of power through a fixed zodiac of constellations.

Victorian astrology books are filled with moral admonition, interpreting the planetary aspects as warnings of fiery consequences should one stray from the appropriate behaviour of the time. Mars was depicted as the penultimate rogue with Saturn as the even more malignant keeper of the gates of the hellish retribution of a dominant, patriarchal and polarized theology. Yet the 'other side' of Neptune showed through the black veils and towards the end of this suppressed era, Alan Leo, Helena Blavatsky and Alice Bailey emerged to plant the seeds of an astrological and spiritual future.

American and European astrology in the twentieth century has had several major trends. Since the 1930s there has been a great increase of psychological approaches to the delineation of the natal chart and to the integration of certain methods of healing and therapy in counselling situations. Jung's work with archetypes lends itself very well to humanistic, astrological interpretation as does Assagioli's work in Psychosynthesis. As in traditional and fundamental astrological teachings, both these psychological systems deal with the 'law of correspondences' (or 'as above, so below') and strive to relate the macrocosmic and microcosmic in terms of the human existence.

The 1960s and 1970s brought in a great many experimental approaches to horoscope delineation while the advent of the computer age totally expanded and revolutionized methods of astrological research and the codification of data. This period also saw the birth of a heightened interest into the more spiritual and esoteric aspects of astrology. In this respect, Eastern religions and philosophies found their way into an astrology that was already taking a decidedly occidental, metaphysical and humanistic turn.

The history of astrology is but representative of the history of the development of human consciousness. A new astrology is emerging today because humanity is evolving rapidly enough to need and utilize such a system. In this respect, the mind has to objectify the unfolding nature of humanity's subjective reality. This reality is currently focused on the relationship between the Soul and the personality. The current task, and what is giving rise to a worldwide heightening of spiritual awareness in a myriad of forms, is the building of the link between the two both on an individual and on a collective level, a theme expanded in my new book *Soul-Centred Astrology: A Key to the Expanding Self* (1988).

Until quite recently, the majority of published astrological work of even a very refined and erudite nature (of which there has been a great deal in the past twenty years) has been geared to the life of the personality and the urges and needs of the outer life. Hardly any mention is ever made about the nature, structure and energy of the life-force which informs the externalized expression of itself. And even less has been written about the life and reality of the Soul, or higher self, which is the intermediary between the two and who together form the primary trinity of human existence. Yet to paraphrase Hugo, the time for the power of the reality of this idea (the Soul's link with and its presence in the consciousness of our daily life) has come!

The definite slant of the majority of astrological work has been, up until now at least, focused upon the need to clarify counselling techniques involved in the resolution of such personal problems as arise in this preliminary phase of the individuation process. This phase is intimately connected to the characteristics of the ego-lower self and in those situations which arise from the many egocentric confrontations with life. In effect, this is an astrology based upon the exoteric significances of the Ascendant and its ruler, Mars, Venus and the Moon. At best (and some very fine and useful astrology has been published in this genre), this orientation leads to the synthesis of the personality and is a major step towards individual growth.

One of the best contributions which psychological, personality-centred astrology has made is to encourage people to take an objective look at themselves through the universal archetypes contained in astrological symbology. Each natal chart reveals one's fundamental energy patterns: blockages as well as creative potentials. Professionally executed humanistic and psychological astrology definitely helps one to become clearer as to the nature and relationships existing in one's component parts.

Personality-centred, exoteric astrology when practised by highly trained astrologers certainly facilitates the understanding and integration of the pieces of ourselves. Modern humanistic and psychological astrology works to allow us to see our individual (lower) self as an expression of a series of energies and forces which give rise to certain modes of response and behaviour. We are even taught to look a bit more universally and certainly more *impersonally* at ourselves and at others so that judgement may eventually be fused with a more universal outlook. We are asked to envision a bigger picture of life than that blindly seen through our navels. Or at least, if we insist on staying at the navel point, to see that our umbilicus is connected to the world mother and the family of man.

A strong and integrated ego structure is essential to a healthy life and of primary importance to spiritual growth in our time. The outer life of the physical body and its associated feelings and thoughts, i.e. the fundamental trinity of the structure of the ego, is the vehicle of expression of the human Soul. It is the Soul which is that essential, inclusive and intelligent love principle which when joined and fused with the lower self, creates a whole person who is greater than the sum of his/her parts.

Our task is not, therefore, just to individualize our egos but to unite the ego of the lower self with the Soul in order to create people who, in the words of the Tibetan Master, Djwal Khul, are 'Soul-infused personalities'. Once this process takes place, a person sees life in a very different manner than one totally focused in the glamours of the lower self. As this 'infusion' takes place, one begins to perceive the world increasingly as parts of a whole. The relationship between the one and the many, between the macrocosm and the microcosm becomes increasingly self-evident.

This is the 'Path of Synthesis' and it is accomplished in our era through serving humanity and those lives who inspire humanity's unfolding potential. These words are not meant as poetic euphemisms but are attempts at giving some indication of the frame of reference and the quality of such individuals, and their numbers are ever growing, who are currently finding themselves on this path. The process is rightly called the 'Path of Discipleship' and it is as much, and perhaps even more, alive in this, the cusp of the New Age, as it was in ages past. Magic and magicians have not gone out of life, only the forms of that white magic of transformation have changed. The same may be said of the externalization of the teachers and initiators of the ancient mystery schools. The essential nature of the evolutionary/involutionary schemata changes minutely throughout the ages as compared to the outward manifestations of the mutating forms of the expressions of life. The archetypes upon which modern astrological science are based were set down primarily in early Atlantean times. The forms and applications of astrological interpretation have constantly changed to meet the needs of the civilizations and eras which gave birth to both the astrologers and their techniques.

The crises, tensions, and opportunities of our current civilization plus the response from the inner life to the sincere aspirations of humanity, have given rise to a vast number of people who are neither exclusively personality oriented nor egocentric. Such individuals have achieved varying degrees of personality and Soul infusion and are heartily at work consciously serving others in a multitude of ways. This vast network of brothers and sisters has worked, and is working, not only to discover a person's place and function in their lover's life, or in their professional life, or in their family life. The latter are all very important but so is the search and the realization of one's place and function in the *planetary life!* So many of us and our contemporaries are sincerely aspiring towards those pathways which will show us how to share and serve each other. Thus we may better learn how to contribute effectively to the wellbeing of the collective life, and by so doing, discover the meaning of that group unity for each of us.

As we approach the end of this century, not only do we begin a new millennium, but we also cross the cusp of two world ages. These transitions have resulted and will continue to result in an increase in personal and world tensions. The juxtaposition of forces and forms of expression inherent in the passing Age of Pisces and those of the coming Age of Aquarius directs our attention to the tremendous polarizations which have manifested in our lives. In addition to the change of world ages, Pluto is in Scorpio until late 1995, focusing current strains and pressures into almost every aspect of the processes of personal and collective transformation.

There is the very real threat of total, planetary annihilation as well as the seemingly neverending stream of moral and physical pollution. At the same time, we are living in a period in which global, spiritual awareness and the positive, creative opportunities which this brings to humanity, have never been greater. Never have separatist egos, thoughts, feelings, and actions been so threatening to world peace. And never has humanity demonstrated more convincingly the power of group endeavour, collective goodwill and the urge for spiritual unity.

There is a way to resolve the tensions indicated by celestial events manifesting through the current state of the polarized nations and their conflicting political systems. This way is called variously: the Path of Synthesis, the Third Way, the Way of the Disciple, or simply, the Way of the Soul.

In our study and practice of astrology, this means the creation of a system which serves the needs of those individuals who are seeking (and finding!) their place in a more planetary and collective orientation to life. For such individuals the question: 'How may I more effectively serve my community, nation, and world through fulfilling the true and inner purpose for my life?', have become more important than asking: 'If I am a Capricorn and my boyfriend is a Libra how can we better get along?' There is nothing whatsoever wrong with such a question. It is one of the most natural and in its way, one of the most beautiful questions one could ask. It is hoped that the 'two of them' will get along, unify, and resolve any polarities into a creative synthesis. Once that takes place, then perhaps they will ask: 'How may we better serve humanity and the Plan?'

It is to that increasing group of people who are aware, in an active sense, that they are more than just their thoughts, desires, and physical body; it is to that group of emerging Souls that another focus of astrology is required. I believe that this astrological frame of reference may be found in the ancient wisdom teachings and in their commentaries written by the hierarchy of masters and teachers of humanity.

As the current age begins to unfold, certain aspects of these ancient teachings are being adapted for our use and benefit. In his treatise on esoteric astrology, the Tibetan master D.K. outlines a method of approach to the natal horoscope which provides an opening into a more Soul-centred astrology. Yet the Tibetan states that his work on esoteric astrology is actually part of his greater five-volume series on the Seven Rays, i.e. the primary septunate of energies and forces behind all manifestation.

> If, in the presentation of this vast subject (astrology), and in the process of indicating the attitude of the Ageless Wisdom to this new and coming (yet very ancient) 'science of effective energies', as it has been called, I may present a new approach . . . I am hoping that some astrologers may be found who will be sensitive to that which is new. I believe that there are investigators along astrological lines who will be open-minded enough to recognize possible hypotheses and then to make fair experiment with them . . . I am looking for these fair-minded astrologers to make fair experiment with the factors and suggestions which I may indicate.
> *Esoteric Astrology*

The present writer is one of these experimentative, 'fair-minded' astrologers of which the Tibetan speaks. There are quite a few of us amongst the many thousands of the students of D.K.'s works. My own first conscious contact with the energy of this Master came about in 1967 and then with much greater emphasis in 1973. At the present time, my life and work centre around D.K.'s teachings and writings, not only in terms of astrology but in the larger framework he outlines in *Serving Humanity*.

In recent years, I have followed the hints and suggestions which the Tibetan gives and have also conferred with my fellow students from several countries, in order to present to the general readership a method of approach to the delineation of the natal chart along esoteric lines. What follows is just a very broad introduction to some of the major factors and principles of 'Soul-centred astrology'. The latter is a term I have coined to indicate the more practical applications of exoteric astrological studies. A great body of work in this area has been emerging in the past decade and many more volumes, including some developed work by this writer will be forthcoming.

Soul-centred astrology is certainly not the future of astrology although the externalization of the Soul fused with personality is the future for a great portion of humanity. But there is a growing place for Soul-centred astrology in astrology's future, as more and more people determine their true reality, exercise the freedom of their consciousness, and establish their own and humanity's purpose for incarnation.

The application of the principles of Soul-centred astrology in terms of the delineation of the natal horoscope are not valid for everyone. They will have virtually no meaning in the lives of people who live exclusively 'below the diaphragm', i.e. whose lives are completely centred in personal thoughts, desires and feelings. What would be far wiser and certainly more effective for such individuals would be to read the horoscope from the established, traditional perspective. This will determine the nature of the personality and reveal those issues dealing with the lower self. The astrologer who is trained in the more esoteric approach can keep his/her insights in mind when reading such a chart. Such inner information can help the Soul-centred astrologer to guide his/her client towards revealing the true Soul purpose in life and still give all the necessary advice in terms of the concerns of the personality.

A delineation based on the teachings of esoteric astrology is only applicable to those individuals who are already working on Soul levels, who are active aspirants or higher, and whose awareness of service is at the focal point of their lives. The 'urge to serve' reveals the Soul's presence in the life. The concern for and the awareness of others, the need to individualize in order to participate more fully in the collective, and the willingness to find a 'field of service' to accomplish these tasks are other clues. The Tibetan stresses the need for the astrologer to harness and develop his/her intuitive faculties in order to perceive the level of consciousness of the person before him/her so that the horoscope may be interpreted accordingly. Today, a Soul-centred reading of the natal chart is valid for a very large number of people; tomorrow this will become a multitude.

The appropriateness of a Soul-centred approach to delineation and counselling increase with the expansion of consciousness. This reaches a point at which an individual is so totally centred in his/her Soul, the Soul having become so integrally fused with the personality, that a traditional rendering of the horoscope reveals little or no association with the individual in question.

The majority who find Soul-centred astrology useful are those who find themselves in the duality of having a foot in both camps. This is the tension which arises in one's life due to the simultaneous magnetism of both the higher and lower selves. It is a wonderful, though not necessarily a pleasant, tension as it only serves to create a greater awareness of both worlds. Thus the qualitative differences and the necessary choices one has to make become crystal clear. Besides, it is a most *natural* state to find oneself in after one has chosen to tread the Path. It is a state towards which we have been striving to attain both in unconscious and, increasingly more, conscious ways. So let everyone keep up the tension! It will and does become resolved through the process of synthesis and service as the duality of one's being merges into the One.

One of the primary purposes of human evolution is for the unfolding of the Soul, which externalizes through the personality. The medium of exchange between the two is the 'Rainbow Bridge', although its Sanskrit name in the ancient wisdom teachings is the 'Antahkarana'. It is through this bridge that the involutionary arc of the Soul and the evolutionary arc of the personality travel. At this time in history, not only are individual Antahkaranas being built but the collective Antahkarana of humanity is being stimulated and strengthened. The result of this interchange is a heightened sense of the spiritual and an externalization of the many pathways and techniques for spiritual achievement which have manifested in the past two decades.

The path of human evolution can be expressed astrologically. The Soul matures through its contacts with the material world. The majority of younger Souls (constituting a large segment of humanity) are motivated in their development through the focus of *desire*. Their incarnations tend to move clockwise around the zodiac from Aries to Taurus via Pisces. This is the pathway of the precession of the equinoxes or what is called in the teachings, 'the Great Illusion'. This desire manifests in the four triplicities as follows:

(a) The desire for recognition (fiery signs)
(b) The desire for security (earthy signs)
(c) The desire for new experiences (airy signs)
(d) The desire for response (watery signs)

Desire mutates to *aspiration* in terms of average humanity up to, including and going beyond those people said to be on the 'Path of Probation'. It is in the lives of these 'aspirants' wherein such motivations are expressed in the most refined and spiritual manners. Reincarnation also moves here in the clockwise ordering of the signs with the opportunity to reverse the wheel. The purpose of lives spent with this orientation is to move the focus of attention from below to above the diaphragm. This requires the re-orientation of the energies of the solar plexus chakra to move to the heart centre. It also requires the movement of the energies of the sacral (or sexual) centre to the throat chakra and the vital centre at the base of the spine to travel to the crown centre at the top of the head.

The quality of aspiration needed to create such transformations is out-lined as follows in terms of the signs:

(a) The aspiration of the fiery signs manifests through ideas
(b) The aspiration of the earthy signs through art, business and the various professions
(c) The aspiration of the airy signs through communications
(d) The aspiration of the watery signs through ideals

Once an advanced state of discipleship is attained, *spiritual attraction* becomes the motivation for evolutionary development. The movement of the wheel of incarnation reverses and the progression is anti-clockwise around the zodiac from Aries to Pisces via Taurus. These incarnations lead to the expression of:

(a) Higher degrees of initiation in the sign of Capricorn
(b) Wider fields of World Service in the sign of Aquarius
(c) The Path of the World Saviour in the sign of Pisces

In terms of the delineation of the natal chart, Soul-centred astrology uses the traditional planetary rulers of the twelve signs as well as the esoteric rulers of the zodiac. The use of different rulerships and the ascribing of additional 'powers and forces' to the planets is of major importance to a Soul-centred interpretation of the natal chart. These esoteric rulers are as follows:

Aries – Mercury
Taurus – Vulcan
Gemini – Venus
Cancer – Neptune
Leo – Sun
Virgo – Moon
Libra – Uranus
Scorpio – Mars
Sagittarius – Earth
Capricorn – Saturn
Aquarius – Jupiter
Pisces – Pluto

In traditional astrology, the Sun-sign is seen as the spiritual centre of the chart and the delineation is based upon it and its planetary ruler or dispositor. The rising sign is seen as the externalized manifestation of the temperament or personality. The position of its ruler is vital in determining the area (house) and means of expression (sign) of the ego in its confrontations with life. In effect, we would call the Sun the future while the rising sign and its associations would be termed the present. We are taught that as a person matures, he/she begins to transform his/her orientation from that of the Ascendant to one's 'true nature', that of the Sun sign.

In Soul-centred astrology, the orientation is completely the reverse. The delineation is based upon the Ascendant and its *exoteric ruler's* position by house and sign — although the sign position concerns us more. The rising sign represents the future of the Soul in its expression on the earth. An analysis of the rising sign, its ruler and the dispositor of its ruler (using the esoteric planetary assignations) reveals the purpose of the incarnation *for one who has already awakened to the presence of the Soul as a living reality*. For all other individuals, the traditional interpretation of the rising sign is quite accurate.

The Sun and its exoteric ruler is seen to represent the personality in a Soul-awakened individual. In this respect, the Sun-sign conditions the present and indicates the basic, inherited equipment which a person brings into incarnation. The Sun certainly indicates the 'Spirit' in a person. Yet the revelation of the significance of the Spirit's presence in the life can only come once the Soul has fused with the personality; the Soul functioning as it does as the intermediary between the highest and lowest points on the involutionary/evolutionary arc. The Sun indicates the point achieved in terms of the unfolding of the Soul qualities of one's life. The rising sign indicates the struggle of the spiritual man or woman to continue from that point into the greater sense of spiritual achievement.

Space does not permit, nor is this the right vehicle to explore a longer treatise about Soul-centred, esoteric astrology. The Tibetan has done this in his primary source book, *Esoteric Astrology*. The reader would be well advised to research this volume and the many fine secondary sources about this subject. Esoteric astrology as a serious discipline has only been studied for a relatively brief period. It is still an experimental field and an exciting one (for this Aries at least), as esoteric astrologers are still at the initial point of working to create systems of delineation of the natal and other charts in light of this particular approach. This to me registers very harmoniously. We are indeed on the cusp of a new World Age as well as at the birth of a new phase of human consciousness. It is only right then that there be a new (yet ancient) branch of astrology for humanity to take into the future.

Astrology is essentially the purest presentation of occult truth in the world at this time, because it is the science which deals with those conditioning and governing energies and forces which play through and upon the whole field of space and all that is found within that field . . . When this fact is grasped and the source of those energies are better comprehended . . . the relationship between individual, planetary, systemic and cosmic entities will be understood and we shall then begin to live scientifically.

Esoteric Astrology

BRUNO HUBER

29 November 1930   12:55 pm CET   Zurich, Switzerland

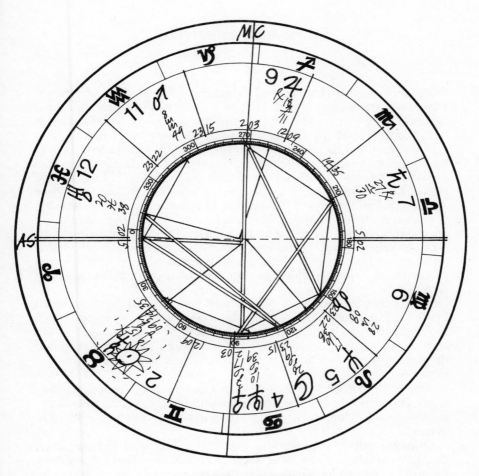

LOUISE HUBER

10 May 1924   3:15 am CET   Bamberg, Germany

Bruno and Louise Huber

Bruno Huber's early background includes the formal study of physics, astronomy, psychology and philosophy and it is in the latter subjects that his and Louise's interests combined after their marriage in 1953, though both had been studying astrology for some six years prior to this.

Whilst continuing to study the history of religions and parapsychology they began their early investigative work into astrology. During the period between 1956 and 1958 they helped with the foundation of the Arcane School in Geneva before going to Italy to work as assistant to Roberto Assagioli at his Psychosynthesis Institute in Florence. Here they were able to intensify their astrological research because of the amount of psychological comparison that was available.

By working with a great number of cases it became obvious to them that astrology and psychology were closely interrelated, and through subsequent work a clearly defined concept to translate one into the other was developed.

In 1962, they moved back to Switzerland and founded the Astrological Psychological Institute (API), all the time continuing to develop further techniques for psychological counselling through the birth-chart. In 1968, they started teaching, originally as a side activity, but their success brought dramatic growth and an ever increasing demand on their time and expertise.

Now, with more than thirty-five years of accumulated experience they have refined a technique for uniting growth psychology and astrology, and their counselling, teaching, research and writing activities continue to expand.

Although most of their work is centred in Switzerland and Germany, they have run seminars and workshops in England and the USA and have more than 8,000 students with whom they are in contact all over the world, many of these being professional men and women engaged in the medical, psychological or social fields.

Since 1981 they have been involved in organizing the World Congress of Astrology held in Zurich.

Bruno and Louise Huber Bibliography

The Astrological Houses: A Psychological View of Man and His World (1978)
Life-Clock I: Age Progression in the Horoscope (1982)
Life-Clock II (1986)
Reflections and Meditations on the Signs of the Zodiac (1984) by Louise Huber

12

The Future of Astrology

BRUNO and LOUISE HUBER

Just as new developments have taken place in every science, in education, psychology and medicine, many new methods, ideas and changes have also come about during the last twenty years in astrology. The greatest concern of the future in astrology must be to create new methods of delineation in line with the growing interest in dealing with the human being as a whole, as a free individual, as a spiritual entity.

In order to gain more insight into the growth of astrology, we have first to consider the deeper meanings of the different methods which have been used in astrology to interpret the past, the present and the future. If we can consider these methods in accordance with the different levels on which human beings can focus their consciousness, we find that astrology can be of help on every level. Astrology has an expansive concept of the universe that describes different laws on each level and places them in analogy with the different stages of development in the human race. In this fashion we can find a new cooperative attitude towards each other. It is the ladder of evolution which we must consider and which expands our view of life and our consciousness, bringing about a sense of inclusiveness. With this new attitude we can fulfil our part in the future and work for the sake of the whole. These ideas shed new light on the different methods as well as on the different levels of consciousness on which a person may be seeking help.

In the future we must strive towards a deeper understanding of universal laws in order to get a more holistic picture of nature, of life, of creation, of the universe. This is also the special question we must put to astrology in the future. These questions are quite different from those of earlier times, and therefore the methods must also be different.

According to the development of human consciousness we must call for solutions to very different problems. It is no longer a question of dividing methods into right and wrong but a question of their effectiveness in serving a specific need. We can then cultivate a new, more holistic, psychological and inclusive attitude. According to this concept of different levels we will now divide the applications of the horoscope into four stages, attempting to describe the possible results. These levels do not stand on their own, but are intermingled. These levels will be analysed thoroughly as four different applications of the horoscope:

1. *In the Past* (Using the chart for determining the future, prognostics, prediction and fortune-telling) (Physical Level)

In this approach life is predetermined and predictable from the beginning – a fatalistic approach characteristic of an undifferentiated attitude. These methods are event-oriented, finding out lucky and bad positions in the chart. This approach contains an unconscious acceptance of fate at the level of simple self-preservation, living as a mere creature, taking orders from stronger persons. One living at this level has no idea that he can liberate himself from his chains: he accepts them as given. His attitude is one of reverence as well as an attempt to gain favour with those more powerful than himself.

From overevaluation of single components in the natal as well as in the progressed horoscope we can easily develop a fear of the future, of 'bad aspects' or 'bad transits'. The compulsion of self-fulfilling prophecies is a danger of prognostic astrology as is the tendency to misplace the blame for personal failures, be it on Mars, on Saturn or on some other planetary influence. This attitude makes us weak, fatalistic and vulnerable to every sort of prophecy. Such an approach to astrology contains no concept of the human being as a free individual, capable of finding solutions to pressures and problems through discrimination and personal decision-making.

2. *The Present* (Using the chart as a diagnostic instrument for character analysis and therapeutic help) (Emotional Level)

At this level astrology makes use of the teachings of psychology, recognizing that astrology is not only the world's oldest science but the oldest psychology as well, a fact of which few people are aware. More and more astrologers are eager to integrate modern psychological knowledge with traditional astrological thinking. Serious astrologers are working to develop new, useful, and reliable methods for using the horoscope as a diagnostic tool in psychological counselling and therapy. Astrology has always made use of the astrological symbols to analyse the weaknesses and the strengths of a person. We can use many psychological methods in order to acquire the ability to begin systematic efforts to change character. Many are using astrological and psychological techniques to unfold latent abilities, to correct faulty character traits and to eliminate destructive propensities. For this reason astrologers can combine astrology with, for example, Jungian psychology, psychosynthesis, transactional analysis, gestalt, bioenergetics and others. One important new psychological method for analysing conditioning or traumatic childhood experiences is the Age-Point method of progression (Life Clock in the Chart). With one glance at the chart one can examine the planets in the first quadrant (houses one to three) as well as the client's age at the time of the Age-Point's passage over these planets. The AP-conjunction with a planet in this area of a chart nearly always indicates traumatic experiences on which the therapist and his client can immediately begin to work, thus sparing a great deal of time.

Thus, astrology can also give back something to psychology. Many helping professions have become interested in astrological knowledge in their pursuit of creative solutions to existing human problems and where old approaches are no longer satisfactory. Psychologists often find themselves at a dead end: they are looking for new ways to understand the human psyche in order to offer effective help to their clients. In this light more and more psychologists, social workers and educators are turning to astrology and its reservoir of wisdom for insight into the human condition. On this standing of astrology in our present time, we are entering the door into the future of astrology.

The next two levels deal with astrology in the future.

3. *Present and Future* (Using the chart as a means to self-knowledge and self-realization) (Mental Level)

The synthesis of astrology, psychology and spirituality will be the goal of the future on this level. It is of benefit to all parties concerned. The combination offers a complete and holistic portrait of the human being and is extremely useful in finding solutions to psychological problems and conflicts. On this level people will begin to have a conception of their own potential power of self-liberation and self-healing. The progress of individuation demands that they grow into a deeper understanding of life and their motivations will change according to the expansion of their consciousness. It then becomes natural that such a person strives towards a task in life, towards true vocation. Such people are able to take responsibility for themselves in a stepwise process in order to liberate themselves from outside influences.

Furthermore, they are drawn by inner forces to become creative in one way or another. They are no longer interested in how they are 'determined' by the factors in their charts but are concerned with the process of growing beyond such limitations. Such questions demand new methods. Astrologically educated people begin to become creative individuals capable of looking at their charts in a different way; they create something new, acting according to the organic laws of nature. For them, astrology is only adequate if it includes a theory of spiritual development and a process of personal growth. They are looking into their charts in order to uncover the hidden causes in their lives, they want to know what stages of development they will reach in this life and what kind of karma they must work through. They enter into the intangible, yet everpresent and potent factors in life – they discover the spirit within the chart, within the astrological symbols and within themselves. Looking into their charts in this way they will come to find a joyful acceptance of life, a new quality in living, courage for self-fulfilment and powerful initiatives to help other people, to serve mankind in one way or another. Such individuals thus become one with their chart and can identify with them, they can accept their life-conditions positively and become more and more able to create a new world for themselves and for mankind. The age-old·concern of astrology to understand the human being as a microcosm in relation to the macrocosm will for these individuals become a reality.

This approach necessarily calls for new methods, different from traditional and from analytical, mercurial attitudes. On this level it is no longer a question of seeing a person as an agglomeration of numerous psychological mechanisms or as an ambivalent and unstable bundle of energies, divided into good and bad traits, but as an organic whole with a potent, spiritual centre containing the power of free will. The chart is used as a tool for self-realization. Here the methods of astrological psychosynthesis enter in. The most important and significant new point is that, looking into a chart, one must see it as a whole, as a potency of the inner Self, the very cause of existence. To see the chart as a whole, one must employ one's awareness and sensory perception.

For this reason the Huber Method draws the aspects in the chart in specific colours, leaving free the circle in the centre which allows a non-definable inner realm of the human being, the higher self, the Soul. The use of colour is an age-old tool to evoke inner pictures, visions, intuitions. One must evoke the sense of awareness, to feel or see the colours as radiating streams of energy, which together make up the 'aspect-structure'. This automatically creates a holistic, intuitive and living approach to the chart and to the individual. When one sees the chart as a complete picture one absorbs with the senses the qualities of the other person. One begins to read the chart not by analysing the individual planetary positions but through looking at it – seeing the interlocking of all the parts – a more jupiterian and less mercurial approach. At this point one is communicating with the innermost nature of the person, the hidden qualities of the Soul. This provides far more information on the real being than any other approach.

In the Huber Method this is the very beginning of chart-reading, a kind of withdrawal from the knowledgeable little ego which claims to know everything. To open up the space for higher awareness one must dis-identify oneself from the lower ego, and for that reason it is worthwhile to meditate first and in this way to give space to the other. Only then does one have the right attitude for going into the details of the chart.

4. *Spiritual Development* (The Goal in the Future: New Rules for Astrology) (Soul Level)

Of the highest significance for astrologers is the possibility of spiritual development: a state in which a person is striving towards an ever-increasing realization of his oneness with the Soul and with the Greater Cosmic Whole. Astrology deals here with the qualities of the Soul and its influence on the personality and thus becomes a spiritual science, leading to a new experience of religion. For many people astrology can be of help in finding out about the inner goal of incarnation, in acquiring knowledge about the tests, difficulties and special tasks on the spiritual path. This expansion of consciousness brings astrology into a much wider orbit. It deals with our earthly span of life as a segment of a greater evolutionary cycle. Each life has in itself the power of growth, a dynamic impulse to become one with what is hidden in the Soul. A combination with the Seven Rays of Alice Bailey's *Esoteric Astrology* is now being created, and here also we have created new rules for finding the rays in the individual chart.

To learn more about inner integration, alignment and the will of the Soul, transformation and sublimation of energies is necessary. People must therefore know more about the laws governing this process of growth. For many this issue provides the major impetus to deal with astrology. Every single detail in the chart is seen from a different point of view, as the possibility of transforming determining factors into greater freedom. Many values are reversed. What is good for the personality may be bad for the Soul, what is good for the Soul may be difficult for the person. A change of values can sometimes cause a great deal of psychic turmoil. The path to one's centre puts all one's problems into a different light. Finally, the entire outer world is seen as a reflection of the inner world. The Soul – symbolized by the circle in the middle of the chart – is realized as the eternal source of life in every human being. Therefore, a new consciousness, a new feeling of identity can be manifested on the Soul-level at which all differences can be transformed into oneness.

This is a new method of self-healing and of healing others through Soul-energies in evoking and respecting the inner entity as the self-healing centre in each human being. Many young people in our time are looking to astrology to find guidance for spiritual growth, transformation and transcendental consciousness leading to universal mind. It is the spiritual path which interests them, with its stages to be reached, its practices and techniques, the esoteric knowledge, the Seven Rays, the Ageless Wisdom, the Laws of Initiation, the Stages of the Ladder of Evolution and the Crises of Consciousness. All these must be considered in the interpretation of a chart in the future, because more and more individuals are following the spiritual path and are preparing themselves for initiation. They must therefore go through crises in the transformation of consciousness and need help, understanding and knowledge about the laws of spiritual development. They must know about the difficulties in shifting consciousness from one level to another. It is our responsibility in the future to develop new astrological and psychological methods to clarify these crises of consciousness.

The Huber Method includes the teachings of Roberto Assagioli's *Psychosynthesis*, which deals with the process of spiritual growth and its inevitable psychological disturbances. Entry into the spiritual realms is not easy but for spiritually oriented individuals it is the most fervent interest in life. It is a turning from the outer to the inner world. To work on the unification of these two worlds is a life's work and is the source of many psychological disturbances. Here the Huber school has developed a new method, the house-horoscope, which, in relation to the natal chart, indicates the discrepancies between these two worlds and the possibilities of integration.

A further aspect lies in the change in one's life motivation. When an individual lives more from his centre, he feels at one with the whole and must therefore contribute something to the whole, otherwise his life is meaningless. He becomes creative and able to build for himself and for others a new reality, a new world, attaining more and more liberation from determining factors. Such a person will find more freedom in his horoscope. He discovers the power of the Self and real love and begins to escape from the chains of narrow materialistic egotism. He tries to live in harmony with the universal consciousness. It is the phase of positive self-acceptance and identification with the true will − spiritual psychosynthesis.

Horoscope Meditation

One technique for achieving union with the Soul is meditation on one's own chart. This is an exercise in guided imagery, similar to psychosynthesis techniques, with a very high capacity for freeing the creative potential of the individual. In this exercise one pictures oneself as standing in the middle of one's chart, with a radiant sun in the centre, and to the left is the ascendant, to the right, the descendant, the IC below and the MC above. Having stabilized this vision one can meditate on each planet, sign, house, aspect, etc. One must be completely aware of the finest reactions in one's inner pictorial. One may see colours and archetypal visions, or experience physical reactions, such as sensations of cold and warmth in the body. After such a meditation a group of individuals might for example exchange their experiences while examining the individual charts. Very important is a detached attitude in the group and especially in the group leader. One must respect the truth of these pictures and work out the hidden message to the person examining this chart.

The Three Higher Planets

In the Huber school the three new planets, Uranus, Neptune and Pluto, are connected with the development of higher consciousness in man and have a transpersonal quality, concerned not so much with the individual as with the whole of the human race. We look to the new higher planets for their power of transformation, for they offer three different means of spiritual growth: Uranus, a scientific search for the unknown; Neptune, universal love and the experience of mystical union; and Pluto, vision and power. The energies of these higher planets will either come into our lives at an unconscious level in the form of collective images, super-egos, catastrophe, etc. scourging and punishing, or we can evolve to a more conscious and self-aware state where the energy can enter at the transpersonal level and be used for the benefit of the whole. There is a sense in which we have to learn to allow the energy of the higher planets to act on and through us, just as a healer is taught to act as an open channel. While we are still struggling to solve problems at the level of our egos any attempt to control or use these higher energies can be disastrous. The ego might inflate to the point where it is overthrown by the higher transpersonal energy leaving behind an inhuman terrorist, false guru or dictator.

The Sign Meditation

Each month at the time of the full moon the possibility exists to enter into the inflow of energies to earth from spiritual sources – an ongoing process since the origin of humanity. When we relax and turn within ourselves in meditation, we penetrate to the 'unconscious' in which archetypal symbols exist as well as the images of the signs of the zodiac. Here all religious metaphors, reflections of God and processes of becoming, arise. Here consciousness awakens to new dimensions which allow penetration to the deeper meanings of the qualities of the signs. We can consciously unlock these energies as they pour in and thus build a channel to substances on the level of ether, providing direct access to the spiritual meaning of the signs. The aspirations of each individual are strengthened in group meditations; the channel becomes broader, more open, so that one can come more easily into contact with these energies. One can of course meditate alone on the signs of the zodiac in a quiet room but groups exist throughout the world which meditate every month at the time of the full moon. In some of these groups the zodiacal texts of Louise Huber's *Reflections and Meditations on the Signs of the Zodiac* are used.

Chart Delineation in the Future

The Three Charts – The Whole Person
In the Huber school we use not only the natal chart, but two others as well: the house and the nodal chart. According to esoteric astrology the three charts must be seen together: (1) The nodal chart as the essential mirroring

165

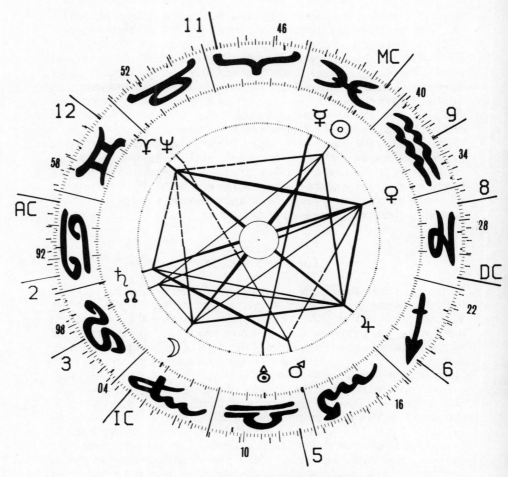

Figure 12.1 The House Chart of Roberto Assagioli

of past incarnations; (2) the natal chart, showing the present situation, the inner task and; (3) the house chart, showing the conditioning factors.

(1) *The Nodal Chart and its Shadow Function*

The nodal chart, mathematically calculated from the natal chart, essentially concerns our desire-nature, all the mastered and unmastered elements of our psyche in the past, stored in the Moon's node system. In esoteric terms it symbolizes our astral body. It is the so-called mirror-sphere where our motivations, wishes and actions from the past (our earlier life-experiences = karma) are projected in the present.

Expressed in terms of depth psychology, the nodal chart makes visible the shadow in our personality. We all have an invisible sector in our minds containing drives, wishes and projections. Because those are not accessible to our waking consciousness we usually suppress them as unusable or even dangerous in our normal everyday life. Thus, this shadow in us is usually designated as negative or 'black'.

However, there are also positive contents just as there is also good karma. Spiritual contents for example can be totally suppressed when they fail to fit into the dogmatism of our thinking or when they seem anachronistic; the result is that these character traits remain unlived. Still, they are part of our being. Modern reincarnation therapy deals with these contents, attempting to make them conscious and to reveal non-causal factors.

(2) *The Natal Chart*

This chart shows us the orientation of our present life and indicates the individual goal of this incarnation. The aspect-structure as a whole shows the individual and social-contact urges as the basis of one's motivation in life as well as one's characteristic goals. The way towards greater self-awareness is indicated by the north node in the chart. Its position by house and sign and its aspects indicate how one can resolve personal difficulties and begin to develop the highest qualities of one's ascendant sign.

(3) *The House Chart*

The house chart is also derived from the natal chart. Our subjective view, seen from the place of birth, gives a distorted view of the ecliptic (this 'worm's eye view' of the heavens is reflected in the natal chart in the well-known, unequal size of the houses). We do not, however, subject the signs to the same treatment – at least when using the tropical zodiac – and we thus end up with signs of equal size, i.e. 30 degrees. But if we were to take a strictly subjective view of the ecliptic we would then have houses of equal size and the signs would become distorted. In this house chart we acquire an objective view of the houses in the chart as well as an objective view of the individual, i.e. how he or she is seen by the outside world. The way in which we see this person determines how we will behave towards him or her. In the natal chart the zodiac is the scale of measurement but in the house chart the houses become the yardstick. (See Figure 12.1.)

167

Comparisons and Free Choice

From the house chart we can see what the world tried to make of us in our formative years – the effects of the influence of family, education and environment. The natal chart shows our inherited potential while the house chart shows how we were moulded and what we became through education. By comparing the two charts we can discriminate between what was originally there and what the environment attempted to make us. Psychologically speaking, a major part of the problems of human beings derive from that seemingly insurmountable contradiction between what we want and what we need. The house chart, therefore, points to a possible, predictable future, to the degree that one allows oneself to be determined in his actions and attitudes by the behaviour and superego conditioned in childhood and adolescence. By comparing with the natal chart we can see where transformation has occurred as a result of the different demands in earlier incarnations, as well as what is needed now for the clearing of the karma.

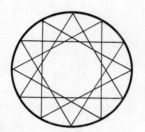

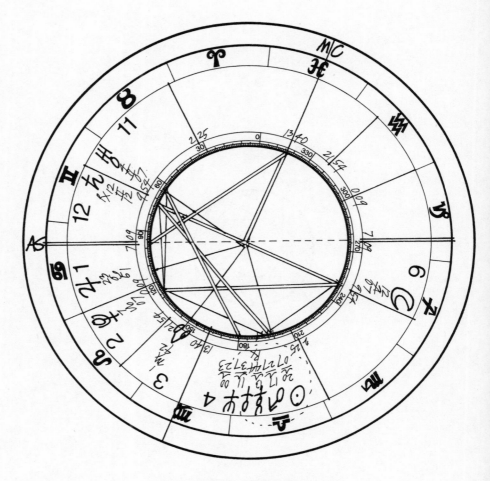

BARRY LYNES

13 October 1942   10:22 pm EWT   Springfield, Massachusetts

Barry Lynes

Barry Lynes was in military service from 1962 until 1965, and received a Bachelor of Arts degree from Boston University in 1967. From 1968 to 1981 he has been a practising astrologer with special research in history, economics, politics and science. In the 1980s he has concentrated his work on climate research, particularly the cover-up of the world cooling phenomenon by 'warming' advocates. Since 1983 he has published the newsletter *The Watchers on the Horizon* and has been president of AstroAmerica Inc, with offices in Massachusetts and Washington, D.C. In 1984, he was authorized by Lionel Day with the responsibility of bringing his work involving astrological archetypes to the mainstream public. Since then he has worked with Jungian therapists to validate Day's controversial theories which unite the discoveries of Freud and Jung and 'put the floor under astrology'.

Barry Lynes Bibliography

Astro Economics (1975)
The Survival of Civilization (1980)
Climate Crime: The Tree War Assembly (1985)

13

Trust Betrayed

BARRY LYNES

The formulation of a problem is often more essential than its solution, which may be merely a matter of mathematical or experimental skill. To raise new questions, new possibilities, to regard old problems from a new angle, requires creative imagination and marks real advance in science.

Einstein and Infeld, *The Evolution of Physics*

The title 'Trust Betrayed' refers to a particular kind of political, economic, and scientific moral failure. In its simplest form, it is a contempt for younger generations and future generations.

This article is concerned with the scientific truth of astrology, the economic cycles which were ignored by politicians, economists and journalists in permitting the 1985–98 world deflation to hit without warning or planning, and the climatic catastrophe which looms unless a world mobilization is initiated. America has not had leaders it trusted for a long time. Its leaders have betrayed trust. The result has been not just a 'play-it-safe' mentality which has spread throughout the society, but a frightening failure to exercise personal responsibility when faced with moral choices affecting the lives, health or economic well-being of millions of people.

An obvious example would be President Jimmy Carter's sacrifice of the health and lives of millions rather than oppose the political power of the tobacco growers. In 1978, Carter's own Department of Health, Education and Welfare began a direct assault on smoking. The facts were grim: (1) more than 320,000 Americans died every year from smoking; (2) more than 75 per cent of all adult smokers were addicted before they reached age 21; (3) nicotine was known to be more addictive than heroin.

Yet when Carter had to choose between moral leadership or surrendering to North Carolina political interests, he surrendered.

Millions will suffer and die as a result of that cowardice. Like the young who were sacrificed in Vietnam by political and military leaders who chose expediency over principle, Carter betrayed future generations – children and unborn – by backing down to a murderous economic interest.

President Ronald Reagan continued the betrayal at the highest level. Only his betrayal was a wholesale sell-out – a moral failure on a level which dwarfed all the political 'compromises' of Kennedy, Johnson, Nixon, Ford and Carter together. Reagan was the grand culmination of two and a half decades of self-deception about the inevitable price of trust betrayed.

According to polls in late 1984, the young generations loved Reagan, but older men had a responsibility to give meaning to language and symbols because the young men were 'helpless'. They didn't know any better. And Reagan betrayed that trust. He distorted facts and language. He misled. He encouraged racism. He ignored the climate and environmental danger. He told the country about a wonderful economic recovery, encouraging the American people to go into debt just before the most massive contraction of the century would force horrible adjustments worldwide.

During the 1984 campaign, he flew into Charlotte, North Carolina and stoked old racial hatreds and fears by condemning school busing for integration, calling it a 'failure'. Charlotte had a model school busing programme built over many years by patient efforts of conservatives and liberals from both races. As an editorial in the *Charlotte Observer* noted the next day:

> Mr President, you flaunted your ignorance, and if you had set out deliberately to upset the people of this community you couldn't have come up with a more disturbing statement . . . through the appointment of several Supreme Court Justices, you might force this community to dismantle its integrated school system. That would be a tragedy for those who have invested so much hard work, good will and loving care in building it, and for future generations of our children.

Future generations were the issue. Thomas Jefferson had written about America's responsibility to 'generations unborn'.

Reagan had betrayed that trust in Charlotte, North Carolina. He also betrayed that trust with his monstrous budget deficits and lies about recovery. Henry Wallich of the Federal Reserve Board openly declared that the Reagan deficit was plain and simply 'one generation stealing from another'.

Trust betrayed between generations – in Vietnam, grovelling before the tobacco industry, in stoking racial hatred, in condemning future generations to mountainous debt – is what pollutes the psyche of a nation. The time when any man or woman has power and responsibility – or the time any generation has them – is limited. When the trust is betrayed and future generations are misled, brutalized or used, a process of dehumanization and degeneration is begun. And unless it is halted and the rot cut away, the malignancy spreads, metastasis follows and breakdown is the inevitable result.

Now what does this have to do with astrology? It is the betrayal of trust at the highest political level which creates a negative mood, a cynicism or a dark subconscious in a nation. Criticism is muted. Problems are swept under the rug. The prevailing political, scientific and economic views are shamelessly parroted. The traditional dogma is never challenged.

The truly radical new discoveries which transform entire industries, entire sciences and entire societies are repressed, censored, squelched. Sometimes this happens because of powerful interests who are on the watch for what threatens them even if it would benefit society. Sometimes it happens because of widespread insecurity and a reluctance to risk one's career. The reality is the same. Trust betrayed at the top produces trust betrayed throughout society.

And this brings us to astrology and its handling by the media, academia, economic think-tanks, political advisers and all who help shape a nation's policies, accepted 'truths' and permitted areas of concern – what is fashionable, safe, etc.

The truth of astrology has been known by numerous intelligent, scientific, responsible professionals and just common citizens for at least fifteen years. Hard evidence of various kinds has existed throughout this period. Incontrovertible facts which explain and define the most important economic turning points have been published for at least four years. Television network personnel have known about economic and political turning points weeks or months in advance. White House aides have consulted astrologers. Numerous and scrupulous examinations by psychologists and psychiatrists who sought to discredit a breakthrough astrological 'floor' for a new psychology have proved futile. Panels of experts have found a little-known, but testable and provable astro-psychology which explained their toughest cases. These were not proponents of astrology. They were antagonists.

Yet no mainstream recognition has been permitted. A black-out persists. The majority of astrology books published by the large publishers continue to be drivel. Nothing on the economic links, the political links, the verifiable psychological links or the new, emerging climate links has come forth. In fact, the major American publishing houses refuse to read the serious astrology material, but continue to disgorge the babble.

Even worse, but not surprising in a twenty-five-year cycle characterized by 'trust betrayed', evidence has been manufactured and facts manipulated by opponents to prevent the recognition of astrology. One committee dominated by Professor Paul Kurtz of the State University of New York at Buffalo, Professor Marvin Zelen of Harvard, and Professor George Abell of UCLA falsified the results of a major test conducted in 1976. Not until 1983 did they admit in a published 'reappraisal' that they had 'erred' and the procedure used by the astrology advocate 'appears to have been vindicated'.

The real truth was that in October 1981 one of their former colleagues had published the tale of their 'deliberate cover-up' and effort to change the test results (proof exists in writing). All their later manipulations – accusations about the honesty of their tests subjects (later retracted), their ability to control the review in the magazine *Psychology Today* about a book published in England which criticized their techniques (they omitted that portion in their review), their silencing of the whistle-blower at a press conference – were motivated by their need to hide what they had done. What was the effect of this seven-year cover-up? Astrology was kept from mainstream acceptance. Countless potential studies and uses were delayed. And in the real, dirty world of mass suffering, political conflict, and war, astrological contributions which might have saved millions or made their lives somewhat more tolerable never were attempted. Iran and Iraq began a war which killed untold numbers of children at a time when – if the dominant planetary patterns had been understood and used – a mutually beneficial compromise might have been arranged. The death of Egypt's Anwar Sadat, with its enormous repercussions for negotiating differences between nations, might have been prevented if the critical planetary patterns had been studied and acted upon by Western policy-makers and peace-makers worldwide. Numerous top media communicators had information (and acknowledged its significance) concerning the political dangers of the assassination period months before the event. They stayed silent, ignoring their primary duty, as expressed by legendary journalist I. F. Stone, which is 'to inform the public and police the government'. And, because of the astrology taboo, monumental changes in the US–USSR arms race were delayed.

The seemingly small 'wrongdoing' of three academics has had enormous ramifications – as the suppression of any major new truth in the dominant nation of the world obviously can. Yet the academic communities have taken no action against the men who perpetrated this deed. Scientists in other fields who have committed similar frauds have been publicly censored and stripped of academic positions – as a warning to those who might be tempted to 'cook the books' and break the scientific code of objectivity, truth, referees, etc.

The press wouldn't even report the fraud. *The Washington Post* managing editor, Howard Simms, knew the facts and refused to print them. Yet the national and international implications of 'astrology proved' were obvious and earth-shattering. As world-renowned English scholars H. J. Eysenck and D. K. B. Nias declared in their objective study *Astrology: Science or Superstition*: 'Predictive astrology can also concern itself with broader issues, such as the fate of nations . . . If there is truth in any of this, then its significance for science, let alone life, is obviously enormous.'

So the 'fate of nations' is ignored because editors of leading newspapers prefer to play it safe and the ethical committees at leading universities look the other way. Trust betrayed becomes a cancer affecting the whole of society, but its most obvious examples are in the positions of responsibility. Because of the astrology black-out by the media, the Paul Kurtz-led CSICOP group which had committed fraud was still delivering its lies and half truths to an unsuspecting public as late as July 1985. On 19 July 1985, the *Wall Street Journal* carried a favourable front page story on CSICOP – no mention of their past misdeeds. On 26 July 1985, CSICOP member and UCLA Physics Professor Bernard J. Leikind appeared on the enormously influential late night talk show of Johnny Carson. Leikind lied to America by saying 'astrology was not based on anything . . . scientific tests have been made . . . we never find anything'. They found something, and they altered the results rather than admit their self-serving assumptions were wrong. History will judge them. And some day the American people will find out about the enormity of the deception which Kurtz, Leikind, Randi, Zelen, Abell, Fraknoi, and others have perpetrated.

The economic cycles were the easiest to recognize as validating astrology. The twelve signs of the zodiac are divided into four elements – fire, earth, air and water. Every 54–55 years, the planet Neptune leaves a fire sign and enters an earth sign where it remains for 14 years. Every 54–55 years, there is a massive 4 or 5 year contraction of the money supply, a depression, and then a 13–14 year deflation period. The planetary-economic link 'works'. It is not debatable. Neptune's earth-sign passages were: 1820–34, 1875–88, 1929–42, November 1984–November 1998.

> The stock of money reached a peak in 1875 from which it declined by some 9 per cent to a trough in early 1879. . . One must go more than half a century forward from 1879 all the way to 1933 to find another 12-year period within which the money stock declined in as many as 5 calendar years.
>
> Milton Friedman and Anna Jacobson Schwartz,
> *A Monetary History of the United States*

> No one actually believes we could experience a depression on the scale of the 1930s. Guess what? During the 1930s that was exactly how people felt about the depression of the 1870s. During the 1870s they felt the same about the depression of the 1820s.
>
> Robert Beckman, *Downwave: Surviving The Second Great Depression*

In August 1929, Neptune's entrance into an earth-sign set the stage for a worldwide economic 'grounding'. But what was the trigger? Neptune's arrival in direct alignment with the Venus (resources and value) position at America's birth. It happened on 24 October 1929. The stock market crashed that day. Economic, political and media leaders cannot arbitrarily dismiss such precision and expect to be considered responsible by future generations – not with the stakes involved.

177

Neptune aligned again with America's natal Venus in May 1931. On schedule, the European banking collapse resulted and was followed shortly by the American banking collapse. International trade went dark for a decade.

Then, on 8 July 1932, Neptune in an earth-sign aligned with the Jupiter position at America's birth, the stock market reached bottom and began a slow expansion. Once again, the precision of these rare alignments – marking to-the-day historic–economic shifts – cannot be dismissed by experts who hope to maintain the respect of future generations.

The Neptune cycle and the 1929 crash are only samples of an extensive series of astrological patterns which define with great precision every major economic shift in American history. These have been outlined in my books and articles.

What does this 'new factor' in economic planning mean? It means that when astrology is recognized, crashes and depressions may be preventable. It means that the same patterns which caused misery in the past could be used to time needed economic restructuring or at least establish safeguards. *We are not at the mercy of predestined events, but we do have to learn the principles of a new science.*

The 'trust betrayed' of President Ronald Reagan in the years 1981 to 1984 can be plainly seen. Economists have long been familiar with the Kondratieff Cycle – a recurring deflation–depression every fifty or sixty years. But they had no explanation for it. They did know that a tax cut and 'secondary prosperity' or economic recovery 'illusion' just before the long debacle was a recurring phenomenon. So what did President Reagan – who had access to the best economic historians in the nation – do in the years preceding the scheduled return of the Kondratieff plunge? He cut taxes and crowed about a great recovery while the hard-eyed analysts saw deep structural economic problems. He misled a trusting public – trust betrayed.

The recognition of astrology could have forced national economic preparation for a difficult transition in 1985 as a long deflation cycle got underway. By late 1984, the signs of the looming disaster were obvious. *Business Week* on 29 October 1984 quoted Leyland S. Prussia, Chairman of the Bank of America Corporation as follows: 'When you get into this kind of disinflation or deflation, the financial implications are very significant. And it's across the board.'

Were there those who could have sounded an alarm, but out of self-interest or lack of nerve failed to do so? There were legions of them.

Germany's top economic think-tank is The World Economic Institute. In 1980, at a meeting in Paris of top leaders from Japan, Germany, France, Kuwait and Switzerland, Herbert Giersh, founder of The World Economic Institute eloquently argued that the public's role was central if positive economic changes were to be realized. As Jean-Jacques Servan-Schreiber reported in *The World Challenge*, this was Giersh's stated position: 'Only a public from whom one hides nothing of the truth will be capable of gathering the courage and the will to act to pave the way for the renaissance of a united world.'

Yet in 1982 The World Economic Institute was given information describing the deflation cycle. One letter from the institute stated the information 'was not taken lightly in this house'. Another declared the information was 'stupefying'. Yet, after a flurry of interest, the economists went back to their more predictable cycles. Astrology was outside the 'fashionable' boundaries. Even preventing a world depression wouldn't arouse them to break that barrier.

The European economists were not alone. Federal Reserve Chairman Paul Volcker had the information in August 1980. In September 1980, he wrote that he hoped the astrological correlations and deflation cycles could be avoided in the future 'through sustained financial and fiscal discipline'. Volcker had 400 PhD's in Economics working for him in Washington, D.C. alone, not to mention access to the most advanced computers, best minds and most extensive resources in the world. He had been given a unique, precise explanation for the worst economic collapses in American history and the timing for the next one. The information was sufficiently detailed and relevant for him to answer in a personal reply. Yet he refused to act on it – even after the all-time interest rate peak occurred four months later on the dates predicted, the historic Reagan tax cut occurred exactly on a turning point date pinpointed for July 1981, and the economy collapsed in October 1981 as forecast. Trust betrayed. The welfare of future generations worldwide was sacrificed for short-term political caution.

The economic cycles were published in 1981. In following years, numerous 'investors' called or visited the author. All sought special information and special arrangements to make a fortune for 'good works'. None had any plans for warning the public or helping change national policies. Wall Street newsletter publishers learned of the cycles. Well-known street forecasters purchased books explaining the cycles and the coming debacle unless social preparation was undertaken. *Barron's Financial Weekly* even described the cycles in a May 1984 article. The *Wall Street Journal* even heard the rumblings and said in an editorial on 11 July 1984: 'These economic calamities are not due to our stars or to some mysterious Kondratieff cycle.' Maureen Orth, a NBC News journalist, contacted me the same month – more than three months before the critical 1984 election. She had heard about my information from a Washington D.C. source. I had lectured there in January 1984, to an audience of Washington 'insiders', Treasury Department employees, the wife of an ex-Chairman of the Federal Reserve System, and many others with responsibilities to the American public. Orth and I talked for more than half an hour. The cycles and their implications were carefully explained to her. Material was sent to her in the hope that the knowledge could be given to the American public before the election. It was ignored. Trust betrayed.

Millions faced another great depression because a careerist played it safe.

And while those who could have broken the silence chose not to do so, playing it safe despite the fact that immense suffering for millions of innocent people were the stakes, President Reagan crowed about controlling inflation. A misinformed public applauded. News commentators analysed. The truth was, he either didn't understand the looming disaster or he was consciously misleading the nation. Either way, he deserved to be impeached.

As economist Alan Reynolds explained in an article titled 'The Fed Flirts With Deflation' which appeared in the 12 July 1984 *Wall Street Journal*: 'No inflation in the history of the world has been presaged by falling commodity prices and a rising currency . . . These are classic warning signs of an imminent overcooling, not overheating.'

As economic newsletter writer Donald J. Hoppe explained in an October 1984 analysis, excess euphoria and optimism have always described the last stage public attitude before the great financial panics. Didn't President Reagan, the media and others have an obligation not to mislead the public into another tragedy? Or was the short-term goal of Reagan getting re-elected and the networks keeping their advertisers happy more important than the long-term well-being of the nation? As Hoppe commented:

> the euphoric mood of 1929 was perhaps more destructive than the stock speculation mania itself, as it left almost everyone, the public, business and government, totally unprepared for the disasters that were to follow. And being unprepared led to hastily improvised counter-measures that often did more harm than good.
>
> (*The Donald J. Hoppe Analysis*)

So we return again to the question of trust betrayed and the question of trust between generations. Responsibility is implied. In a democratic, scientific society, two qualities are especially needed in those who are in positions of responsibility from which they can speak out. The first quality is open-mindedness. The second quality is courage.

When three professors from leading American universities conspired in their fraud to discredit astrology, a number of their associates resigned from the committee. One of the more outspoken investigators who condemned the three and continued objectively to analyse astrology was Dr Marcello Truzzi of the Center for Scientific Anomalies Research in Michigan. It seemed he might be willing to warn about the terrible economic contraction.

Unfortunately, his reply was standard academic posturing. He suggested articles to economic journals in which the astrology was omitted. He also recommended entering a contest to 'prove' astrology. There was even a financial 'prize', he added. He was sorry he could offer no further help.

Have we as a nation gone mad or just become so accustomed to caution and non-involvement that we can risk millions of lives without even trying? 'Trust betrayed' applies to people on all levels, not just the political, military and economic leadership levels. Truth sought and truth championed – political truths, scientific truths, social truths – are not just pretentious words for politician's speeches, but essential for national progress and survival.

In the August 1983 *TV Guide*, Mary Murphy described top producer Gary Marshall's contention that the TV networks consciously censor astrology in order to avoid controversy. Marshall stated: 'Half the people in this country totally believe in astrology. The other half thinks it's crazy. So either way, if it goes on television it is sure to offend half the people in this country. No network wants that.'

The élite newspapers are no better. Astrology is a taboo subject even when disturbing facts throw light on the most serious international conflicts. For example, Pluto takes approximately 265 years to complete one cycle through the zodiac and return to its position at a nation's birth. When it reaches the quarter points in its orbit – an extraordinarily rare occurrence – dangerous events affecting great masses can occur. On 25 October 1973, Pluto reached a quarter point in the Soviet Union's birth-map. On 24 October 1973, the US–USSR crisis over the Middle East began when the Soviets threatened to send troops into the Egypt–Israel war. US troops were put on full alert. For one day – 25 October 1973 – the two superpowers were eyeball-to-eyeball, with nuclear weapons.

Ten years later, on 31 August 1983, Pluto reached the critical quarter point in America's birth-map. On that day a Korean commercial airliner with a number of Americans aboard was shot down by the Soviet Union after 'straying' into Soviet territory.

On these two occasions – during just two days in a ten year period – the world held its collective breath as the superpowers stared into the dark abyss of pure power, murderous instincts and nuclear nightmares.

The New York Times refused to print any description of these facts, even though every scrap of information pertaining to the Korean jet tragedy was routinely disgorged to the public for days.

These two dates and their extraordinary linkage to a planetary cycle warn us to break the taboo against a serious, twenty-first-century astrology and to break it fast. There is incontrovertible evidence which will stand up under the most sceptical examination and which suggests a road map exists to a peaceful transformation of the long superpower conflict. To prevent astrology from making its case to the American public and the world at large is to be censoring out of hand what will be the story and the breakthrough of the century. When that breakthrough happens – when astrology is recognized as a real science even if the 'why' remains a mystery – Western science and Western philosophy will begin to be utterly transformed.

What we lose by suppressing the knowledge that astrology works cannot be measured. Not only will the recognition of astrology as a science provide a gateway to a new economics, a new politics, a new psychology, a new medicine and more, but it can make the difference between survival of civilization or catastrophe and the death of millions.

For example, on 25 October 1984, when the Sun and Pluto joined in Scorpio – the sign associated with mysteries, degeneration and regeneration, mass death, etc. – it signalled the beginning of a very important month. Twelve years of Pluto in Scorpio lay ahead. One of the greatest struggles in the history of the planet faced humanity.

Astrological knowledge – understood and used widely – could have provided a blueprint for responsible action and public education. Ignored or misunderstood, Pluto in Scorpio promised terror, resource wars, class wars, mass death, climate catastrophe and possibly mass nuclear contamination from sexual plagues, weapons or other sources – the horrors of all time culminating in a twelve-year period.

What would a world aware of the astrological significance of 25 October 1984 have recognized immediately as a warning, which the critical Sun-Pluto-Scorpio alignment signalled? A Congressional Study appeared on that day which warned that the next crisis was a hidden and gradual pollution of drinking water.

Of course, doomsday warnings have been so common in recent decades that they tend to be ignored. It was not simply a case of letting the government technicians handle it. Only a national effort, involving millions working cooperatively on national and local levels, and including rigorous new controls on industry, could prevent what soon might be a catastrophe.

It was the sure knowledge of the science of astrology which provided the clear warning. It was the use of astrology combined with other professional expertise – political wisdom, economic organization, scientific discipline, communication mobilization – which offered a chance for averting tragedy.

But the general ignorance of astrology, the suppression of any discussion of astrology's scientific validity, the censoring of open examination of the astrological indications of coming crisis . . . meant humanity was in for a rough future until the current political leaders, economic leaders and communication leaders were replaced by a new generation capable of exercising responsible and courageous leadership.

Beyond the water problem lay the food problem. Ever since the middle 1970s, American climate genius John Hamaker had been warning that the soils were demineralized. As a result, trees would begin to die, earthquakes, volcanoes and tornadoes would increase, and accelerating carbon dioxide in the atmosphere would trigger a new ice age. The growing seasons would shorten, winters would become more harsh, and drought (and famine) would increase worldwide.

Six months before his death, world renowned multidimensional scientific thinker R. Buckminster Fuller came out in support of Hamaker's work, and top advisers to the British government began circulating Hamaker's book *The Survival of Civilization* in 1982.

By 1983, Hamaker's predictions were being fulfilled. The trees in Europe and America were dying – precipitously. Germany's *Stern* magazine for July 1984 was an emergency issue describing and illustrating what a horrible, tree-less future meant. The winter of 1983–84 broke all records for cold in America and elsewhere. And by October 1984, America's western states were under intense December–January type snowstorms.

Hamaker claimed a world mobilization to remineralize the entire planet was necessary or the world would starve to death by the 1990s. And, the remineralization had to begin by 1985 or it would be too late.

Top ecologists could recognize the sudden shift of the climate, but without the astrology, they wouldn't recognise the accuracy of Hamaker's timing and solution. Neptune entering Capricorn in November 1984, for fourteen years, marked not only the beginning of a long deflation cycle, but it also timed the opportunity for a new world order (Capricorn), and cooperation – one centred around grinding and spreading gravel dust to remineralize the world. Only this fundamental approach to saving the trees (Germany – 8 per cent dying in 1982, 33 per cent in 1983, 50 per cent in 1984) and the crops, and pulling the carbon dioxide out of the atmosphere would reverse the climate wallop that was building.

And Neptune in Capricorn – for those who knew how to read the signs – described perfectly the mountainous, disciplined, collective journey ahead as the glacial till was spread into the rivers and forests, as the rocks were ground, and the resulting dust dumped from the air, as nations and cultures that hated each other were forced to structure a new way – or die.

Hamaker's truth had also been censored. Establishment scientists knew years of erroneous advice would be uncovered by the acceptance of Hamaker's programme. Politicians temporized – as usual putting off the hard decisions. The communication media élite blacked out the information. (Top media and political people in America had personally communicated with me about the Hamaker warnings, but none of them had the nerve to break the truth to the public.) Trust betrayed.

Astrology works. Soon it must be recognized and utilized in a coming world mobilization, or civilization will not survive – most of humanity will die.

On 5 June 1947, Uranus conjoined the Mars position at America's birth. An extraordinarily rare and brief opportunity existed for a revolutionary (Uranus) creative, initiative (Mars) which could advance human understanding and cooperation. On that day, Secretary of State George Marshall proposed the Marshall Plan – the rebuilding of Europe after the Second World War. It was the greatest humanitarian initiative of the twentieth century.

Slightly less than six years later, Neptune aligned with the Neptune position at America's birth. Neptune can time grand illusions, deceptions of various kinds and other collective tragedies (such as the beginning of the Second World War, as Neptune precisely aligned with the Soviet Union's Neptune and the infamous Nazi–Soviet Pact was signed). But Neptune also can time great human advances, especially when political leaders step into the unknown in order to make ideals real or advance the collective good – transcending political barriers in the process.

On 16 April 1953, with Neptune precisely aligned with Neptune's position at America's birth, President Eisenhower called for an end to the arms race. The response was overwhelming. According to Eisenhower biographer Stephen E. Ambrose, 'messages from American embassies around the world reported the greatest enthusiasm to any statement by an American since George Marshall outlined the European Recovery Program'.

In the speech titled 'The Chance for Peace', Eisenhower declared:

> The cost of one modern heavy bomber is this: a modern brick school in more than thirty cities; two electric power plants, each serving a town of sixty thousand population; or two fully equipped hospitals. We pay for a single fighter plane with a half-million bushels of wheat. We pay for a single destroyer with new homes that could have housed more than eight thousand people.

Eisenhower closed by asking the Soviets to show by deeds that they were ready for peace. If so, he promised the United States would devote:

> a substantial percentage of the savings achieved by disarmament to a fund for world aid and reconstruction . . . to assist all peoples to know the blessings of productive freedom. The monuments to this new kind of war would be these: roads and schools, hospitals and homes, food and health.

In 1960, Neptune precisely aligned again with the Neptune position at the Soviet Union's birth. At this time, instead of beginning a war – as occurred twenty-one years before – Khrushchev and the leaders of the Soviet bloc went aboard a boat and collectively sailed to America where they participated in the greatest gathering ever of world leaders at the United Nations.

Both Eisenhower's call for peace and Khrushchev's pilgrimage demonstrate the power of astrological timing. Neither man was aware of the planetary alignments occurring when each separately broke with the past and took a leap of faith. Only partial progress resulted, but as historic guidelines they offer us a chance to use comparable future alignments in a conscious, daring, breakthrough way. Or else we die.

Neptune's shift into the earth and cardinal sign Capricorn describes the most monumental world management shift in all of history. Neptune was only discovered in 1846. Never before has Neptune moved into the sign associated with rocks, minerals, mountains, arduous endeavours and ordered change on a world scale, while humanity consciously knew of Neptune's existence. The opportunity for a conscious, coordinated effort exists.

Hamaker's call for a worldwide mobilization to prevent a new glacial age has the cyclical evidence of past glacial periods, carbon dioxide acceleration, the forest crisis, and several outstanding scientific studies to support it. But what is overlooked is that Hamaker's emergency blueprint, combined with a verification of astrology (would happen overnight if the communication channels investigated), offers the world a practical reason to begin cooperating overnight and to start talking united action and then begin taking united action. The dead-end conflict between different world systems could be transcended because of a greater, common purpose. The long-sought light at the end of the twentieth century's dark tunnel of mass violence could be Hamaker's greatest contribution.

But no world mobilization or cooperation will occur while the current political, economic and communication leadership exists. Trust betrayed describes the misguided reign of second-rate leadership.

Unless a major breakthrough happens soon and astrology is openly recognized and then practically used in creating new international, cooperative policies, along with fundamental change in the political leadership, tragedy looms.

ROGER ELLIOT

25 June 1937   3:15 am BST   Torquay, Devon

Roger Elliot

Roger Elliot is a jolly, roly-poly kind of astrologer who attempts to bridge the chasm between popular and serious astrology. At the popular end, he has written columns for most of Fleet Street, including the *TV Times* and *News of the World*, not forgetting *The Fisherman* and *Banking News*. He once wrote a whole New Year issue of *Sunday* magazine in two days. His best joke was calling himself, as first astrologer to *Cosmopolitan*, by the pseudonym Andromeda, which means in Greek 'the enchained woman'.

For the past seven years he has published an annual series of Zodiac paperbacks, giving forecasts for each sign, and his latest venture is Star-line, a daily telephone horoscope series.

To produce this material he employs many computers – eleven to date – which he programs himself. His Starlife service produces personal written reports on astrology, reincarnation, biorhythms and financial investment, and he does major research into horse-racing, stock market price movements and indeed any data that is susceptible to astrological analysis. He is developing computerized analysis programs that can be applied to any and all kinds of human phenomena.

He lives with his Australian wife Suzie, plus his teenage children Mark and Stephanie, in a Somerset manor house that's mentioned in Domesday Book. It burnt down five years ago, when he had his Saturn half-return, but with Jupiter in attendance he got all his insurance.

Jupiter on his Midheaven has played a dominant role in his career. Everything he touches turns to gold – 9 ct gold plate that eventually comes off on your fingers. But he keeps trying. His greatest ambitions: to wear a bright woolly, and develop enough self-confidence to write his own biographical description.

14

Binary Stars

ROGER ELLIOT

To the question 'What is the future of astrology?' I'm tempted to reply: 'Don't ask me, I'm only an astrologer!'

For in recent years the idea that astrology is a *'predictive'* craft has fallen out of favour. Nowadays most nice, sensible astrologers – er, sorry, cosmobiologists – see their profession as a branch of psychotherapy. The horoscope – whoops, birth-chart – is a diagram of the psyche, and, if it has a meaning, it refers to the development of the inner life. Only marginally can it relate to outer events – ideally in the past and viewed with hindsight, rather than the future, as forecasts.

This educated, rational liberal astrologer seeks approval and recognition from fellow-workers such as clinical psychologists, Samaritans and agony aunts. This kind of astrologer wants to be part of a holistic welfare state, a society where 'telling people what to do' is replaced by 'suggesting valid alternatives'.

This astrologer favours free will, self-motivation and balance – a nice, harmonious balance between your inborn nature, whether genetic or astrological, and your brought-up nurture, such as family influence and the pressures of your environment. These acrobatics are controlled by the Self, the conscious, grown-up part of your personality who can, indeed should, try to override Destiny. All the astrologer does is put you in touch with your Self, point out the imbalances and challenges of your task, and leave the rest to you.

I am such an astrologer. But even more recently, a new – or perhaps very old – kind of astrologer has resurfaced, wallowing and spouting, from the depths of the collective unconscious. This is the Young Fogey astrologer, more conservative than the Tories, sporting a plenitude of old-fashioned astrological terms and techniques. Never a *birth-chart*, only a *nativity*. And never mind midpoints, harmonics and other suburban rubbish, let's stick to good, solid seventeenth-century judicial astrology, with its lords and rulers, querents and ends of the matter.

These astrologers – actually, they'd prefer to be called *divinators* – often use horary techniques, casting a figure, as they say, for the moment you, the client, pose your question. An analysis of this map of the sky yields the appropriate answer according to a complex set of rules established by William Lilly some three and a half centuries ago.

To consult a horary astrologer, you must formulate a precise question. It can be as general as: Will I marry soon? but the more detailed the better, for horary astrology is well suited to answer the minutiae of life. Thus the Elizabethan, Simon Forman, drew up a comprehensive list of rules governing all romantic possibilities. How rich was the proposed bride? Was she really in love? Was she sincere, or an adventuress? and so on.

To such questions, the latter-day horarists seek to give precise answers. Olivia Barclay, for instance, is proud that she could predict that a missing cat would be nearby, but high up, in a closed room, alive but weak – an answer that echoes the prognostications that Lilly himself would give to seventeenth-century problems: Where is my lost cow? When will my ships return? How will Charles II relate to the Cavalier Parliament? And many more.

There is a growing tension between the Young Fogeys and the Wets, to adopt current political slang. Whereas the Wets believe in a loose-limbed kind of astrology, where technical rules will yield, if necessary, to the exigencies of common sense, the fusty Fogies pay homage to a more ancient art – of magic, seership, hierophancy. They are recreating the vocation of *divining*, and, were they writing a contribution to this book, might well steal the Spielberg title *Back to the Future*.

If the Wets believe the human spirit capable of transcending little local difficulties – indeed, require it to, in the name of progress – the Fogies take a quiet stoic pleasure in the acceptance of fate. Just as Asian astrologers would say that you cannot flee from your karma, so the Fogies respect the inevitability of life and its conformity with the richly varied but *ordained* planetary patterns.

I caricature, of course, but in Britain at least astrologers are assembling into opposing camps. Perhaps a happier metaphor is a pair of binary stars, warily circling each other – each trying to radiate its own truth but, regrettably, seen at a distance by non-astrologers as a single, slightly eccentric phenomenon.

We could imagine other polarities, for the astrological universe is rich in diversity. We could picture the siderealists circling the tropicalists (an ancient war between those who use a zodiac based on the actual constellations versus those who base their zodiac on the point where the Sun crosses the Equator northwards). Or else there's the trinary battle between traditional planetarists (out to Saturn), the modern planetarists (to Pluto) and the neo-modernists (trans-Plutonic, hypotheticals and teeny-weeny asteroids). Above all, there are skirmishes and gang warfare between proponents of different House systems, ranging from the plainly Puritan

Equal House supporters to the numerous Cavalier regiments of Campanus, Moranus, Albertius, Placidus and old Uncle Regiomontanus himself.

In no other system of thought is there such vigorous debate and practice over the basic tools of the trade. To this extent astrology resembles Renaissance theology, with its constant arguments about theories that are difficult, if not impossible, to prove, rather than Renaissance science that gradually left astrology, along with alchemy, behind in its progress along the path of inductive reason.

Whereas the cosmos of modern science is analogous to a series of blaze-trailing comets – Einstein and Planck and Crick and Watson – astrology seems a circulatory universe, an eddying backwater where ideas are dropped, revived and dropped again; where each concept has a season of growth and decay; and where opposing notions gain a kind of static strength from each other instead developing enough momentum to soar off into new dimensions.

Whew! It's time to leave this overworked metaphor and devise a fresh meaning for my title 'Binary Stars'.

In recent years, an entirely new factor has entered astrology as much as any other craft or science – namely, computers. This simple invention of binary gates, basically an electronic device to enable a current to pass, or not to pass, has transformed modern thinking. Allied to increasingly miniature yet detailed microchips, this invention enables man to achieve what alchemy or religion could not: the creation of a God, or at least a superman, in our own image. A reliable superman, sophisticated beyond most men's dreams, a mixture, like Jesus and the Buddha, of servant and master, ape and angel – for pull the plug on this living God and he quickly lies doggo.

People are tired of computer-freaks hyping their new deity, much as medieval townsmen must have got sick of imagining what the new cathedral would eventually look like. So let us examine some humbler structures, the little Saxon churches where computer astrology was first worshipped.

The first kind of computer astrology is the most common, and the most boring, and was probably started by Neil Michelson when he ran Astro-Numeric Services, later to become Astro-Computing Services of San Diego, California. This uses a computer to calculate astronomical positions and display them as a list of planetary positions, later as a graphical horoscope such as an astrologer might draw, and later still with all the bells and whistles of midpoints, harmonics, various progressions and directions and what you will.

This is using a computer as a calculator and layout artist. The computer can work much faster than a human, and so tasks that were neglected by the astrologer because they were so time-consuming, such as primary progressions, or intractable, such as heliocentric positions, soon become commonly available. This kind of mail-order service became available in the early 1970s and is now offered by a variety of main-frame or mini-computer operators. There are also dedicated microcomputers, even portable calculators, that can be bought ready-programmed to perform and print the necessary calculations. And of course, along with the growth of ordinary business or home microcomputers, there has been a corresponding surge of off-the-shelf programs from Matrix, Astrolabe, AstroCalc and others, enabling astrologers all over the world to calculate charts and transits and print them attractively, to a uniform style, for their own use or for sale to clients.

No doubt this service will expand into glowing colour, pinpoint laser accuracy and, in time, into 3-D simulation. This is a development that I am helping, bloodied cheque book in hand, to advance, for like all true believers I buy my indulgences from the Holy Cathode Church in the shape of newer, ever more expensive computer hardware. The software, sadly, has to be fashioned oneself, like a hundred Hail MS-DOSes before breakfast.

A principal barrier to more widespread acceptance of astrology has always been its visual jargon. The intelligent layman has never mastered those arcane hieroglyphs for planets and signs – or at least, he may recognize the notation, just as I can tell a crochet from a semi-breve, but he cannot infuse those markings with the inner melody. Yet a practised astrologer can, although not as well as he should. Few, if any, can sight-read a chart confidently through the fourth dimension of time. Fewer still can immediately overlay one chart with another, spotting all the major links and tensions between the people concerned. Partly it's a lack of training; if you're brought up on plainsong, why meddle with counterpoint? But mainly it's the unexpected way that astrological information crops up. A Sun-Saturn square, or Capricorn rising, or Pluto on the tenth house cusp all tell much the same story, yet they appear in different parts of the chart. More subtle factors, such as midpoint combinations, are not visible at all; they must be refined from the raw materials, and that's where the computers can greatly help.

New graphic presentations of the horoscope can transform our grasp of astrology. Faced with a traditional chart, today's astrologer resembles someone setting out on an unknown journey without a map but has instead a collection of eccentric traveller's tales. 'Look, there's a mountain over there – no, sorry, it's over *there*. Or is it a lake? It doesn't look dangerous – ah, but I'm wrong, I've just seen this Mars-Uranus square, it's *very* dangerous – well, sometimes it is.'

Tomorrow's astrologer will have much more reliable guides to the landscape. At the touch of a key he will get colour maps to all the regions he wants to visit, not simply the topological scenery but statistical information about the life, customs, industry, health and habits of the people living there. Put plainly, the computer can analyse and sort and sift and syn-

thesize all the astrological information and represent it in easily understood ways. The raw materials of planetary positions will be left far behind;
only the refined products, portrayed in user-friendly fashion, will show.
Instead of asking 'How strong is Saturn?' the astrologer will want to know:
'Can the client hold down a responsible job? What are his strengths and
weaknesses in dealing with people? What is the likelihood of developing
rheumatoid arthritis?'

At this rate we will soon no longer need an astrologer at all. The
computer may soon be analysing the chart directly, without expert intervention, so that the client himself can consult the computer, pay the
computer its fee, and leave the computer consulting room happy and
fulfilled.

This is the fear of Zip Dobyns, matriarch of the American Wets. She does
not want a computer to think for her; she wants it solely to present the evidence in a form she can quickly grasp. Thereafter it is her skills and experience that will transform this material into psychological truth.

There's no doubt that push-button astrology can take the humanity
away from the astrologer-client relationship. Just as today's astrologer,
gazing at hieroglyphic squiggles, has only an occasional perception of the
lumps of rock or gas out there in space that form the basis of his horoscope,
so tomorrow's astrologer will be even further removed from even the
names of planets. The whole astrological vocabulary may be automatically
translated into psychological language. He will have become purely an
explainer, a communicator, no longer an interpreter or analyst. At the last
resort, the astrologer as a living presence is obsolescent, and maybe fast
becoming obsolete.

At this level, tomorrow's astrology will have more in common with
Fogeyism than Wetness. Under the pressure of technology, astrology will
revert to the anonymous authority of the Delphic oracle. Take it or leave it,
baby. You can't question me beyond the prewritten list of queries on
Touchscreen Two. No, you cannot see my software – what a disgusting
suggestion! I'll have the Thought Police after you.

Which brings us to Astrotalk, the term coined by Michael Erlewine for
the use of computers to mimic the astrologer's consulting technique. I have
been a leader in this field since the early 1970s, when I launched a written-
report service in Britain through Mercury Marketing Ltd. In those days the
computer – an IBM main-frame belonging to Tate & Lyle we moonlighted
with – acted purely as a word-processor. If you had Mars in Taurus, you
got paragraph forty-five. There was no subtlety, no real astrological
analysis. But with microcomputers coming on to the market in the late
1970s, I determined to go solo with a computer and software of my own.

Michael had just taken delivery of his Commodore PET in the spring of
1978 when I visited him at Ann Arbor. Enthused beyond measure by the
awesome power of this 8K RAM machine, I bought one myself, quickly
followed by a 64K Cromemco processor and two heavy-duty dot-matrix

printers. Within nine months I had taught myself BASIC, adapted the computational programs of James Neely and Michael Erlewine, and developed a Solar Arc analysis that is still the heart of a twelve-month forecast I sell as a Birthday Horoscope.

At first this program analysed the chart – admittedly in considerable detail, using harmonics and midpoints – and brought forth a plenitude of paragraphs. But the technique was soon refined, partly by myself but also by Terry Dwyer in England, who produced a densely packed character analysis program called Starword, and later by Maritha Pottinger of Astro-Computing Services, among others. Here the technique is to correlate English syntax with astrological syntax. Take a simple statement like: *Venus in Scorpio in the fourth house square Saturn in Leo in the first house and trine Mars in Cancer in the twelfth house but sesquiquadrate Uranus in Gemini in the eleventh house.* This can translate, item by item, into prose like: 'You are capable of intense affection, in a cosy and possessive fashion, but this conflicts with your outer manner which can be proud, haughty and rather unattainable. Yet beneath your somewhat cold, snobbish outer demeanour there's a deeply caring sexuality that is intuitive and living somewhat in fantasy-land. No harm in this, but this sense of unreality in your real inner feelings can make actual relationships a bit unstable.'

If it were Pluto instead of Uranus in Gemini, the final three words of the passage would be switched by the computer to something like 'very fraught and obsessive', while for Jupiter the words might be 'a bit fly-by-night, as you're always searching for the perfect man but rarely finding him'.

Thus squares and other hard aspects correspond with *buts* and *on the other hands* while trines and soft aspects are represented by *what's more* and *in addition.*

The problem with this technique is that the eventual prose can become too cluttered for comfort. What's more (there must be a trine about), the eventual report must always be written to a strict format. The computer is still carrying out a series of fixed orders, like a freshly trained servant, instead of thinking for itself like a true Jeeves.

My own line of development has been interactive Astrotalk. Anyone receiving a written horoscope from a Matrix-generated report-writer, for example, will recognize only two personal references – one to the name and address on the title page and the other to his or her gender.

My own reports take into consideration a mass of information given by the client. What work does he do? What would he like to do? Is he happy with his present firm, or does he want to move? If so, where does he fancy – elsewhere in Britain or abroad, to a larger firm, to a new field altogether, or does he want to start his own business and if so, has he the money, know-how and experience to do so?

This calls for detailed data-storage – believe it or not, the above information can be packed into four computer bytes – and even more detailed software to extract and absorb this data into the finished report. But the results are gratifying. Comedians speak of the five basic jokes from which all others flow; playwrights talk of the seven basic plots; and I know there are fifteen basic questions that people ask about their love lives. Given the right circumstantial details and a proper analysis of the birth-chart, each question can be amplified into an (almost) comprehensive answer.

Well, it sounds comprehensive, anyway – and there's the rub. Are we Astrotalkers simply massaging egos and, by the by, finding a pretty way to turn a penny? Are we *understanding* anything and, by extension, passing on any real understanding to our clients? For make no mistake: these techniques will develop, and develop fast, into expert systems that can be applied to any human activity. Wanna make money on the Stock Exchange? Tune into Stars & Shares, your very own interactive computer-aided investment analyst service. Feed in your birth-data, and presto! – buy IBM, sell AT&T, hold on to ICI but cut your losses on BL, BTR and BA Fool.

Wanna man for tonight? Dial Stardate, punch in your details, and presto! – our deeply caring, deeply sharing Data General computer will link you *live* with the man we say is astrologically suitable for your bed. No guarantees, no refunds, no explanations.

Each of these expert systems, due to be here quicker than the day after tomorrow, will be based on impeccable astrology. The intricacies of your birth-chart will be matched with the horoscope for the formation of ICL, founded as a private company on 22 November 1915. Transits to that horoscope will be compared to previous movements of share-price. If the links are good, buy, buy, buy! This isn't, after all, so different from the computerized buy-sell instructions that are already such a feature of the American stock exchanges and commodity markets. And what's the difference between Stardate and Dateline or any other computer-assisted mix-and-match romance service already in the market-place? The people out there are looking for love – give 'em what they want. Don't be so prissy.

Years ago I wrote a piece for *The Astrological Journal* called 'Town v. Gown', in which I argued the case for prostituting astrology instead of keeping it forever in the ivory towers. My main point, I think, was that if astrologers don't do it, other less qualified and even less scrupulous people will. In addition, who can tell where serious astrology ends and pop stars begin? Each of us, from Geoffrey Dean to Sidney Omarr, is happy to talk Sun-sign astrology in private conversation. Why not do so in public, and pay the next mortgage instalment?

By extension, I also asserted that all publicity is good publicity. If Lucky Stars columns keep astrology in the forefront of the public imagination, well and good. They may not be brilliant astrology, but they can lead the punters to what is good and truthful and wise.

Today, fifteen years later, the scene is more muddled still. Many of the serious astrologers, like Julia Parker, who attacked pop astrology in those days have become ardent popularizers themselves. Everyone is much more aware of the marketable side of astrology. It may still be a spiritual science, but I have a wife and two kids to support and there's another point: research, once the proud bastion of the Gowns, is increasingly used by Towners for their nefarious money-making aims.

Computers have helped here, of course. In tomorrow's world, astrologers will all have access to a vast, growing data-base of facts correlating astrological information with all kinds of phenomena – health, careers, accidents, sexual proclivities, you name it and astrologers will have it on compact disc. Data that has taken decades to collect, compute and clarify will be at everyone's GET command. We are moving from amateur to professional standards. People at last are prepared to finance research, simply because they see a profit at the end of it all. This may be personal profit in the City, or community profit through medical astrological research. Whatever the cause, computerized research, done by scientific methods, will become much more widespread.

Is this good? No, cry the Fogies, curmudgeonly to the last. It's not that they distrust knowledge (and research results are only organized knowledge, after all) so much as *mechanical knowledge*. Like quantum physicists, they claim that astrology, like a subatomic particle, is changed by the manner in which it is observed. Studied by sympathetic humans, astrology can blossom into a life-enhancing vision of how the cosmos works. Measured by machines, the same data withers on the vine; the evidence dies or contradicts itself, and nothing fruitful can come of it.

Maybe, say the Wets. They are all for more knowledge, but they don't want to be overwhelmed by systems that they cannot comprehend, facts they cannot absorb. They yearn, like the British astrologer Dennis Elwell, for comfortable results – nothing too dry or rigorous, but facts that can stimulate your imagination or suggest new avenues of thought. He wants a computer as an *aide-mémoire*, so that at the touch of a button he can be reminded of this piece of research, or prompted to explore that particular idea.

Expert systems are being developed for many fields – in medicine especially – but there is a great difference between artificial intelligence in astrology and in any other field. Compare, in a few year's time, the medical diagnostic computer in many a doctor's surgery with a similar device in the astrologer's study. The medical computer will ask for your symptoms; it will quiz you about when, where and how you developed signs of illness, and will consult your medical history already stored in memory. If the illness is familiar and straightforward, the computer will print out the necessary prescription. If not, you will be referred to the correct human specialist.

Now such a system, or something similar, could go through all the motions in the astrologer's study – with this difference, that whereas medical knowledge is widespread, accepted and built upon, astrological knowledge is partial, often unique to one astrologer, and incapable of development. It is a series of anecdotes, research based on too small a sample or hypotheses built on too slender an axiom. It remains science.

Hang on, cry the Wets, you're comparing us to physical scientists. Why not align us with the social scientists, such as psychologists and economists, whose axioms are as slender as a gazelle's neck and whose samples are often as tiny as its toes.

A good point – but there's a further objection. Social scientists of all persuasions manage to build their profession on knowledge that is testable, capable of replication, able to be accepted by peer-groups in other fields. Why are astrologers so insular? Why do we treasure our truths like a miser's hoard, saying in so many words that my truth is perhaps similar to Russell's truth or Rob's truth or Charles's truth but is basically a *much better*, more truthful kind of truth. No wonder we are linked more often with patent medicine quacks than leaders in real professions.

It's interesting that computerization, far from reducing personal aggrandizement, seems to foster it. Sometimes we try to make the computer aspect of our trade almost transparent, as though it weren't there, so that our original, unique and personal insights still shine through.

Yet a true science of astrology would pay scant attention to the personalities involved. A true profession like the law or medicine actively discourages any stress on personal qualities over and above those of professional qualification.

So what of the future of astrology? I have trod this path before. In 1970, at the first-ever Astrological Association conference, I forecast to the assembled weirdoes and matrons what the 1980 conference would be like:

> I hope there will be 500 of us, not the mere 100, and that everyone holds a recognized qualification in astrological science. Obviously, too, the professional consultants among the delegates will hold a current licence issued by the Home Office or local authority.
>
> The conference will be organized by a single body. It may be called the Association or the Faculty, or the Lodge or the Federation, but more probably there will be an entirely new organization within which our separate communal identities will have long since merged. We will have our own premises in London, with a permanent staff. This body will act as trades union, workshop, university, law court and parliament for all astrologers in this country. It will be a respected institution.
>
> Now to the delegates themselves. There will be far more, proportionately speaking, already fully qualified in other disciplines: scientists of all kinds, social workers, doctors and psychologists, management consultants, administrators and so forth.
>
> The actual astrology we shall practise in a decade's time will either be very similar to our present brand – a mish-mash of traditional precepts

interpreted in the light of modern psychology and leavened by a few new techniques which are really just variations on an old, old theme – or completely different. If it is different, I doubt whether many, or any, of us here today will understand much that will be said. There will be a new vocabulary to cope with new concepts; and a bookful of jargon from other disciplines too. We shall have to be well versed in computer technology and, probably, medicine, general systems theory and more complicated mathematics that you and I can handle at present.

Well, my forecasting was pretty good those seventeen or eighteen years ago. Like my literary style, some things have distressingly failed to progress. We are still stuck with astrological techniques that have not been honed by much fresh research or experimentation. We are still awaiting premises in London, to say nothing of the Home Office licences.

But some factors have changed as I indicated. In Britain, the Urania Trust promises to become the unifying force in astrological institutions, and the premises, permanent staff and all, are becoming a real focus instead of a mere blur on the horizon. In the United States, new groups such as AFAN or NCGR have linked to supersede the outworn American Federation of Astrologers. And we have indeed been infiltrated by experts in other fields.

Will these trends continue? Only if astrology delivers. Our science must take a more decisive step beyond personal belief into public recognition, and this can happen only if we gather a body of knowledge that the open-minded, intelligent layman will accept as valid. Everything else – computers, professionalism, theories of all kinds – fade into insignificance before the overwhelming need to show that astrology works.

Until then, astrology and 'real' science resemble binary stars endlessly circling each other, each an echo or mirror image of the other, first one and then the other gaining prominence. Look at the Science section of popular bookshops today and half the books are proto-science – anything from the Turin Shroud to numerology to spacemen building the pyramids. Our world today is yearning for this sexy, kinky sort of science. We distrust and fail to appreciate the science that builds bridges and undertakes brain surgery. In every astrologer's heart, there is this division between the real and the unreal, the world that analyses and the world that imagines. To those who have built the Apollo spaceship, reality is measured, exact and undeniable. To those that flew in her, reality has become something more. To those who live wholly in this world, there is no other. To those who have a smattering of cosmic consciousness, 'this world' will never quite seem real again.

Personally, I work on one star and take my holidays on the other. But I can never remember which is which.